The Rise of German Industrial Power
1834-1914

W. O. Henderson

THE RISE OF GERMAN INDUSTRIAL POWER
1834-1914

UNIVERSITY OF CALIFORNIA PRESS

Berkeley and Los Angeles, California

University of California Press
Berkeley and Los Angeles, California
© 1975 W.O. Henderson
Maps drawn by T.A. Bicknell
ISBN 0-520-03073-7
ISBN 0-520-03120-2 paperback
Library of Congress catalog card No. 75-17293
First Paperbound edition, 1975
Printed in Great Britain
by J.W. Arrowsmith Ltd, Bristol

Contents

III *The Industrial Giant, 1873-1914*

To
W. H. CHALONER

Author's Note

The author wishes to thank Dr B. M. Ratcliffe of the University of Manchester for his helpful comments on the chapter on the banking revolution and also for his help in reading the proofs. Mrs Jeanne Lockett has typed the manuscript with her accustomed efficiency.

W O H

Notes on currencies

The following list shows the approximate value of the currencies referred to in this book, giving in each case the number of units equivalent to one pound sterling:

Thaler (Prussian): 6½
Florin or Gulden (Austrian): 12
Mark banco (Hamburg): 13
Mark current (Hamburg): 17
Mark (gold standard): 20

List of maps

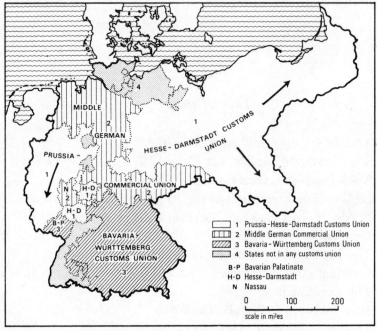

The three Customs Unions of 1828

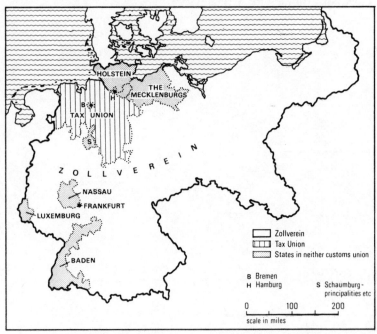

The Zollverein and the Tax Union, 1834

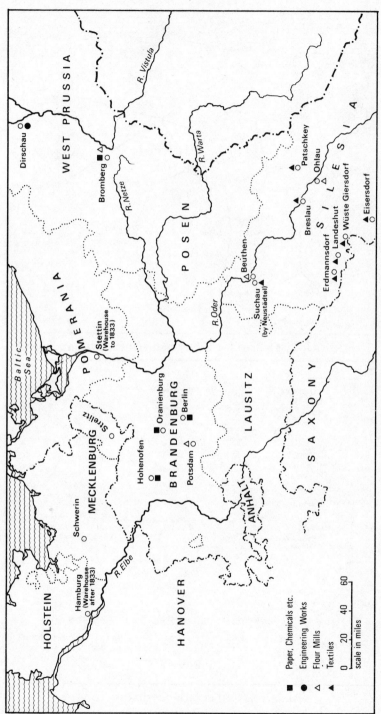

Seehandlung enterprises in the 1840s

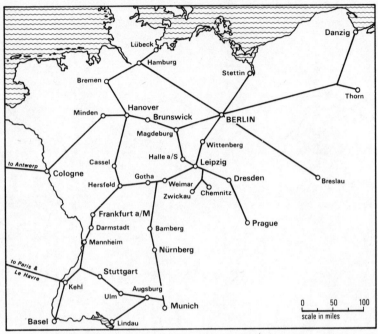

Friedrich List's plan for a German railway system, 1833

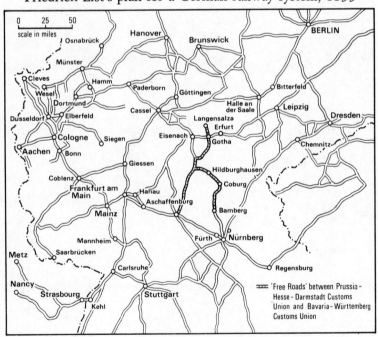

Main roads in central Germany, 1834

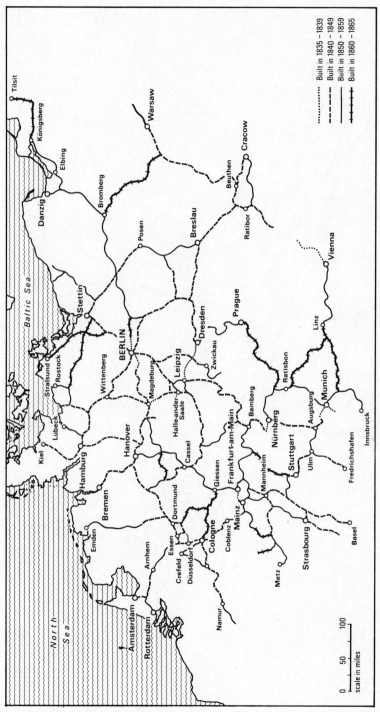

German railways, 1835-65

Built in 1835 - 1839
Built in 1840 - 1849
Built in 1850 - 1859
Built in 1860 - 1865

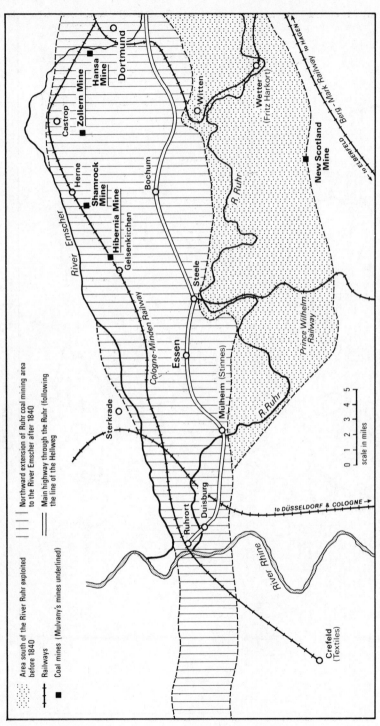

The Ruhr in the middle of the nineteenth century

Legend:

Area south of the River Ruhr exploited before 1840

Northward extension of Ruhr coal mining area to the River Emscher after 1840

Railways

Main highway through the Ruhr (following the line of the Hellweg)

Coal mines (Mulvany's mines underlined)

Labels on map:

Dortmund
Hansa Mine
Zollern Mine
Castrop
Witten
Wetter (Fritz Harkort)
Herne
Shamrock Mine
Hibernia Mine
Bochum
Gelsenkirchen
New Scotland Mine
River Emscher
Steele
R. Ruhr
Cologne–Minden Railway
Essen
Mülheim (Stinnes)
Prince Wilhelm Railway
Sterkrade
R. Ruhr
Ruhrort
Duisburg
to DÜSSELDORF & COLOGNE
River Rhine
Crefeld (Textiles)
to ELBERFELD
Berg–Mark Railway
to HAGEN

scale in miles
0 1 2 3 4 5

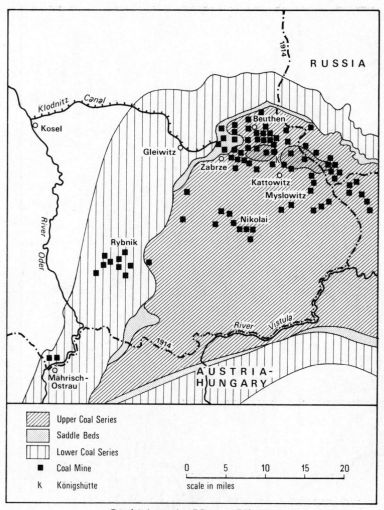

Coalmines in Upper Silesia

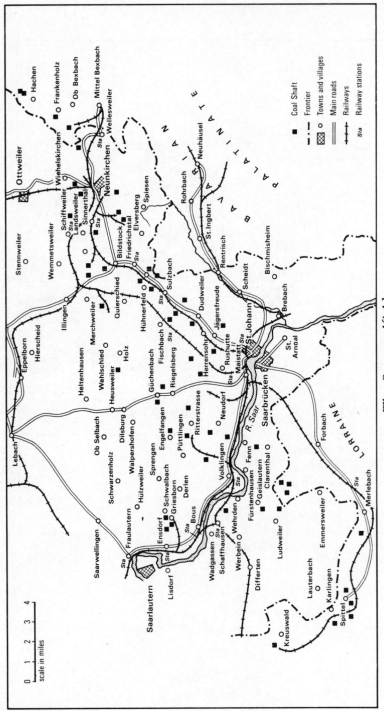

The Saar coalfield

Legend:
- ■ Coal Shaft
- ○ Towns and villages
- — Main roads
- Railways
- Sta Railway stations
- Frontier

Places labelled on map:

Hachen, Frankenholz, Ob Bexbach, Mittel Bexbach, Welfesweiler, Neuhäusel, Ottweiler, Wiebelskirchen, Neunkirchen, Spiesen, Rohrbach, Stennweiler, Schiffweiler, Landsweiler, Sinnerthal, Elversberg, St. Ingbert, Wemmetsweiler, Bildstock, Friedrichsthal, Rentrisch, Bischmisheim, Eppelborn, Hierscheid, Illingen, Merchweiler, Quierschied, Hühnerfeld, Sulzbach, Dudweiler, Scheidt, Brebach, Heitenhausen, Wahlschied, Holz, Fischbach, Güchenbach, Herrensohr, Rushütte, St. Johann, St. Arnoal, Heusweiler, Riegelsberg, Maistatt, Lebach, Ob Selbach, Dilsburg, Engelfangen, Güchenbach, Ritterstrasse, Neudorf, Saarbrücken, Schwarzenholz, Walpershofen, Sprengen, Püttlingen, R. Saar, Forbach, Saarwellingen, Hülzweiler, Schwalbach, Derlen, Volklingen, Fenn, Clarenthal, Fraulautern, Ensdorf, Griesborn, Bous, Wadgassen, Wehrden, Fürstenhausen, Geislautern, Ludweiler, Emmersweiler, Merlebach, Saarlautern, Lisdorf, Schaffhausen, Werbeln, Differten, Lauterbach, Karlingen, Spittel, Kreuswald

PALATINATE
BAVARIAN
LORRAINE

scale in miles
0 1 2 3 4

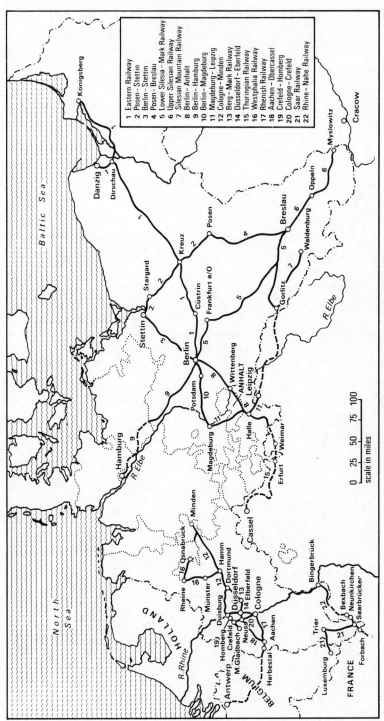

State railways in Prussia, 1848-70

1 Eastern Railway
2 Posen – Stettin
3 Berlin – Stettin
4 Posen – Breslau
5 Lower Silesia – Mark Railway
6 Upper Silesian Railway
7 Silesian Mountain Railway
8 Berlin – Anhalt
9 Berlin – Hamburg
10 Berlin – Magdeburg
11 Magdeburg – Leipzig
12 Cologne – Minden
13 Berg – Mark Railway
14 Düsseldorf – Eberfeld
15 Thuringian Railway
16 Westphalia Railway
17 Rhenish Railway
18 Aachen – Obercassel
19 Crefeld – Homberg
20 Cologne – Crefeld
21 Saar Railway
22 Rhine – Nahe Railway

0   25   50   75   100
scale in miles

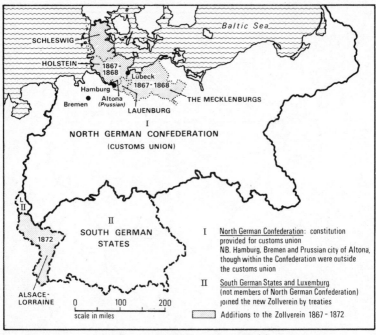

The new Zollverein, 1867

Within the first map:

Baltic Sea

SCHLESWIG

HOLSTEIN — 1867-1868

Lübeck 1867-1868

Hamburg

Altona (Prussian)

Bremen

LAUENBURG

THE MECKLENBURGS

I

NORTH GERMAN CONFEDERATION

(CUSTOMS UNION)

II

SOUTH GERMAN STATES

II

1872

ALSACE-LORRAINE

0   100   200

scale in miles

I North German Confederation: constitution provided for customs union
NB. Hamburg, Bremen and Prussian city of Altona, though within the Confederation were outside the customs union

II South German States and Luxemburg (not members of North German Confederation) joined the new Zollverein by treaties

Additions to the Zollverein 1867–1872

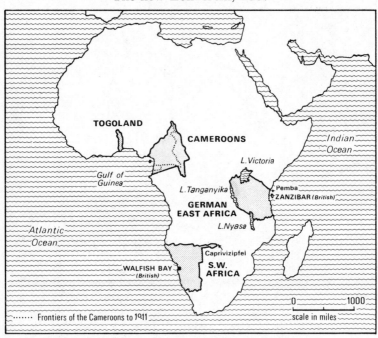

Within the second map:

TOGOLAND

CAMEROONS

Indian Ocean

L. Victoria

Gulf of Guinea

L. Tanganyika

Pemba

ZANZIBAR (British)

GERMAN EAST AFRICA

L. Nyasa

Atlantic Ocean

Caprivizipfel

WALFISH BAY (British)

S.W. AFRICA

0   1000

scale in miles

.... Frontiers of the Cameroons to 1911

German colonies in Africa, 1914

I
The Dawn of the Industrial Era
1834-1851

1 Introduction

The establishment of the customs union on 1 January 1834 and the opening of the Nürnberg-Fürth railway on 7 December 1835 heralded the dawn of the industrial era in Germany. At that time Germany was still a predominantly agrarian region and three-quarters of the population lived in villages and small market towns. Industries, such as the manufacture of textiles and metal goods, were still largely in the hands of craftsmen, while large units of industrial production were quite exceptional. Eighty years later, on the eve of the First World War, Germany had become one of the leading industrial states in the world, with an output of iron and steel that was exceeded only by that of the United States.

The fall of many tariff barriers and the building of railways between 1834 and 1850 enabled German trade to move much more freely than before and stimulated the growth of modern industries. But the genesis of the industrial revolution in Germany can be traced back to a much earlier period. In the second half of the eighteenth century, when England was forging ahead to become the 'workshop of the world', German industry and agriculture were also making some progress, though on a much more modest scale.

Certain changes in the size and distribution of the population usually occur during an industrial revolution — an increase in population; a movement from rural to urban districts; and the appearance of large towns. All this took place in Germany in the eighteenth century. In Prussia the population rose from 2,380,000 to 5,750,000 in Frederick the Great's reign, while the population of Berlin grew from 29,000 to 141,000. At the same time peasants from the country districts and craftsmen from abroad were moving into industrial regions. In Silesia — a centre of the linen industry — some 200 villages were founded in 1740-83 and 13,000 foreigners were brought into the province. The growth of the textile and metal industries and the establishment of luxury industries — such as silks and porcelain — were features of the expansion of the Prussian economy in the second half of the eighteenth century.

A growing population could be fed only if agricultural output rose. Expanding industries needed the raw materials — wool, flax, hemp, hides, madder, timber — drawn from the farms and the forests. In Germany some progress was being made in agriculture in the eighteenth century, though this did not occur everywhere. There were backward districts such as the Eifel and the Senne, where farming standards were low and the peasants were very poor. But in certain parts of the country new crops — clover, beet, hops, tobacco — were introduced; unproductive land was reclaimed; fields formerly left fallow were cultivated; there was an improvement in the quality of horses, cattle and sheep; and more cattle were fed indoors in the winter. East of the River Elbe the junkers (owners of large estates) were farming more efficiently. They extended the acreage they cultivated themselves by farming smallholdings formerly cultivated by peasant tenants (*Bauernlegen*), by seizing waste land and common land, by draining marshes and by cutting down forests. Large fens that were reclaimed in Prussia included the *Oderbruch*, the *Warthebruch* and the *Netzebruch*. Some German landowners introduced new English agricultural methods on their estates. Caspar Voght, for example, transplanted English practices to Germany when he laid out his model farms, park and gardens at Klein Flottbek and Gross Flottbek in Holstein at the end of the eighteenth century. The agrarian sector of the German economy not only produced food for a growing population and raw materials for industry but also helped the craftsmen by providing them with new markets. When agriculture flourished, those who made a living on the land were able to increase their purchases of iron goods (farm implements, horseshoes, nails) and leather goods (footwear, saddles, harnesses) and textiles (clothing).

The invention of new machines and processes was another feature of industrialization. On the whole few contributions to the advancement of technical knowledge were made in Germany at a time when revolutionary changes were taking place in England in the textile industries by the introduction of the mule and the powerloom and in the metal industries by the invention of the charcoal blast furnace and the Huntsman process for making cast-steel. German inventions in the eighteenth century included a new water-pressure engine by Winterschmidt and new dyes by Diesbach and Barth. Advances were being made in higher technical education in the 1760s with the establishment of a commercial college at Hamburg and mining colleges in Freiberg (Saxony) and Clausthal (Harz). German governments and entrepreneurs were able to take advantage of English technical progress by sending their agents to inspect some of the new iron-works and engineering plants. Freiherr vom Stein, for example, succeeded in inspecting a Boulton and Watt steam-engine at Barclay and Perkin's brewery in London in 1789. In addition Englishmen visited Germany to install modern machines and teach German workers how to use them. The coke-smelting process was introduced into Silesia by William Wilkinson and John Baildon.

Dramatic changes in industrial organization take place in the early stages of an industrial revolution. Large units of production replace small workshops run by craftsmen. Although there were no modern factories with machinery driven by steam-power in Germany in the eighteenth century there were some large establishments using machines operated by hand or by water. And by running such under-takings entrepreneurs gained experience in training and handling a labour force that was working under new conditions. The state porce-lain factory at Meissen in Saxony employed 730 workers in 1765 and a similar establishment in Berlin had 500 workers in 1783. Count von Waldstein's woollen mills at Oberleutensdorf on the Bohemian side of the Erzgebirge employed over 400 operatives in 1773. Such 'manufactories' (*Manufakturen*) were an intermediate stage between the domestic system and the modern factory system. The 'manufac-tories' employed far more workers than the craftsmen, but they lacked the steam-power that was an essential feature of later factories.

Good communications to speed up the movement of raw materials to the factories and of finished manufactured products to consumers were essential for industrial expansion. Transport facilities in Germany were poor in the eighteenth century, since the roads were not properly maintained and there were many tolls on the rivers. But some progress was made. Philipp Jakob Klump, Major Günther and Freiherr vom Stein made considerable improvements in the network of roads in Württemberg, Saxony and the County of Mark. Stein's highways in the Ruhr district linked Herdecke, Siegen, Meinerzhagen and Soest. The inland waterways of Prussia were extended by the construction of the Finow, Plauer, Templin, Fehrbellin, Bromberg and Klodnitz canals. The waterways of the Mark Brandenburg — a system of rivers, lakes and canals — linked the Elbe to the Oder and promoted the growth of Berlin as a centre of commerce in the eighteenth century.

An industrial revolution needs money as well as entrepreneurs, workers, machinery and transport facilities. In England much of the capital that was required was raised by manufacturers themselves, who ploughed profits back into their enterprises. But capital was also secured from outside sources such as landowners and merchants. Germany was a poorer country than England in the eighteenth century and it was often difficult to find capital for industry. Some noble landed families financed various manufacturing enterprises. In Saxony the Lauchhammer ironworks were set up at Müchenberg by the Löwendal family, while in Silesia feudal magnates — such as the families of Pless, Ratibor, Henckel-Donnersmarck, Tiele-Winkler, Renard and Hohenlohe — founded collieries and ironworks on their estates and actively encouraged the expansion of the rural linen industry.

There were examples of German entrepreneurs who started with very little capital. In 1712 David Splitgerber and Gottfried Daum established themselves as commission agents in Berlin. At first they operated from two small rooms. Then the dowry of Daum's wife provided them with the finance they needed to expand their business. They secured the patronage of Frederick William I and Frederick the Great and became wholesalers, financiers and industrialists. They successfully managed several state-owned metalworks and arms factories. J. E. Gotzkowsky, who began his business career as a dealer in a small way in haberdashery, jewellery and trinkets, became a leading merchant, financier and entrepreneur in Berlin in Frederick the Great's reign. He described his business activities in his memoirs. Although he played an important part in establishing the manufacture of silks and porcelain in Berlin he died a poor man, harassed by his creditors.

The availability of credit facilities through banks and other financial institutions is a factor favourable to industrial progress. In the eighteenth century German banks were financial institutions of a more rudimentary character than those of England, Scotland, Holland or Switzerland. Indeed the function of the private banker was only just beginning to be differentiated from that of the merchant. But the Bank of Hamburg was growing in importance as a major institution for financing commerce in northern Germany, in the Scandinavian countries and in the Baltic region. This bank established a form of 'bank money' known as the 'mark banco'. This mark was not a coin or a note. It was a unit of value that was used for accounting purposes in commercial transactions. As there were many currencies in Germany at this time — some of which fluctuated in value — traders found it convenient to make out invoices and bills of exchange in mark bancos rather than in thalers or florins.

Since it was difficult to raise capital in Germany for new industrial undertakings, the governments of the various states invested money in certain private manufacturing enterprises and established nationalized mines and workshops. While English entrepreneurs in the eighteenth century were expected to stand on their own feet and to set up new undertakings without government aid, German industrialists frequently received privileges, grants and loans from the State. And while there was no nationalized sector of the economy in England, the German states established and operated manufacturing enterprises of various kinds. The policy of German governments to encourage industrial growth between 1740 and 1815 — to some extent a traditional mercantilist approach — was being affected by events in England. Some entrepreneurs and civil servants saw that a new kind of industrial economy, based upon machines driven by steam-engines, was developing across the North Sea. They appreciated the connection between industrial growth and national wealth. They believed that German industry could expand as English industry had expanded. And so the traditional assistance given by German governments to industry was modified to encourage industrialists to follow the example of English entrepreneurs.

German governments were particularly interested in fostering the development of armaments as well as the manufacture of luxury goods. Since it was essential to make adequate provision for national defence it was natural that the State should own ironmines, forests and foundries for casting cannon as well as workshops to manufacture smallarms, gunpowder and ammunition. Luxury industries, producing silks, porcelain and glassware, were fostered for a different reason. They were encouraged because the export of such products could earn foreign currency and so improve the balance of payments in international trade. Gustav Schmoller considered that the silk industry, fostered by Frederick the Great, turned Berlin into 'an important factory town, and the town whose inhabitants were distinguished by the best taste in Germany'. In Prussia, in the second half of the eighteenth century, the State operated ironworks at Malapane, smallarms workshops at Potsdam and Spandau and a porcelain factory in Berlin. A nationalized lead-silver mine was opened at Tarnowitz, while coalmines were established at Königshütte and Zabrze. Rulers of small states followed the example of their larger neighbours. In the Saar district, for example, a number of ironworks at Fischbach, Geislautern, Sulzbach and St Ingbert were publicly owned during the reign of Prince Wilhelm Heinrich of Nassau-Saarbrücken.

Another feature of industrialization is the geographical concentration of manufactures in particular districts and the specialization of industrial regions in particular products. As early as the last quarter of the eighteenth century certain German regions were already becoming industrialized. Berlin was — with some exaggeration — described in 1800 as 'the principal manufacturing city in Germany'. In Silesia the linen industry was expanding and the number of looms in the province rose from 19,800 in 1748 to 28,700 in 1790. Claus Friedrich von Reden, head of the regional mining office at Breslau in 1779-1802 and later in charge of the whole mining administration in Prussia, founded nationalized mines and engineering works in Upper Silesia and introduced steam pumps and coke-smelting into the district. At the end of the eighteenth century the Ruhr produced nearly 400,000 tons of coal and the Saar 30,000 tons. In the Siegerland, the Sauerland, Nassau and other districts numerous iron-ore deposits were being worked. The Duchy of Berg, in which the Ruhr was situated, has been described as 'one of the most advanced industrial countries of the Continent' in 1800. In the valley of the River Wupper the twin cotton towns of Elberfeld and Barmen were described as 'a miniature England' in 1809, while the cutlery centres of Remscheid and Solingen had long enjoyed a reputation for high-quality workmanship in steel. Specialization was already in evidence. Krefeld was known for its silks, Augsburg for gold- and silverware, Aachen and Burtscheid for needles, Stolberg for brass articles and Chemnitz for cotton goods. Hamburg and Bremen had developed — particularly after the Americans threw open their ports on gaining their independence — into major ports for the import of 'colonial wares' and the export of manufactured goods such as linens. Frankfurt-am-Main, the headquarters of the Rothschilds, had already become an important centre for banking and entrepôt trade by the end of the eighteenth century, while Leipzig had long been famed for its international fairs at which goods from all over the world were offered for sale.

In the second half of the eighteenth century a wind of change was blowing through the Germany of Frederick the Great and other of the eighteenth century, while Leipzig had long been famed for its gave the country a lead by promoting schemes for expanding industry and commerce. Private entrepreneurs — Splitgerber and Gotzkowsky in Berlin and the feudal magnates in Silesia — responded to this stimulus. Population growth encouraged farmers and industrialists to increase their output. For the German princes and their advisers and for those engaged in manufacturing or agrarian enterprises, the industrial revolution and the rise of scientific farming in England provided a challenge. The hope of emulating England's prosperity spurred the Germans to take steps to modernize the economy and to expand production.

Industrialization brings with it social problems. When workers leave their homes to work together under one roof they are subject to a new and often irksome discipline. Long hours and low pay are other grievances apparently inseparable from the early factory system. Even before the machine age, the dependence of domestic workers upon a capitalist entrepreneur and the establishment of large workshops led to social discontents. In Silesia, for example, the linen weavers were in open revolt in the spring of 1793.

In view of the progress made by German industry in the second half of the eighteenth century, more rapid advances might have been expected in the early nineteenth century. But various other factors retarded industrial growth. The division of the country into numerous independent states — each with complete control over its own economic affairs — and the existence of numerous tariff barriers and river tolls restricted internal trade. At the same time foreign commerce was hampered by the high tariffs of neighbouring states such as France, Austria and Russia. The fact that important manufacturing regions — the Ruhr, the Saar, Upper Silesia, Saxony — lay on the periphery of the country made it virtually impossible to develop them properly until a network of railways had been built. The trade of Danzig was hampered because Denmark controlled the Sound, while Hamburg and Bremen were not so favourably situated as Liverpool or Le Hâvre to trade on the North Atlantic route.

The wars of the French Revolution and Napoleon delayed Germany's economic progress. The Continental System, which attempted to keep English goods out of the territories controlled by Napoleon, throttled Germany's international trade. Men who were called up were lost to the labour force. French requisitions and levies drained the country of its material and financial resources. There was an alarming increase in national and local debts. The small town of Erfurt, for example, had a municipal debt of 300,000 thalers (6½ thalers = £1) in 1816. And there was an equally alarming increase in the number of homeless beggars who roamed the countryside. From an economic point of view Germany became a French satellite. Admittedly Germany gained some advantages in the years when Napoleon dominated the country. New frontiers, involving the disappearance of many small states, improved opportunities for internal trade. So did the building of some military roads and the regulating of the navigation of the Rhine, which reduced the number of toll stations on the river. The work of French engineers, such as Héron de Villefosse in the Harz and the Ruhr, fostered the expansion of the mining industry in Germany. And some German branches of manufacture, like the textile industries of Saxony, were saved from competition from cheap English goods by the protection afforded by the Continental System. Heckscher declares that 'of all manufacturing countries on the Continent there is scarcely one which developed so powerfully under the Continental System as Saxony'. Despite the assertion of the economist Friedrich List that 'German manufactures of all and every kind for the first time began to make an important advance in the Napoleonic era' it may be doubted whether the advantages that the Continental System conferred upon particular industries or regions outweighed the serious damage it did to the German economy as a whole.

2   The Customs Union

After the Napoleonic Wars Germany became a federation of thirty-nine states which varied considerably in size. A number of them did not have compact territories. There were some isolated provinces and it was not uncommon for enclaves of one state to be embedded in the territory of another state. There were two great powers — Prussia and Austria — and several medium-sized states, of which the most important were Bavaria, Württemberg, Baden, Hanover and Saxony. There were also numerous small territories and four Free Cities. North of the River Main Germany was dominated by Prussia, which had considerably extended her territories after the Napoleonic Wars. Prussia was divided into two groups of provinces separated by Hanover and Brunswick. The eastern and central provinces were Brandenburg, Pomerania, Posen, Silesia, East and West Prussia (united 1824-78) and the province of Saxony. The two western provinces were Westphalia and the Rhineland, which included some of the most advanced industrial regions in Germany. South of the River Main lay Bavaria, Württemberg and Baden. Their territories were compact except that Bavaria had an isolated province (the Palatinate) west of the River Rhine. The map of Germany was most confused in the centre of the country and in the Rhine valley. This part of the country was split up into a medley of medium-sized states (Saxony, Brunswick, Nassau, Hesse-Darmstadt, Hesse-Cassel) and tiny territories in Anhalt and Thuringia.

All these states, from the largest to the smallest, controlled their own economic and social affairs. Customs and excise, communications, coinage, banking, gilds and so forth were regulated by the states and not by the Confederation. No German state hesitated to injure a neighbour's economy if it thought that any advantage could be secured by doing so. Each state used its geographical position and natural resources to become as independent an economic unit as possible. Sometimes this led to tariff wars or to road building deliberately designed to attract transit trade from one state to another. Small terri-

tories sheltered nests of smugglers. English manufactured goods
were smuggled into Germany through Frankfurt-am-Main and the
Anhalt duchies. Most states found, however, that economic prosperity
could not be secured within the narrow limits of the political frontiers
of 1815 and they learned by bitter experience that attempts to inflict
economic injury on a neighbour frequently recoiled on their own
heads. The formation of a customs union in 1834 and its subsequent
expansion was a recognition of the fact that the political frontiers of
Germany could not survive as customs frontiers if serious economic
progress were to be made.

A customs union could have been founded in one of two ways.
First all the German states could have agreed on a new tariff and on
a common customs administration. This might have been done under
Article 19 of the Federal Act of 1815, which stated that 'the members
of the Confederation reserve for the first meeting of the Federal Diet
at Frankfurt-am-Main discussions on trade and communications
between the various Federal States, as well as shipping, on the basis
of the principles laid down at the Congress of Vienna'.

At the spring fair at Frankfurt-am-Main in 1819, a number of
merchants formed an association 'to promote German trade and
industry'. On their behalf the young economist Friedrich List drew
up a petition to the Diet of the Confederation advocating freedom of
internal trade in Germany. List declared:

> Thirty-eight customs boundaries cripple inland commerce, and
> produce much the same effect as ligatures which prevent the free
> circulation of the blood. The merchant trading between Hamburg
> and Austria, or Berlin and Switzerland must traverse ten states,
> must learn ten customs tariffs, must pay ten successive transit
> dues. Anyone who is so unfortunate as to live on the boundary
> line between three or four states spends his days among hostile
> tax-gatherers and custom house officials; he is a man without a
> country . . . . Only the remission of the internal customs, and
> the erection of a general tariff for the whole Federation, can restore
> national trade and industry and help the working classes.

Shortly afterwards a group of merchants from the Rhineland suggested to the king of Prussia that it would 'be advisable to encourage
a revival of German industry by removing all customs barriers within
Germany and by simply levying duties on land frontiers and at ports'.
But all attempts at this time to raise the question of a customs union

in the Federal Diet and at meetings of representatives of the German states at Carlsbad and Vienna had no practical results.

The second way in which a customs union could be formed was for all the German states to accept the tariff of one of their number and to enter its customs administration. It was in this way that Prussia built up the *Zollverein* on the basis of her own tariff. Prussia worked for her own interests, but it happened that, on this occasion, Prussia's interests coincided with those of Germany as a whole. In the year before List drew up his petition on the need to abolish internal customs duties in Germany, Prussia had undertaken a drastic reform of her own tariff. Its author, Karl Georg von Maassen, had no intention of drawing up a tariff that would one day prove to be suitable for the whole of Germany. He was concerned with devising a tariff that would produce sufficient revenue, give Prussian manufacturers some protection against foreign competition and reduce smuggling to a minimum. He rejected the prohibitions and high duties that had been features of Prussia's tariff in Frederick the Great's reign. Instead he introduced a liberal tariff that swept away some sixty internal duties, abolished prohibitions, admitted raw materials free of duty and levied import and consumption duties of only 10 per cent on manufactured goods and 20 to 30 per cent on colonial goods and wines. Duties were specific — levied by weight or some other appropriate unit — and were not levied according to value. Special provisions applied to salt and playing cards, which were state monopolies. A less liberal feature of the tariff was the transit duty of ½ thaler a hundredweight on goods crossing the country. Foreign countries naturally complained about this levy on international commerce. Despite the transit dues the Maassen Tariff was the most liberal in Europe in the 1820s. Huskisson, speaking in the House of Commons, summarized the main features of the Prussian Tariff and declared: 'I trust that the time will come when we shall be able to say as much for the tariff in this country.' But 20 years elapsed before Peel's fiscal reforms gave Britain a tariff as liberal as that of Prussia.

Soon after the introduction of the new tariff the civil servants in Prussia responsible for the administration of customs and excise began to tackle the problem of the enclaves. These were lands of other German states that were surrounded by Prussian territory. From them foreign goods were smuggled into Prussia. To stop the smuggling the Prussian government tried to persuade the states concerned to allow their enclaves to be administered as part of the Prussian customs system. The first negotiations to be successfully concluded were with Schwarzburg-Sondershausen. Two-thirds of this little state were an enclave in Prussian territory. It was agreed that the enclave should form a customs union with Prussia. Between 1819 and 1830 Prussia made similar arrangements concerning all the other enclaves. The Anhalt duchies proved to be the most obdurate, but eventually they were persuaded to fall into line. The enclave treaties contained provisions that were later applied to larger states that became part of the Prussian customs system. The customs revenue, for example, was divided according to the size of the population of the states that joined the Zollverein. In the negotiations concerning the enclaves the Prussian civil servants gained valuable experience, which stood them in good stead in subsequent negotiations with larger German states. They learned to respect the determination of even the smallest territory to safeguard its sovereign independence. They learned how to persuade small neighbours to overcome their deep-rooted suspicion of Prussia's policy.

Meanwhile the failure of the Confederation to set up a German Zollverein was followed in the 1820s by attempts in southern and western Germany to establish a smaller regional customs union. For 5 years — from 1820 to 1825 — meetings were held in Darmstadt and Stuttgart between representatives of Bavaria, Baden, Württemberg, Hesse-Darmstadt and some smaller states. When these negotiations failed, Bavaria and Württemberg formed a southern German customs union in January 1828.

Three weeks later a northern German customs union was established between Prussia and Hesse-Darmstadt. Motz, the able Finance Minister of Prussia, was anxious to bridge the gap between the eastern and western provinces of Prussia by persuading Hanover, Brunswick and Hesse-Cassel to join the Prussian customs system. But these states were determined to maintain their economic independence. Then the government of Hesse-Darmstadt approached Prussia with a view to the establishment of a customs union. Although the adhesion of this state to the Prussian customs system would not link the eastern and western provinces of Prussia, Motz felt that a customs union between the two states would increase Prussia's influence in northern Germany. The negotiations were successfully completed and Motz had taken the first step towards the establishment of a German customs union based on the Prussian tariff. Treitschke wrote that 'at all the courts the first vague intelligence from Berlin was received with indescribable alarm, the news falling into the diplomatic world like a bombshell'. Many of the smaller German states feared that the customs union between Prussia and Hesse-Darmstadt would be the first step towards the extension of Prussia's economic and political power over her smaller neighbours. Foreign governments — particularly those of Austria, France and Britain — did not relish any extension of Prussia's commercial influence.

With Metternich's blessing a third customs union was set up in Germany in September 1828. This was the Middle German Commercial Union, which was deliberately created as a rival to the union between Prussia and Hesse-Darmstadt. It was formed by Hanover, Brunswick, Hesse-Cassel, Nassau, Frankfurt-am-Main, Saxony and the Thuringian states. The Middle German Commercial Union had two aims. The first was to prevent any extension of the Prussian customs system and to stop the forging of any link between the northern and southern unions. To this end the members of the Middle German Commercial Union pledged themselves not to join any other union. The second aim was to keep open routes for international trade that did not cross Prussian territory and therefore avoided paying the transit dues that Prussia levied on through traffic. The Middle German Commercial Union proposed to build new roads that would enable trade to flow from the North Sea ports of Hamburg and Bremen to Leipzig and Frankfurt-am-Main, which were important commercial centres, famous for their international fairs. The British representative at Frankfurt-am-Main cheerfully observed that the Middle German Commercial Union 'would afford immense facilities for carrying on the contraband trade in the dominions of Prussia, Bavaria, Württemberg and [Hesse-]Darmstadt'. No wonder that Treitschke later denounced the union as 'a malicious and unnatural conspiracy against the Fatherland'.

The Middle German Commercial Union failed to achieve its objectives. The projected roads were not built. The members of the union, united only by a common hostility to Prussia, were jealous of each other. Each feared that a proposed new road would be of greater benefit to a neighbour than to itself. Torn by internal dissensions, the union could not withstand Prussia's implacable hostility. In May 1829 Prussia concluded a commercial treaty with the Bavaria-Württemberg customs union, which provided for preferential trading arrangements between the two tariff regions. Then Prussia effectively turned the tables on the Middle German Commercial Union by persuading two of its members — the tiny states of Meiningen and Gotha — to permit the building of two Prussian roads through their territories to link the northern and southern customs unions. No transit dues were levied on these roads. A firm economic link between northern and southern Germany had been forged. In 1831 the signing of a treaty between Prussia and Holland facilitated navigation on the River Rhine and gave the southern German states an improved route for their overseas trade.

Finally in 1831 Prussia secured the adhesion of Hesse-Cassel to her customs system and so welded her eastern and western provinces into a single economic unit. When a new road between Wanfried and Mühlhausen had been opened — linking Hesse-Cassel and the Prussian province of Saxony — it was possible for goods to be sent from Aachen on the Belgian frontier to Memel on the Russian frontier, without having to cross a single tariff barrier. These events led to the fall of the Middle German Commercial Union. In a memorandum of 11 June 1831 Metternich warned the Emperor Francis I that the creation of a German customs union under Prussian leadership would be a serious challenge to Austria's influence over the Confederation. In a last effort to check the establishment of the Zollverein, Hanover — supported by Austria and Britain — suggested to the Federal Diet that negotiations for the formation of a customs union should be opened on the basis of Article 19 of the Federal Act. But Prussia — with her own customs union within her grasp — was not interested in these discussions and nothing came of them.

Meanwhile Prussia was negotiating with the southern German states and with some members of the Middle German Commercial Union to secure their adhesion to the Prussian customs system. In 1833 agreement was reached with Bavaria and Württemberg in March, with the Thuringian states in May, and with the kingdom of Saxony in October. The treaties linking eighteen states with a population of nearly 23.5 million, came into force on 1 January 1834. Thirty years later Gustav Fischer recalled the enthusiasm with which the Germans had greeted the founding of the Zollverein. He wrote: 'The older generation can still remember how joyfully the opening hour of the year 1834 was welcomed by the trading world. Long trains of waggons stood on the main roads, which till then had been obstructed by tax barriers. At the stroke of midnight every turnpike was thrown open, and amid cheers the waggons hastened over the frontiers which they could thenceforward cross in perfect freedom. Everyone felt that a great object had been attained.'

By the treaties of 1833 all members of the customs union agreed to adopt the Prussian tariff and to allow Prussia to represent the Zollverein in negotiations with foreign countries. Officials of the member states continued to collect duties, the revenues being divided according to population. Changes in the tariff were made at a general congress to be held every 2 years. Since a unanimous vote was needed to pass a resolution at the general congress it was clear that the members of the Zollverein were clinging tenaciously to their sovereign rights as independent states.

It needed all the skill and patience of the Prussian civil servants to overcome the difficulties caused by the existence of the veto at the general congress. Long discussions — and hard bargaining — took place between Prussia and the governments of the member states before each general congress. A meeting of the congress was generally a purely formal affair. Contentious matters did not appear on the agenda and the decisions taken had been previously agreed upon in private negotiations. The Zollverein was not a permanent institution. It was first established for 8 years and was subsequently renewed for two periods of 12 years. When the Zollverein treaties were renewed, Prussia had an opportunity of insisting that other members of the customs union should accept changes that had previously been vetoed by one or more states at the general congress.

Some characteristics of the Zollverein deserve notice. While Austria dominated the Confederation at this time, Prussia was the leading state in the Zollverein. In December 1833, on the eve of the founding of the customs union, the Austrian delegate to the Diet of the Confederation wrote: 'The Zollverein is one of the chief nails in the coffin of the German Confederation . . . . Prussia is now taking over the actual leadership of Germany's policy, Austria's leadership being merely formal'. Prussia's leading position was recognized since the headquarters of the organization were in Berlin and Prussia was responsible for negotiations on behalf of the Zollverein.

Although the members of the Zollverein jealously guarded their sovereignty and did not hesitate to threaten to use the veto at the general congress, Prussia could eventually get her way by refusing to renew the Zollverein treaties when they expired. Recalcitrant members might protest, but in the end they gave way. No state that joined the customs union ever left it. The main reason was that membership of the Zollverein conferred undoubted financial advantages on nearly all the members except Prussia. At a time when indirect taxation — mainly revenues from customs and excise duties — was far more important to a minister of finance than direct taxation, the German states soon realized that their income from customs duties was larger than it had been before they joined the Zollverein.

The Zollverein was not a democratic organization. The delegates appointed to the general congress were not elected but were appointed by the various governments. They voted in accordance with government instructions. Since Prussia had no parliament at this time, there was no way in which public opinion could directly influence the policy of the largest and most important member of the Zollverein. Industrialists and merchants could express their views only through the press or by petitioning their own government. The Zollverein was a national institution, since only German states were admitted. Various suggestions were made that neighbouring states, such as Belgium or Holland, might be persuaded to join, but Prussia refused to agree to such proposals.

The Zollverein was not a common market. It was concerned only with the administration of the customs and with tariff negotiations with foreign countries. Experience showed, however, that the operation of a common tariff led to cooperation on other matters. In 1838, for example, the collection of customs duties in the Zollverein was facilitated by fixing a permanent ratio between the coinages of Prussia and the southern German states. In 1847 agreements were reached on a code governing bills of exchange and on the establishment of the Association of German Railway Administrations. In 1850 a German postal convention made it possible for prepaid letters to be sent to all parts of Germany and Austria by the shortest route.

The first Zollverein treaties, which came into force in 1834, had only 8 years to run. In that period Prussia tried to convince her partners that they had taken the right decision when joining the Zollverein and that they should renew their membership in 1842. Prussia hoped to show her partners that they would gain financial advantages from membership of the customs union and that they would obtain better terms in negotiations with foreign countries than they could secure on their own. In addition Prussia was determined to extend the customs union to include as many German states as possible.

A number of German states did not join the Zollverein when it was founded. They included Hanover, Brunswick, Oldenburg, Mecklenburg-Strelitz, Mecklenburg-Schwerin, Holstein, Hamburg, Bremen and Lübeck in the north and Baden, Nassau, Luxembourg and Frankfurt-am-Main in the west. Baden joined the Zollverein in 1835.

Nebenius, her Minister of the Interior, had for many years been a strong supporter of tariff unification in Germany. Nassau adhered to the customs union in 1835, Frankfurt-am-Main in 1836 and Luxembourg in 1842. France failed to prevent Nassau from joining and Britain was unable to stop Frankfurt-am-Main from joining. The adhesion of these small states increased the population of the Zollverein to over 25 million.

On the other hand Hanover, the three Hansa towns and some other small states in the north of Germany refused to join the Zollverein. In 1834 Hanover and Brunswick formed a rival customs union — the Tax Union — to which Oldenburg and Lippe-Schaumburg subsequently adhered. It lasted for 20 years, though Brunswick's scattered territories were absorbed in the Zollverein between 1837 and 1844. The refusal of Hanover, Hamburg and Bremen to join deprived the Zollverein of direct access to the North Sea. The growing overseas trade of the Zollverein was in the hands of independent ports over which Prussia and her partners had no control.

Prussia's negotiations with foreign countries on behalf of the Zollverein were not uniformly successful at this time. The concessions granted to Holland in 1839 — particularly the reduction of the duty on Dutch refined and partially refined sugar — were, according to Treitschke, 'both a bad blunder, and a departure from the fundamental principles of the Zollverein, which normally rejected all differential duties but on this occasion granted dangerous privileges to an unfriendly neighbour'. Vigorous protests from the sugar lobby forced Prussia to think again. The treaty was allowed to lapse when it expired after three years.

On the other hand Prussia's negotiations with Britain secured undoubted benefits for German merchants and shippers. Austria had gained a valuable concession from Britain in 1838, when Britain had agreed to give most-favoured-nation treatment to Austrian exports from certain ports on the Elbe and Danube that lay outside Austria. These non-Austrian ports — Hamburg for example — were now regarded as 'natural outlets' for Austrian exports as far as the British navigation code was concerned. Prussia demanded similar concessions and got them. In 1841 Britain agreed that the Zollverein, too, had 'natural outlets' beyond its own borders for its overseas commerce. Ships from Zollverein states coming to Britain from North Sea ports between the Elbe and the Meuse were to be treated as if they came from a Zollverein port.

If Prussia's partners in the Zollverein regarded her negotiations with foreign countries with mixed feelings, they were virtually unanimous in expressing satisfaction with the financial results of the Zollverein in the early years of its existence. Bavaria, for example, drew 3,860,000 florins (12 florins = £1) in customs revenue from the Zollverein in 1834, as compared with 2,100,000 florins in 1831-2. Every year Prussia made substantial payments to her partners in the Zollverein except Saxony. At the end of 1839 the Prussian Government stated that 'it had received no declaration from any members of the Zollverein which left any doubts as to their genuine desire to preserve the customs union'. Little was now heard of the fears expressed so vehemently only a few years previously by certain industries and regions that ruin awaited them if they were forced to face competition from neighbouring German states. The Zollverein was renewed in 1842 without difficulty. Indeed Bavaria successfully pressed for the new treaties to run for 12 years, although Prussia had originally suggested 6 years.

Although the industrial development of the country had undoubtedly been stimulated by the founding of the Zollverein, German manufacturers and merchants realized that more rapid progress could be made if other aspects of economic life—in addition to tariffs—could be brought under unified control. In 1843, for example, the *Düsseldorfer Zeitung*, a leading newspaper in the Rhineland, complained that

. . . we have instead of one Germany, 38 German states, almost the same number of courts, as many representative bodies, 38 distinct legal codes and administrations, embassies and consulates. What an enormous saving it would be if all of that were taken care of by one central government . . . Yet far worse than the present waste of money is the fact that in these 38 states prevail as many separate interests which injure and destroy each other down to the last detail of daily intercourse. No post can be hurried, no mailing charge reduced without special conventions, no railway can be planned without each seeking to keep it in its own state as long as possible.

In 1841, the year before the Zollverein treaties were renewed for the first time, Friedrich List's *The National System of Political Economy* was published. This book—the Bible of the German protectionists—and articles that List contributed to the *Zollvereinsblatt* and the Augsburg *Allgemeine Zeitung* heralded the opening of a controversy on fiscal policy in Germany. The controversy was in certain respects different from the struggle between the free-traders and the protectionists in England. While England had a protectionist tariff with high corn laws and a strict navigation code, the Zollverein had the most liberal tariff in Europe. Consequently the English free-traders took the offensive and the protectionists were on the defensive. In Germany it was the protectionists who attacked the existing tariff, while the free-traders defended it and demanded that it should be made even more liberal. In England the agricultural interest — landowners and tenant farmers — generally supported protection, while the manufacturers normally supported the Anti-Corn Law League. In Germany, however, the owners of the great estates east of the Elbe were free-traders, while certain industrialists — many ironmasters and textile manufacturers — were protectionists. In England the free-traders won a decisive victory with Sir Robert Peel's reform of the tariff, the repeal of the corn laws, the ending of imperial preference and the abolition of the navigation laws. In Germany the first phase of the struggle ended in stalemate. By 1848 a few concessions had been made to the protectionists, but most Zollverein import duties continued to be levied at much lower rates than those of other countries on the Continent.

Friedrich List had long been a champion of economic unification and railway building. He denounced the theories of the English classical economists as being too 'cosmopolitan' and argued that the policy of each state should be based upon 'national' economic doctrines suited to its own particular needs. He held that the State was the natural unit of economic production and that the State should stimulate agriculture and industry to increase its own power and to raise the standard of living of its citizens.

In List's view the 'national' system of economics, appropriate to Germany in the 1840s, was one of protection. List paid lip service to the ideal of free trade. He suggested that at some time in the future, when the major manufacturing countries had attained the same level of industrial efficiency, it would be to their advantage to drop high import duties and adopt a policy of free trade. But List argued that when he was writing, Britain (having experienced an industrial revolution before other countries under the shelter of a policy of protection) had become the workshop of the world. Her advanced industries could produce manufactured goods more cheaply than any of her rivals.

There was a grave danger that Britain would dominate world markets completely and crush all rival industries before they had a chance to develop. List argued that, in these circumstances, the German customs union should impose high tariffs on English imports, so as to give growing German industries a breathing space in which to catch up with their more efficient English rivals. This was the 'infant industry' argument in favour of protection and it was hardly surprising that it was enthusiastically supported by those German manufacturers who had most reason to fear competition from Britain.

A General German Union for the Protection of Home Industries was established as a pressure group to agitate in favour of high protective duties. This union made little headway. Its influence was seen in 1847, when the Prussian government put forward a project for founding a Shipping and Commercial Union between the Zollverein and other German states. If Hamburg and Bremen signed the proposed agreement, differential duties could be levied on the goods imported in the ships of countries like Britain, which maintained restrictive navigation laws. But the plan fell through. List's followers also received some support from Friedrich von Rönne, the head of the recently established Board of Trade in Prussia, but his influence was effectively checked by the more powerful Ministry of Finance, which favoured a moderate rather than a high tariff. On the whole the agitation in favour of protection had not achieved much success by 1848.

The free-trade cause in Germany was championed by John Prince Smith, an English schoolmaster who lived in the small Baltic port of Elbing. His pamphlet *Über Handelsfeindseligkeit* was published 2 years after the appearance of List's *The National System of Political Economy*. Prince Smith argued that although the Maassen Tariff had been a liberal one when it came into force, it had become more protectionist in recent years. In 1844, for example, the Zollverein duty on pig-iron—except Belgian pig-iron—had been raised to £1 a ton. Moreover since Zollverein duties were levied on weight or quantity, the fall in prices in the 1830s had automatically increased duties when calculated by value. Dr John Bowring told the Select Committee on Import Duties that German import duties on manufactured goods, which had once been no more than 10 per cent *ad valorem*, had now risen to as high as 'from 60 to 100 per cent'.

Prince Smith argued that the Zollverein should adopt a free-trade policy, since protection led to tariff wars, which injured those who levied high import duties as much as those against whom the duties were directed. 'If England increases the price of bread of its citizens why should Prussia as a reprisal raise the cost of the cotton goods consumed by its people?' Prince Smith also echoed the argument put forward by Cobden and Bright that world free trade would lead to universal peace. Prince Smith became known to a wider public when he drew up an address on behalf of the merchants of Elbing congratulating Sir Robert Peel on the triumph of free trade in England. In his reply Peel claimed that all would benefit from the maximum interchange of goods between the countries of the world. In 1847 Prince Smith set up a Free Trade Union in Berlin and attended an international conference of free-traders in Brussels. Two years later he set up an association of German Free Trade societies. The free-trade movement enjoyed the support of the Prussian junkers, the merchants of ports such as Hamburg, Bremen and Danzig and of inland centres of commerce such as Leipzig and Frankfurt-am-Main, as well as some leading figures in the professions.

The Prussian civil servants responsible for Zollverein affairs had been educated at universities at which the doctrines of the classical English economists were taught. They considered the existing Zollverein tariff to be suited to Germany's economic needs and were opposed to the demands of List and his supporters. In a pamphlet entitled *Der deutsche Zollverein während der Jahre 1834 bis 1845*, Kühne (the Director General of Taxes) observed that in the first 11 years of its existence the revenues of the Zollverein had increased by nearly 90 per cent, although the population had increased by only 21 per cent. Nearly all members of the Zollverein had secured considerably increased revenues from customs duties. In addition the administrative expenses had been halved. By implication Kühne was warning the critics of the Zollverein — particularly the protectionists — that drastic changes in the tariff might have unwelcome financial repercussions. The outbreak of revolution in 1848 halted, for the time being, the controversy between the free-traders and the protectionists.

3 Railways

In 1825—the year in which the Stockton to Darlington railway was opened—Goethe wrote that 'railways, express mails, steamboats and all possible means of communication are what the educated world seeks'. Three years later he declared that Germany's 'good roads and future railways' would one day promote national unity. At this time Britain was the leading industrial country in the world and she had achieved this position without railways. Other forms of communication—roads, rivers, canals and coastal shipping—had met her transport requirements in her early phase of industrial expansion. But in Germany and elsewhere on the Continent the situation was different because it was the construction of railways that promoted the expansion of manufactures. It has been suggested that railway building was 'the most important single stimulus to industrial growth in western Europe'. Unlike Britain—where a network of private railways using horse traction had been laid down in the latter part of the eighteenth century—Germany had little previous experience of railway construction. Only a very few industrial lines (using horse traction) had been built, such as the Clausthal (Harz), Himmelfürst (Ruhr) and Gerhard (Saar) mineral railways, a line in a Berlin foundry and Gerstner's 'salt railway' (Linz-Budweis) in the Salzkammergut in Austria. Lack of technical knowledge made it necessary to use locomotives—such as the *Adler* and the *Pfeil* on the Nürnberg-Fürth line—which had been built in England and were driven by Englishmen.

Soon after the Napoleonic Wars the advantages of railways were recognized by some of the more far-seeing industrialists and civil servants in Germany. Between 1825 and 1835 various railway projects were discussed in the Rhineland, Westphalia and Upper Silesia, where modern industries were already developing. In March 1825 Friedrich Harkort of Wetter, the founder of Germany's first machine-building plant, wrote in the journal *Herrmann* about the Stockton and Darlington Railway. He urged his countrymen to lose no time in building a network of railways themselves. In 1828 he established Germany's first joint-stock railway company, which built a narrow-gauge line in the Ruhr from the Himmelfürst colliery at Überruhr to Kupferdreh, on which coaltrucks were drawn by horses. In the same year it was suggested that a railway should be built to link Upper Silesia with Austria. The plan was submitted by Count Renard to Christian von Rother, the director of the State Overseas Trading Corporation, but it was turned down.

In December 1830 Harkort laid before the Westphalian provincial assembly (*Landtag*) a plan to link the valleys of the Lippe and the Weser by a railway running from Minden to Lippstadt. A similar plan had already been put forward in 1827 by Krüger (an official of the Prussian Ministry of Finance) and in 1829 by the mining engineer Carl von Oeynhausen. Motz, the Prussian Minister of Finance, had been impressed by a report on English railways written by von Oeynhausen and his colleague Heinrich von Decken. At this time Motz was trying to persuade Holland to abolish the dues levied at the mouths of the Rhine. He considered that if he failed it might be possible to provide the Rhineland and Westphalia with a new route to the North Sea—by-passing Holland—by the construction of a railway from Minden to Lippstadt. But the king of Prussia turned down a suggestion that the government might give financial aid to this project, mainly on the ground that the road from Minden to Lippstadt was adequate for existing traffic.

Three pamphlets, published in 1833, showed that there was increasing public interest in the construction of railways in Germany. The best known is that by Friedrich List. It was addressed to 'the highest public authorities in the kingdom of Saxony'. List, who had already been largely responsible for building a 21-mile mineral line in the Blue Mountains in the United States, now advocated the construction of a railway between Dresden and Leipzig, which would form the nucleus of a railway network not only for the kingdom of Saxony but for the whole of Germany. List declared that he 'could not observe the astonishing results of railway building in England and in North America without desiring that my German Fatherland should derive similar advantages from railways'. He argued that the main benefits conferred by railways were to facilitate the movement of raw materials to the factories and of manufactured goods to the shops. Railways would bring about 'an extraordinary expansion in the productive powers of society'. The map of proposed lines that List included in his brochure was a remarkably accurate forecast of the future German railway network.

In the same year Friedrich Harkort wrote a pamphlet advocating the construction of a railway between Cologne and Minden, which would link the Rhine and the Weser. Although commercial considerations were uppermost in his mind Harkort was one of the first to draw attention to the military advantages of railways. He wrote that '150 railway carriages could take a brigade from Minden to the Rhine in a day and a telegraph line from Mainz to Wesel would make it impossible for the French to cross the Rhine'. The third pamphlet, which appeared in 1833, was written by Ludolf Camphausen, a corn merchant who was one of the youngest members of the city council of Cologne. He declared that the future prosperity of the Rhineland depended upon the opening up of a new route to the sea over which the Dutch had no control. Motz had suggested that a line from Minden to Lippstadt would serve this purpose. Now Camphausen proposed the construction of a railway from Cologne to Antwerp. The success of his scheme depended upon the cooperation of the Prussian and Belgian governments to waive transit dues on the proposed railway.

Although several railway projects had been discussed in Prussia and in Saxony, the first German railway to be opened—the Ludwig Railway — was in Bavaria. This was the 4-mile line between Nürnberg and Fürth, a railway suggested by the mining engineer Joseph von Baader as early as 1814. In the 1830s King Ludwig was an enthusiastic supporter of railway projects. He sent the architect Leo von Klenze to study railway developments in England, Belgium and France and he considered various plans for building lines to link Bavaria with Prussia in the north and with Austria in the south. But the king's interest in railways was short-lived and he was soon immersed in plans to build his *Fossa Carolina* —a new waterway to link the Rhine and the Danube.

The money to build Germany's first railway was raised by some of the wealthy citizens of Nürnberg with little aid from the king of Bavaria. Government support was limited to the purchase of two shares at 100 florins each. The driving-force behind the plan came from Burgomaster Johann Scharrer. Many difficulties had to be overcome, not the least being the high cost of land. Bavaria had no expropriation law by which property could be compulsorily purchased for the construction of public works. The line was opened in December 1835 and was served by a locomotive (*Der Adler*) built by Robert Stephenson and driven by an English crew. Unlike early English and French lines, which were built primarily to transport minerals, the Nurnberg-Fürth railway was constructed to carry passengers. No freight was handled for 6 months and then two barrels of beer were conveyed with passenger tickets. The little line proved to be particularly convenient to Jewish businessmen, who worked in Nürnberg during the day but — by ancient custom—did not sleep there at night.

Three years elapsed before two other short suburban lines were opened in Germany. One was the Berlin-Potsdam railway (16 miles) which was built by a private company, and the other was the nationalized Brunswick-Wolfenbüttel line.

Meanwhile in the kingdom of Saxony the government had authorized the construction of a much longer line. This was the 72-mile railway between Dresden and Leipzig that List had recommended. As soon as a company had been floated to raise the necessary capital, List went to Berlin to try to secure concessions for lines to link Berlin with Magdeburg and Hamburg. In his railway journal (*Eisenbahnjournal*) he argued that short-sighted rivalries between German states should not be allowed to prevent the planning of a railway network for the whole country. The advantages gained by cooperation on tariffs through the Zollverein would be greatly increased by cooperation on communications. But List's mission to Berlin achieved no results and he soon found himself at loggerheads with members of the committee responsible for building the Dresden-Leipzig railway. Apart from clashes of personalities, the main difference of opinion concerned the purpose of the line. The committee wanted a railway that would serve the economic interests of the kingdom of Saxony, while List wanted a line that would be the nucleus of a future German network of railways.

List had recommended that the line should run across the Mulde highlands by way of Meissen but, on the advice of an English engineer, an alternative route through Riesa was chosen to avoid as many hills as possible. Even so a tunnel 561 yards long had to be built at Oberau and this was constructed by skilled men from the Freiberg mines. The Dresden-Leipzig railway — Germany's first long line — was opened in April 1839. Stephenson's English gauge was adopted. The first locomotive, the *Comet*, came from England and was driven by an Englishman. The shareholders who (on a single day) had raised the funds necessary to build the line had every reason to be satisfied with their investment. Until it was nationalized in 1876 the Leipzig-Dresden line was one of the most successful private railways in Germany.

The success of the line between Dresden and Leipzig provided the impetus for railway building throughout the country. In the 1840s investors in Germany — as in England — were eager to buy railway shares. The opposition of governments and public officials to the new form of transport was gradually overcome. The attitude of civil servants in Prussia can be seen from a report on railways submitted to the king by Christian von Rother in 1835. He did not go quite as far as Thiers, who declared that although the citizens of Paris could not be stopped from having their railway as a toy, the line would never carry a passenger or a piece of luggage. But Rother clearly had a poor opinion of the prospects of railways. He argued that existing roads and waterways were adequate for the transport of passengers and freight. He dismissed as exaggerations the glowing accounts given by promoters of the success of English and American railways. He considered that the lines already in existence on the Continent had been expensive to construct and were not paying adequate dividends. In his opinion the exchequer would suffer if railways were built, since revenues from road tolls would fall.

In the circumstances Rother advised the king not to sanction the building of state railways or to give financial aid to private railway companies. Nagler, the head of the Prussian post-office was also strongly opposed to the construction of railways. And when it became clear that nothing could stop the advent of railways, some German governments were determined that the new means of transport must be owned and operated by the State. In Bavaria, for example, Minister President Karl von Abel declared in 1845 that the government would in no circumstances allow railways—'whose owners can, up to a point, dominate the country's entire commercial and passenger traffic'—to be run by private companies. Brunswick, Baden, Hanover and Oldenburg—following the example of Belgium—built nationalized railways from the first, while in Bavaria and Baden many of the main lines were run by the State.

In Prussia railway building in the 1840s was left to private enterprise. Joint-stock companies built all the early lines — Berlin-Potsdam in 1838; Magdeburg-Leipzig in 1840; Düsseldorf-Elberfeld and Berlin-Köthen (Anhalt Railway) in 1841; Berlin-Frankfurt-an-der-Oder and Cologne to the Belgian frontier (Rhenish Railway) in 1843; Deutz (Cologne)-Minden in 1847; and Elberfeld-Hagen (Berg-Mark Railway) in 1848-9. It was not until 1852 that Prussia's first nationalized railway was completed. This was a line between Saarbrücken and Neunkirchen in the Saar coalfield.

These developments were hardly in accordance with Prussia's traditions, since the State had been accustomed to control the various forms of communication. The state post-office, for example, was not only responsible for the conveyance of the mail but its coaches carried many passengers on the main roads. But at this time the Prussian government did not have the capital available to build a network of railways, even if it had favoured the rapid expansion of railways. It was not possible for the State to raise railway loans, since the National Debt Law of January 1820 forbade any borrowing by the government in excess of 18 million thalers without parliamentary approval and no popular assembly was called until 1847. All that the government was able to do was to buy blocks of shares in some railway companies to guarantee interest on certain railway shares and loans. The money paid to shareholders when their dividends failed to reach the stipulated amount was generally recovered, since the companies concerned had to contribute to the government's Railway Fund whatever they earned above 5 per cent on their capital. So those who invested in the less successful railway companies were subsidized by the shareholders of the more prosperous companies. The Prussian Railway Fund was established in 1843, its revenues being derived from a variety of sources such as a railway tax and some of the profits from the state salt monopoly. The resources of the fund were used to guarantee the interest on new railway shares and loans. The railways were built in accordance with the Railway Law of November 1838. This assumed that the railway network would be built by private entrepreneurs and it provided regulations for the construction and running of the railways. When the concessions expired, the State had the right to nationalize the lines.

In the 1840s Germany expanded her network of railways more rapidly than any country on the Continent except Belgium. In 1847 Bourgoing, the French representative in Munich, wrote to Guizot: 'The German railway system is being daily extended and completed with an ever increasing activity which enables one to forecast that this country will be far ahead of other continental states in this respect.' Germany had 3,660 miles of railway in operation in 1850, which was nearly double that of France. By 1860 'the German lines formed by far the most impressive network of railway in continental Europe'. While in England and France the major railways radiated from the capital, there was no city that dominated the whole railway system in Germany. The three most important railway centres were Berlin, Cologne and Munich. By 1848, when the revolution slowed down railway construction, railways already radiated from Berlin to Stettin,

Hamburg, Anhalt, Magdeburg and Breslau. Only the line to Danzig was lacking. Berlin was linked with the railways of neighbouring states such as Hanover and Saxony and had direct access to the North Sea, the Baltic and the industrial regions of the Ruhr, Silesia and Saxony. In the Rhineland Cologne was the centre of railways running to Minden (by way of the Ruhr), Aachen (for Antwerp) and Bonn. When the gap between Bonn and Mainz had been closed, Cologne would be linked by rail with Basel and the Swiss railway system. Less progress had been made in the south, but Munich was soon to be linked with Leipzig and the railways of central Germany.

Certain characteristics of early German railway building deserve mention. No joint action for the construction of railways was taken either by the Confederation or by the Zollverein. List's plea for a united railway system went unheeded. There was no overall plan as in France. The German railway system—like the English system—was built up piecemeal. In the early days there was what has been called a 'spontaneous anarchy of petty companies'. There were rivalries between different states over railway building and there were disputes between towns and districts in the same state. There were disputes between Leipzig and Halle-an-der-Saale, Darmstadt and Mainz, Cologne and Aachen. There was no uniform method of running the railways. Some were built and operated by joint-stock companies — with or without government assistance — while others were constructed and run by the State as nationalized lines. Railway construction was rapid and was facilitated by the cheapness of land, rails and labour. The German lines cost much less to build per mile than the English railways. There were few geographical difficulties to be overcome. It was easy to build lines across the northern German plain, where the great rivers proved to be the only obstacle. Many years elapsed before railway bridges were built over the Rhine to link Cologne and Deutz and over the Elbe to link Hamburg and Harburg. In the south the Alps and their foothills were a more serious obstacle to railway building and Bavaria had to overcome difficulties similar to those faced by Austria and Switzerland in constructing their railway networks. The position of Germany in central Europe enabled German railways to handle a profitable international traffic. Freight and passengers moving from France, Belgium and Holland to eastern Europe or from Hamburg and Bremen to southern Europe had to pass through Germany.

The railways soon stimulated Germany's industrial progress. New firms of contractors and a new labour force sprang up to lay the tracks and to build bridges and stations. New engineering firms supplied locomotives and rolling-stock and provided facilities for maintenance and repairs. Iron-foundries were inundated with orders for nails and wheels. At first some railway equipment was imported—particularly from England and Belgium—but Germany soon depended less and less upon foreign supplies. Borsig of Berlin, Henschel of Cassel, Hartmann of Chemnitz, Klett of Nürnberg and Maffei of Munich were some of the engineering firms that specialized in the construction of locomotives and the manufacture of railway equipment.

When a railway was built a new form of transport operated by a new labour force was created. There were new jobs for engine drivers, firemen, guards, porters, signalmen and clerks. The building of new lines brought the contracting industry into existence and gave employment to many skilled mechanics and an army of navvies. Existing industries — coal and iron — were expanded to supply fuel and rails to the railways. New industries sprang up, such as railway engineering and railway telegraphy. The electric telegraph owed much to the inventive genius of Werner Siemens. As the network of railways was extended, new markets were made available for German industrial and agricultural products. Manufactures from the industrial regions of the Rhineland and Westphalia could be exchanged for the farm products of the agrarian provinces east of the Elbe. When the railways reached Hamburg, Bremen, Stettin and Antwerp, goods that had formerly been sold only at home could be exported. It was the railways that promoted the rapid growth of the great cities of the Ruhr and Upper Silesia. The railways quickly turned Berlin into a major centre of industry, commerce and finance. The courtiers, civil servants, professors and students were joined by manufacturers, merchants, stockbrokers and bankers.

Older forms of transport did not at first suffer from competition from the railways. In England the railways put many canal companies out of business, but in Germany the traffic on the roads and inland waterways increased. Indeed some of the early railways — Elberfeld-Düsseldorf, Frankfurt-am-Main — Mainz, Darmstadt-Mannheim — stimulated river traffic by widening the hinterland of inland ports. In 1840s the establishment of two companies to operate steam-tugs on the Rhine greatly expanded the transport of coal and other bulky commodities by barges.

Certain drawbacks to railway development were inevitable. Some of the fairs and markets declined when the railways provided new facilities for industrialists to get into touch with wholesalers and for commercial travellers to call on retailers. The greatest triumph of the German railways was to ensure the success of the Zollverein. By itself the abolition of many internal tariffs might not have immediately given German industry the stimulus needed to promote rapid growth. But the Zollverein and the railways together set Germany on the road to industrial success.

No immediate political repercussions were to be seen from the construction of railways, but in the long run the new means of transport brought Germans close together and helped to break down the local prejudices and the isolationism that had once been a characteristic feature of the various states and provinces of the country. In a Germany served by express trains running from Aachen to Berlin, and from Hamburg to Munich, the Main gradually ceased to divide the north from the south, while the Elbe no longer separated the east from the west. Treitschke declared that 'the railways completed what the Zollverein had only begun . . . . They initiated such dramatic changes that even in the 1840s the German scene changed completely.' For Wilhelm Raabe 'the German Empire was founded with the construction of the first railway between Nürnberg and Fürth', while Karl Beck spoke of railway shares as 'bills drawn upon Germany's future unity'. A generation passed before Bismarck was able to bring the German states together into the Reich of 1871, but the foundations of unity had been laid by those who founded the Zollverein and built the railways.

4   *Industrial Expansion*

The first results of the establishment of the customs union and the building of railways could be seen in Germany between 1834 and 1850, when the output of the cotton, wool, coal, iron and engineering industries expanded. Factories began to be established and some steam-engines were installed in them. The number of steam-engines, including those driving locomotives and river steamships and tugs, rose from 400 in 1834 to 1,200 in 1850. Most of them were in the manufacturing districts of Prussia and Saxony, where they operated pumps, spinning-machines and powerlooms. In the iron industry the puddling process and the manufacture of crucible cast-steel were introduced.

In the early nineteenth century foreigners helped to promote the industrial growth of Germany, just as foreign merchants and middlemen had fostered the expansion of domestic industries in an earlier period. English capital and technical knowledge was represented by the younger William Cockerill, who made machinery for the woollen industry at Guben (Brandenburg) and at Grünberg (Lower Silesia); his brother James, who built similar machines at Aachen; and the operatives from Bradford, who introduced the powerloom weaving of woollen cloth to the *Maschinen-Wollen-Weberei* at Wüste Giersdorf in Lower Silesia. English engineers and mechanics were employed by Harkort at Wetter (Ruhr) and by Gleichmann & Busse at Hamburg. English puddlers were engaged by Remy & Hoesch at Rasselstein and at Lendersdorf, and by Count Hugo Henckel von Donnersmarck at the Laura foundry in Upper Silesia. And in the early days of the railways it was not unusual to find English drivers on the footplates of German locomotives. Belgian enterprise on the left bank of the Rhine included the establishment of a colliery company at Wurm, a machine-building plant at Aachen; and rolling-mills at Eschweiler. A Belgian firm at Aachen constructed the Rote Erde rolling-mills in 1846. Shortly afterwards the English traveller Banfield mentioned the activities of 'young Frenchmen, élèves of the École des Mines at Paris' in engineering plants in the Rhineland.

Coal

In the nineteenth century an expansion in the output of coal and iron was essential if the industrial sector of the economy was to grow rapidly. When the Zollverein was established Germany's output of coal was small — a mere 3,000,000 tons a year. Although Germany still had ample supplies of timber, the demand for coal was increasing in the 1840s, since this fuel was now being used to drive machinery and locomotives and to smelt iron-ore. But neither the public nor the private sector of the coal industry was able to make a quick response to this demand. Most of Germany's coal came from the three main coalfields in Prussia — the Ruhr, Upper Silesia and the Saar — and these produced only 3,200,000 tons in 1846. The deposits of coal lay in relatively remote regions near the frontiers and, particularly in winter, the roads were inadequate for the transport of coal. Only the construction of a network of railways could open up the coalfields. Again the strict application of the mining laws in Prussia discouraged private entrepreneurs from establishing new collieries.

In the valley of the Ruhr coal lay near the surface and it had been mined and quarried on a small scale for many years. Then prospectors discovered that there were hidden and deeper deposits to the north of the river. On 31 December 1838 a seam of coal 54 metres below the chalk and clay was discovered east of Essen, and in November 1839 another seam was found not far away. The Graf Beust mine, opened by Matthias Stinnes in 1841, the Präsident mine near Bochum and other collieries were established to exploit these deposits. From then onwards the history of the Ruhr was one of expansion northwards to the River Emscher. Between 1841 and 1849 twenty-four new pits were opened in the Ruhr. Problems of shaft construction, drainage and ventilation were successfully tackled. Steam-pumps and steam winding gear were introduced. It was found that five types of coal existed in the hidden coalfield — long flame-coals, gas-coals, coking-coals, semi-anthracite and anthracite. Each type could be used for a special purpose, such as smelting iron, driving steam-engines or making gas. The discovery in 1849 of blackband deposits — coal and iron-ore together — near Dortmund was significant for the future development of the Ruhr as a region of iron-foundries as well as coalmines.

The output of coal in the Ruhr reached 1,666,000 tons in 1850. In that year there were already in existence eight mines, each of which produced over 50,000 tons a year. The coal owners of the Ruhr — all private entrepreneurs — had to contend with many difficulties. It was not easy to raise money to establish or to expand mining enterprises and many small firms survived only by ploughing profits back into their business. One reason why local bankers and private investors hesitated to finance Ruhr companies was that in Prussia mining (unlike other industries) was under direct government supervision. Even the day-to-day working of collieries was controlled by mining inspectors. Vincke, the president of the province of Westphalia, argued that methods that had been suitable in the eighteenth century to raise standards of technical efficiency in a backward industry were no longer appropriate. Vincke also complained that taxes on mining were too high. They amounted to 10 per cent on the output — at the pithead — and were double those levied on the left bank of the Rhine. Government control and heavy taxation made it difficult to attract new capital to the Ruhr and this retarded the expansion of the coalfield. Vincke did not secure any reform of the Prussian mining laws but he was able to make some improvements in the communications of the Ruhr district. New highways were built, such as the arterial road from Wesel to Minden, and the navigation of the River Ruhr was improved. Private entrepreneurs — Matthias Stinnes of Mülheim and Franz Haniel of Ruhrort — promoted the transport of coal by water, and steam-tugs drawing coal barges became a familiar sight on the Rhine. When the Cologne-Minden railway company completed its line in 1847 a new era of expansion dawned for the Ruhr coalfield.

In the first half of the nineteenth century the coal deposits of Upper Silesia — part of a coalfield that stretched across the frontiers to Austria and Russia — were the most important in Germany. Coal production rose from a mere 311,000 tons in 1815 to 3,834,000 tons in 1850. There were many obstacles to the industrial development of Upper Silesia. While Lower Silesia had rich farm lands and a flourishing linen industry in the eighteenth century, Upper Silesia was an inhospitable, sparsely populated region of heaths, forests and hills. The nature and extent of its mineral wealth was not fully realized when Frederick the Great annexed the territory in 1742. The remote location of Silesia — between the Sudeten Mountains and the Polish Jura — isolated the region from the rest of Prussia. Facilities for transport by road were inadequate, while the River Oder was not navigable for vessels of any size above Breslau. In the autumn of 1844 the Halemba furnace had to close down for a time because the roads were impassable and supplies of iron-ore and fuel ran out. Moreover hostile tariffs restricted trade between Upper Silesia and Russia and Austria.

On the other hand there were favourable factors that promoted industrial growth in Upper Silesia. This region—unlike the Ruhr—was rich in other minerals besides coal, since it had deposits of iron, zinc, lead and silver. Frederick the Great and his successors had encouraged the economic development of Upper Silesia by establishing state coal-mines and ironworks. Three nationalized collieries were opened between 1786 and 1811 — the *Friedrichsgrube* at Tarnowitz, *Königs-grube* at Königshütte and the *Königin Luise Grube* at Zabrze. Several feudal magnates followed their sovereign's example and invested capital in the exploitation of the mineral resources of their great estates. Contrary to what happened in most modern manufacturing regions, industrial capitalism in Silesia evolved directly out of the former feudal economy. Feudal magnates became capitalist entrepreneurs and their serfs became miners and factory hands. While early mining operations in the Ruhr were run by individual proprietors, partners and companies, the mines of Upper Silesia were in the hands of either the State or the great landlords. As early as 1785, when 243 mines were in operation in Upper Silesia, 205 of them belonged to members of the aristocracy, 20 to the king of Prussia and only 2 to commoners.

The way in which the new labour force was brought together in the coalfield of Upper Silesia was different from what happened in other coalfields. After the emancipation of the serfs—and the process of freeing the serfs in Silesia was a slow one—some of the peasants, who had lost their smallholdings, became coalminers. The fact that many miners were Poles while their employers were Germans made the problem of industrial relations a particularly difficult one. In the early nineteenth century—although supplies of wood were still available—there was an increased demand for coal to smelt the various ores of Upper Silesia. These factors help to explain the boom in mining after the Napoleonic Wars. In 8 years — between 1815 and 1823 — the production of coal rose from 311,000 tons to 1,423,000 tons. A quarter of a century later the output of coal in Upper Silesia was twice that of the Ruhr.

The resources of Upper Silesia, like those of the Ruhr and the Saar, could be fully exploited only when railways had been built. By 1846 the industrial district had been linked by rail with Breslau and Berlin. In the following year the Upper Silesia Railway was extended to join the Austrian line to Cracow. The products of Upper Silesia could now reach the markets of Berlin and Vienna and the output of coal and pig-iron rapidly expanded in the 1850s.

The Saar was the third major coalfield in Germany. Most of the deposits lay in the Prussian province of the Rhineland but a few were to be found in the neighbouring Bavarian Palatinate and at St Avold in Lorraine. While the coalmines of Upper Silesia lay on the eastern borders of Prussia, those in the Saar were on the western frontier. Before the railway age inadequate transport facilities hampered the growth of the industrial region. Roads were poor and the inland waterways — the Moselle and its tributaries — were not suitable for moving large quantities of coal and iron.

As in Upper Silesia there were other minerals in the Saar region besides coal, the most important being iron-ore. While the ironworks were operated by private entrepreneurs, such as the Stumm family, nearly all the collieries were owned and worked by the Prussian State. The Hostenbach mine was privately owned, while the St Ingbert and Mittelbaxbach collieries were nationalized Bavarian mines.

Small quantities of coal had been mined since the Middle Ages in the valleys of the Saar, Fischbach and Sulzbach. The coal lay near the surface and open-cast mining was practised. The territories of the Duke of Nassau-Saarbrücken produced only about 3,600 tons of coal in 1740. Prince Wilhelm Heinrich (1740-68) established state collieries and ironworks in an effort to stimulate the industrial expansion of his dominions. His successor Prince Ludwig, however, fell into financial difficulties and allowed the firm of Leclerc-Joly to handle the export of Saar coal to France, to control the state ironworks and to collect certain taxes. Claude Savoye, the manager of this firm, was a dominant figure in the Saar in the years before the French Revolution. In 1790 the Saar produced about 50,000 tons of coal.

In 1792 French troops marched into the Saar, which remained in French hands for 22 years. The region was one of Napoleon's richest prizes in the territories he annexed east of the River Rhine. Most of the collieries were placed under state control in 1808 and the Provisional Administration of the Saar Mines made strenuous efforts to expand the production of coal. A geological survey of the area was made and a mining school established at Geislautern. It seems unlikely that any students were admitted, since the French engineers in charge — first Duhamel and then Baunier — devoted their energies to improving the efficiency of the local coalmines and ironworks. Again, although plans were made to link the Saar with the French saltworks at Château-Salins and Dieuze by a new waterway, no canal was constructed at this time. When Napoleon passed through Saarbrücken in May 1812, he received reports from his mining engineers concerning the progress that had been made in improving the output of coal and iron. In that year the production of coal in the Saar was 80,000 tons. In 1815 it had risen to 100,000 tons. When Napoleon fell the French Mining Law of April 1810 survived as a legacy of the French occupation.

In 1815 most of the Saar coalfield was incorporated in the new Prussian province of the Rhineland. With one exception the collieries remained under state-ownership and management. Leopold Sello, who took charge of the Mining Office at Saarbrücken in 1816, had to deal with serious problems of reconstruction after the Napoleonic Wars. Napoleon had incorporated the region in his empire and now coal and other products had to surmount a high tariff wall if they were to be exported to France. It was not easy to recover lost markets in Germany, particularly in view of transport difficulties. Sello closed some mines as their output was declining. In others he increased production by sinking new shafts. Some new mines were opened. Collieries were modernized by installing pumps and winding gear driven by steam-engines. Safety measures included the introduction of Davy lamps and improvements in underground drainage and ventilation. Skilled miners from the Harz were brought to the Saar, while the reorganization of the Saarbrücken Mining Academy in 1822 — originally established by the French at Geislautern — ensured that, in future, engineers and technicians would be thoroughly trained. The transport of coal was facilitated by the building of roads and colliery tramways and by improving the navigation of the River Saar. In 1852 the completion of the Saarbrücken Railway linked the Saar with the Rhine port of Ludwigshafen and with Forbach in Lorraine. Saar coal was used locally, particularly in Stumm's ironworks in Neunkirchen, and was exported to France, where it was used in the textile-mills of Alsace and in the ironworks and saltworks of Lorraine. The production of the state-owned collieries in the Prussian part of the Saar rose from 100,000 tons in 1816 to 631,000 tons in 1850.

In addition to the Ruhr, Upper Silesia and the Saar there were some smaller coalfields in Germany that were of some significance for the development of industries in their immediate vicinity. They were the Eschweiler coalfield on the Belgian frontier, the Zwickau coalfield in Saxony and the Waldenburg coalfield in Lower Silesia. It was only after they had been linked to the German railway network — the line from Leipzig to Zwickau, for example, was opened in 1845 — that the output of these coalfields began to expand.

Germany also had considerable resources of lignite. There were some scattered deposits, running from the Harz Mountains through the Prussian province of Saxony to Lower Silesia and Posen. Lignite was also mined on both sides of the Rhine, in Nassau and in Bavaria. In the first half of the nineteenth century the exploitation of lignite was largely confined to primitive workings by peasants who used this fuel to supplement their supplies of wood. In Prussia the output of lignite was only 200,000 tons in 1825, though this had risen to over 1,000,000 tons in 1847.

Iron

Germany had no large ironfields such as those possessed by France in Lorraine or by Russia in the Donetz basin. Her iron-ore deposits were scattered in various parts of the country. In the west iron-ore was mined in the wooded hills of the Siegerland and the Westerwald on the right bank of the Rhine and in the Eifel on the left bank. In central Germany deposits were worked in the Harz Mountains, in Thuringia, in the Swabian Jura and the Franconian Jura. In the east some iron-ore was found in Upper Silesia, though the main deposits in that part of central Europe lay on the Austrian side of the Sudeten Mountains. When timber was readily available for the charcoal-smelting process the ironworks were generally situated near deposits of iron-ore. But as coke gradually replaced charcoal as the fuel for smelting, the ironmasters built their furnaces on the coalfields. By the end of the nineteenth century the smelting of iron had virtually disappeared from southern and central Germany and about three-quarters of the country's blast furnaces were located on the major coalfields.

At the time of the founding of the Zollverein, however, the iron industry was not concentrated in a few regions. There were numerous ironmines, foundries and forges in operation in many hilly wooded districts. Progress was slow. The output of iron-ore rose only from 266,000 tons in 1838 to 545,000 tons in 1850, while the production of pig-iron rose only from 96,600 tons in 1837 to 167,000 tons in 1852. About a third of Germany's blast furnaces in the 1840s lay in the Siegerland and Westerwald districts — the valleys of the Sieg, Lahn and Dill. Much of the pig-iron produced there was refined and manufactured in other regions such as the Sauerland. Here — at Iserlohn, Altena and Lüdenscheid — most of the ironmines had been worked out, but there were hundreds of refineries, forges and metal workshops in which many iron products were made. Remscheid and

Solingen were particularly important centres for the manufacture of cutlery. In the Ruhr the iron and steel industry was developing. Before 1849 — when blackband deposits were discovered near Dortmund — the iron-ore came from neighbouring districts. The *Gutehoffnungshütte* (foundry), Sterkrade, Friedrich Harkort's engineering workshops at Wetter and Alfred Krupp's steelworks at Essen were pioneer establishments in a region that eventually played a vitally important role in the expansion of Germany's output of iron and steel. In 1848, on a visit to the Rhineland, Banfield declared that the ironworks of Haniel, Huyssen and Jacobi at Sterkrade, which used hematite ore from Nassau, 'now rank among the largest in Europe'.

In the Saar district Stumm's ironworks at Neunkirchen were expanding in the 1840s. In central Germany the iron industry was declining in the 1830s and 1840s. The output of local iron-ore was falling and little was being done to increase the efficiency of small charcoal furnaces. In 1850 it was reported that the decline of the industry in Thuringia was due to 'the conservatism of the older men, an unwillingness to progress with the times, and in many instances, a lack of carefully trained and skilled workmen'. In Silesia the Prussian authorities had made great efforts to encourage the exploitation of the mineral resources of the district. The example set by the State in establishing blast furnaces and engineering workshops at Gleiwitz and Königshütte in the 1790s had been followed by some of the great magnates of Silesia, who had set up similar ironworks such as the *Antonienhütte* and the *Hohenlohehütte*. Nearly seventy blast furnaces were in operation in Upper Silesia in 1846.

After the establishment of the Zollverein there was an increased demand for iron and steel products for the railways and engineering plants. Improved transport facilities enabled pig-iron, bar-iron and finished iron products to reach wider markets than before. At first the industry failed to take full advantage of these new opportunities and it did not supply all the needs of the home market. Old-fashioned methods of production continued to be used and many ironmasters were slow to introduce new techniques. In 1834 nearly all Germany's iron was smelted with charcoal. One reason for this was a lack of good coking-coal. Although Germany's first coke blast furnaces had been installed in state ironworks in Upper Silesia at the end of the eighteenth century, many years elapsed before they were widely used. In 1846 Upper Silesia still had only seventeen coke furnaces. In western Germany the iron industry was even more backward. It appears that in the 1830s and 1840s only five coke furnaces were fired. It was not until the middle of the nineteenth century that the first such furnace was in action in the Ruhr. This was at the Friedrich Wilhelm ironworks near Mülheim. With only a little over 10 per cent of their iron smelted by coke in 1850 the German ironmasters lagged behind those of England, France and Belgium. But in the later stages of iron production (the refining process to make bar-iron) greater progress was being made. In the 1820s puddling had been introduced into ironworks at Lendersdorf (near Aachen), Neuwied (near Coblenz) and Wetter (Ruhr). The pioneer work of Friedrich Harkort and the Remy and Hoesch families led to the spread of puddling in western Germany. In 1841 Dietrich Piepenstock used the puddling process in his newly established Hermann ironworks near Hörde. A few years later the English traveller Banfield reported that at Oberhausen the firm of Haniel, Huyssen and Jacobi was running a rolling mill 'round which 37 puddling and reheating furnaces were ranged'. Meanwhile crucible cast-steel was being made in the Ruhr by Alfred Krupp, Jacob Mayer, Gottlob Jacobi and other entrepreneurs. It has been estimated that the output of iron products in Germany increased by just over 60 per cent between 1835 and 1847.

Textiles

There were three main textile industries in Germany in the nineteenth century — the spinning, weaving and finishing of flax; carded and combed wool; and cotton. The oldest were the linen and carded wool industries, both of which used raw materials produced on German farms. The cotton and combed woollen industries were of more recent origin. Linen weaving was largely a rural industry. Many linen weavers worked for part of the time on the land and for part of the time in industry. But (as Clapham observes) 'with cotton and silk the peasant had nothing to do, because he did not produce either . . . . The industries were necessarily more professional and more capitalistic than wool or linen.'

The textile industries were located in three regions — eastern and central Germany (Silesia, the Mark Brandenburg, the province of Saxony and the kingdom of Saxony); the Prussian provinces of Westphalia and the Rhineland; and the three southern states (Bavaria, Württemberg and Baden). The most important of these textile regions was the first. In 1840 it had 62.6 per cent of Germany's spindles and 64.9 per cent of its looms.

The fortunes of the major textile industries varied considerably in the first half of the nineteenth century. The spinning of flax and the weaving of linens was the largest textile industry in the country. The linen looms in 1850 represented 70 per cent of all Germany's looms. The annual output of the industry at that time was about 200 million yards of cloth. Yet this great industry was very slow to establish large spinning-mills and weaving sheds containing up-to-date machines driven by steam-engines. The cotton industry, on the other hand, did see the setting up of mechanical spinning-mills and weaving sheds in which the powerloom replaced the handloom. In all the textile industries the weaving branch lagged behind the spinning branch in changing over from machines operated by hand to those operated by water-wheels or steam-engines. And in the woollen industry the carded wool branch was ahead of the combed wool branch.

The manufacture of linens from home-grown flax had long been of major importance to the German economy and to her balance of international payments. Several regions were famous for their yarns and for their various finished products — fine linens, curtains, thread, sailcloth, canvas. Linen cloth was manufactured in Silesia (in the 'mountain towns' of Hirschberg, Landeshut, Schmiedeberg, Greifenberg, Schweidnitz and Bolkenhaim), in Brandenburg, Hanover, Brunswick, Westphalia, Saxony and Württemberg. Flax, linseed yarn and linen goods were exported from Germany's Baltic ports and from Bremen. A. J. Warden observed in 1864 that

> . . . the linen trade is not only one of the oldest, but it is also one of the most important branches of industry in Germany. It gives employment to an immense number of the inhabitants, and a vast capital is embarked in it. Many of the articles made in the United Kingdom were at first imitations of German linens, and some of them are still familiarly known by their German names, or by the district in Germany where they were manufactured.

The eighteenth century had been the golden age of the German linen industry. Frederick the Great had compared the profits derived from the export of Silesian linens to the wealth that Spain had once secured from the silver mines of Peru. Linen exports from Silesia rose from £500,000 in 1740 to £3,000,000 in 1805, while the export of linens from Prussia in 1799 accounted for a quarter of all her exports. By exporting her linens — particularly to Spain for the South American market — the Germans earned the foreign currency with which to buy 'colonial goods', such as sugar, coffee, tobacco and cotton.

At that time the manufacture of linens was a domestic — and largely a rural — industry regulated by gilds and local authorities. Some of the spinners and weavers were full-time linen workers, while others were part-time workers, whose main occupation was farming on a small scale. In central, southern and western Germany the linen industry was generally organized on the outwork system (*Verlagsystem*), but in Silesia many spinners and weavers were nominally self-employed (*Kaufsystem*), though in practice they were under the control of their feudal lords and of capitalist clothiers. An English observer wrote that in Silesia 'the artisan himself purchases the yarn, weaves the web, and brings it to market as a merchant . . . . Thus he is never certain of gaining a farthing, for he is exposed to all the vicissitudes of the market.' Moreover the Silesian linen workers had to pay a 'weaver's tax' (*Weberzins*) to their feudal lord, as well as dues in lieu of rendering labour services. Towards the end of the eighteenth century the standard of living of the linen workers declined because the price of linen did not rise sufficiently to meet the increased cost of food and raw materials. In the spring of 1793 there were serious riots among the linen weavers of Silesia.

The disruption of international trade during the revolutionary and Napoleonic Wars caused the linen industry to decline. Although linen manufacturers were protected in the home market by the Continental System, they lost their overseas markets to foreign competitors, who were replacing handlooms by powerlooms. When peace was restored prosperity did not return. Foreign competitors could now produce linens more cheaply than German manufacturers. In addition linen cloth had to face increased competition from cheap calicoes. J. Russell, who travelled in Germany in the early 1820s, declared: 'On the return of peace, Silesia endeavoured, but in vain, to regain the ground which it had lost; it found Britain firmly established as a successful rival in the markets of the new world; in Russia and Poland it was opposed by Bohemia; and the export, I was assured, is not one third of what it amounted to before this calamitous period.'

When the Zollverein was established the German linen industry was failing to meet the challenge of a new era. The output of flax was falling, the manufacture of linens was widely dispersed and units of production were small. Traditional methods of production were still used. In 1816 the Prussian government sent an agent (Neubauer) to Britain 'to collect all the necessary information concerning the progress made in England, Scotland and Ireland with regard to flax

spinning machinery'. But the information he obtained does not appear
to have been put to any practical use. Linen workers refused to become
factory operatives if this involved moving to a town and losing their
smallholdings. Little success attended attempts to establish power-
driven flax spinning-mills and in the 1840s there were only twenty-two
of them in all Germany. There were still over 100,000 hand spinners
and handloom weavers in Silesia alone. In that province mules driven
by water-power or steam-engines had been set up at Waldenburg,
März-Wernersdorf and Erdmannsdorf. The Erdmannsdorf factory had
been erected by command of the king of Prussia, after he had visited
Silesia in 1840 and had seen for himself the depressed condition of the
textile workers in the province.

In 1841 the Prussian consul in Hamburg wrote that he doubted
whether the linen industry would 'ever again attain the important
position that it enjoyed for so many years in trans-atlantic markets . . . .
England, with her enormous factory industry, has been making linen
cloth by machinery and has been able to drive Germany's handmade
linens not only out of colonial markets but even from the markets of
the Continent.' The linen industry survived by paying very low piecework rates to the workers. The hardships suffered by the impoverished
handloom weavers led to unrest in Silesia in 1844, when the premises
of the firms of Zwanziger and Dierig were destroyed in Peterswaldau
and Langenbielau. Troops were called to the district to restore order.
Three years later hundreds died of hunger typhus in Silesia.

The production of woollen and mixed cloths was also an old-
established industry. With over 8,250,000 sheep in Prussia alone in
1816 Germany had ample supplies of the raw material. Cloth, made
from carded wool, had long been produced in various parts of the
country such as Silesia, the Mark Brandenburg, Saxony and the
Rhineland (Aachen and Monschau). Cloth made from combed wool
was of more recent (seventeenth-century) origin and it was manufactured in only a few districts, of which the Eichsfeld was the most
important. In the reign of Frederick the Great merino sheep were
introduced into Prussia, but no new breed was developed from them.
The elector of Saxony, however, achieved greater success with the
merino sheep that he brought from Spain to his estates at Hohnstein and
Stolpen. The wool from these 'electoral sheep' found a ready market
both at home and abroad. The output of cloth in Germany increased
and by 1788 Prussia produced nearly as much woollen cloth as linen
cloth. Yet the growth of Germany's flocks of sheep, the expansion of
the home clip and the increased output of cloth was not sufficient to

meet the demand at home and in 1799 Germany's imports of English woollens were valued at 4,400,000 thalers.

At this time cloth making was still mainly a domestic industry and the craftsmen were organized in gilds of spinners, weavers, shearers, fullers and drapers. Many craftsmen had lost their former economic independence and were now virtually wage-earners employed by entrepreneurs (*Verleger*) who gave out the raw material and paid the workers at piecework rates. Some of these entrepreneurs were already operating on a large scale in the eighteenth century. In Berlin Johann George Wegely, a Swiss, had established a woollen manufactory in 1701 which grew into a large and flourishing business, while in 1713 Johann Andreas von Kraus had founded a wool warehouse with the aid of a royal subsidy. Kraus employed many weavers in the Mark Brandenburg — in Brandenburg, Neuruppin and Treuenbrietzen for example — to make cloth for the army. At Monschau (Montjoie) in the Eifel district Bernard Schreiber manufactured fine cloth on a large scale and established a considerable reputation for himself both at home and abroad. He considered that one factor that contributed to his success was the absence of restrictive gild practices in Monschau. In 1787 Schreiber's output was valued at 1,500,000 thalers.

The various woollen industries in Germany were affected by the Revolutionary and Napoleonic Wars in different ways. In the territories on the left bank of the Rhine, which were annexed by France, the gilds were abolished and manufacturers gained access to the French market. The woollen industry of Aachen prospered and several mechanized spinning-mills were established. In 1814 the Prussian factory inspector, J. G. May, reported that during the war there had been a considerable expansion in the production of woollen and cashmere cloths in Aachen, Eupen, Verviers, Monschau and neighbouring hamlets. In other parts of Germany there was an increased demand for coarse cloth from the military authorities. On the other hand the industry lost its overseas markets when the Continental System was in force.

After the Napoleonic Wars the cloth industry was faced with severe competition from English woollens. It might have been expected that German manufacturers would have met this challenge by establishing factories with power-driven machinery. But — except for the fulling mills — the mechanization of the woollen industry was a slow process. Spinning-machines were introduced more rapidly than powerlooms. And the carded wool branch of the industry adopted modern machinery more quickly than the combed wool branch. As early as 1799 Count von Einsiedel had established a wool spinning-mill at Wolkenburg in

Saxony. The working of the jennies was supervised by an English engineer. After 1815 the power for the mill was provided by an iron waterwheel. Before 1800 the mechanics Hoppe and Tappert were building hand machines in Berlin to card and to spin wool.

During and immediately after the Napoleonic Wars mechanized mills for spinning carded wool were established at Cottbus and Guben in the Mark Brandenburg, at Grünberg in Lower Silesia and at Aachen in the Rhineland. Many of these machines were made by members of the Cockerill family. Shearing machines were also installed at this time — for example in Lennep in 1804 and in Aachen in 1818. The earliest example of a mechanized mill to spin combed wool appears to have been one at Langensalza in Thuringia. This factory had been established by Johann Christian Weiss in 1802 to spin cotton, but when the Continental System came to an end it was turned first into a flax-mill and then into a combed wool-mill.

Powerloom weaving came rather later. In 1835 experiments in the weaving of wool with an American powerloom were conducted at Luchenwalde with the aid of a subsidy from the Prussian government. Shortly afterwards some powerlooms were introduced into weaving sheds in the Rhineland in Saxony and at Gera. In 1842 the Maschinen-Wollen-Weberei — aided by the state-sponsored Prussian Overseas Trading Corporation — was established at Wüste Giersdorf in Lower Silesia.

The progress made by the cloth industry in the Aachen district after the Napoleonic Wars showed how the challenge of foreign competition could be met by determined entrepreneurs. The woollen industry of Aachen was now situated in Prussia and not in France and a high tariff made it very difficult for the manufacturers to sell their cloth in Paris. But they soon recovered some of their old markets both in Germany and overseas.

In 1828 a tribute to the progress made by the German industry came from a factor at Blackwell Hall, the chief market for cloth in England. He declared that 'Prussian cloths were manufactured with a great deal of address and I think they are our most powerful rivals'. The growth of the woollen cloth industry in Germany may be seen from the fact that the annual consumption of raw wool rose from 300,000 tons in 1821-30 to 490,000 tons in 1841-50. But this expansion took place in small workshops using machines operated by hand rather than in large factories using power-driven machinery. In 1840 wool-combing was still a manual process. In 1846 there were only 1,372 powerlooms in the German woollen industry, as compared with 47,290 handlooms. Berlin in that year had 5 woollen spinning-mills (3 for a combed wool and 2 for carded wool) and they employed only 205 workers altogether. Again, in 1846 there were only 53 steam-engines (538 horse-power) in all the woollen factories of Saxony.

In the cotton industry more spinning-mills and weaving sheds were established and more machines — particularly spinning-machines — driven by steam-engines were installed in the early nineteenth century than in the linen and woollen industries. The manufacture of a mixed cloth(*Barchent*) — which had a linen warp and a cotton weft — had been an important industry in Germany in the Middle Ages. Cotton goods were made in southern Germany (Augsburg, Regensburg, Ulm) and later in Saxony and Jülich. Most of the raw material came from Cyprus and Syria. The industry collapsed during the Thirty Years War and revived slowly in the eighteenth century, when the main centres of production were Elberfeld and Barmen in the Duchy of Berg, München-Gladbach and Rheydt in the Duchy of Jülich, and Chemnitz, Zwickau and Plauen in Saxony. And the new industry was not organized on a gild basis, which proved to be a factor favourable to expansion in the future.

Towards the end of the eighteenth century German governments and manufacturers began to realize the significance of the inventions that were revolutionizing the cotton industry in England. In Saxony spinning-machines were installed at a mill at Ernstthal (1782), while powerlooms were installed in a weaving shed at Mittweida (1790). In 1791 Baumgärtel visited England to examine the new cotton-machines and on his return to Saxony he constructed both a mechanical shuttle and a cloth-shearing machine. In 1794 Johann Gottfried Brügelmann of Elberfeld installed spinning-machines, driven by water-power, in a cotton-mill at Kromford near Düsseldorf. In 1796 Lancashire cotton goods sold well at the Leipzig fair and the cotton manufacturers of Saxony became alarmed at the prospect of increased English competition. Karl Friedrich Bernhard established a cotton spinning-mill at Harthau, which was run by three skilled English operatives, while Wohler installed a water-frame in his mill at Chemnitz. At about the same time Tappert, aided by a grant from the king of Prussia, was building cotton (as well as woollen) spinning-machines, which were based upon English models. Tappert became a leading cotton spinner in Berlin in the early nineteenth century.

The Continental System affected various German cotton regions in different ways. In Saxony, despite some difficulty in obtaining the raw material, the industry expanded because dangerous competition from

Lancashire vanished. There was an astonishing increase in the number
of mule spindles in Saxony. In 1805 there were only 13,200 but in
1814 there were 283,713. Cotton goods were made in two districts —
in the Voigtland (Plauen), which produced muslins, and the Erzgebirge
(Chemnitz), which produced calicoes. During the Napoleonic Wars
the output of muslins declined but the great increase in the manufacture of calicoes more than made up for this loss. In the territories on
the left bank of the Rhine (Roer Department), which were annexed to
France, the opening of the Paris market led to an expansion in the output of cotton in München-Gladbach and Rheydt, just as it stimulated
the growth of the woollen industry in Aachen. In the valley of the River
Wupper — in Elberfeld, Barmen, Cronenberg, Vohwinkel, Ronsdorf,
Beyenburg — a flourishing cotton industry had developed in the
eighteenth century. The first cotton spinning-mill to be driven by
water-power in this district had been erected in 1785 and — according
to Banfield — was 'managed by some English spinners'. Napoleon
incorporated the valley of the River Wupper into his Duchy of Berg, a
territory that Heckscher considers 'suffered nothing but injury from
the Continental System'. The cotton manufacturers were faced with
a shortage of their raw material and they were cut off from the French
market on the other side of the Rhine, and from the ports on the North
Sea. Economic activity declined in the valley of the Wupper and some
skilled operatives migrated to the Roer Department to find work in
the flourishing textile towns of Aachen, München-Gladbach and
Krefeld.

After 1815 the German cotton manufacturers had to face severe
competition from Lancashire. In Prussia they complained that the
Maassen Tariff of 1818 did not give them adequate protection against
cheap foreign imports. Nevertheless the cotton industry made greater
progress than the other textile industries. First in spinning — later
in weaving — factories replaced workshops and steam-engines replaced horses and waterwheels. In 1825, for example, Karl August
Milde founded at Breslau the first German machanized cotton spinning-
mill to be set up east of the River Elbe. The founding of the customs
union and the building of railways extended the home market for cotton
goods. The labour force was increased as flax-spinners deserted their
declining industry and found work in new cotton-mills. Cotton manufacturers adjusted their output to meet the needs of their customers.
In Gladbach they now made cloth for men's coats and suits. In Elberfeld
and Barmen they made fashion articles in imitation of French products.
In Saxony, however, the cotton manufacturers showed less enterprise

and continued to use machines originally installed at the time of the Continental System. J. E. Tennent, who gave evidence before a parliamentary enquiry in 1841, stated that cotton operatives in Saxony could not cope with modern machinery. He observed that 'the use of the powerloom is so imperfect in their hands that it becomes a much dearer instrument of production than the handloom itself'. He added, 'I actually saw machines of English construction standing idle in the workshops of calico printers in Chemnitz, who stated to me that they were unable to employ them to advantage and that they found it cheaper to continue the old system of hand labour. 'On the other hand the hosiery industry in Saxony was largely mechanized by the 1840s. By the middle of the nineteenth century some large cotton-mills were at work in Germany — such as the firm of Jung in Elberfeld, which had 20,000 spindles and a cotton factory in Augsburg, which operated 12,000 spindles and 300 powerlooms. The expansion of the cotton industry could be seen by the increase in the consumption of the raw material. This rose from a mere 7,000 tons a year in 1821-30 to 490,000 tons a year in 1841-50.

The manufacture of silks was the least important of the German textile industries. It was situated in two regions — in and round Berlin and Krefeld. The silk industry of Berlin and the Mark Brandenburg had been established by Frederick the Great and had been fostered by subsidies and privileges. Foreign silk workers had been brought to Prussia and the importation of silks from abroad had been prohibited. The merchant Gotzkowsky had established a velvet manufactory in 1746 and he had then managed several silkworks in Berlin. When he went bankrupt in 1763 his silkworks were taken over by two Jewish entrepreneurs. Subsequently the king encouraged the founding of new silkworks in Potsdam and elsewhere in the Mark Brandenburg. The silk industry prospered in the 1790s, when the silk industry of Lyons was in temporary difficulties during the French Revolution. In a few years — between 1794 and 1796 — the number of silk looms increased from 3,700 to 4,500. The Continental System caused the Berlin silk industry to collapse. Only 979 looms were in operation in 1815. Eventually — particularly after the founding of the Zollverein and the building of railways — there was some recovery and in the middle of the nineteenth century the Berlin silk industry had 2,138 looms — but only 213 of them were powerlooms.

The second region in which silks were manufactured was in the Rhineland — mainly in Krefeld and Elberfeld — and this industry flourished in the nineteenth century, while that of Berlin and the Mark

Brandenburg was stagnant. The Krefeld silk industry, situated near the Dutch frontier, was largely in the hands of the Van der Leyen family, which dominated production in this district. Unlike the Berlin industry, which had been supported by state subsidies, the manufacture of silks in Krefeld had expanded in the eighteenth century without any help from the Prussian authorities. Indeed Mirabeau, in his book on the Prussian monarchy, argued that the silk industry in Krefeld had prospered simply because it had been left free to 'run along natural lines'. One reason for the expansion of the manufacture of silks in the Krefeld district was the availability of labour. When their own industry declined the skilled linen workers readily found employment in the silk industry. Silk weaving was done in the workers' homes on the out-work system, while the finishing process was carried out in the firm's factory.

It was some time before the Krefeld silk industry recovered from the effects of the Napoleonic Wars, when overseas markets had been lost, and meanwhile markets on the Continent were dominated by the manufacturers of Lyons. In the 1830s the establishment of the Zollverein extended the home market for silks, ribbons, tapes, velvets and satin, while the opening of a weaving school helped to raise standards of workmanship in the industry. By 1846 the Krefeld district had 8,000 silk looms (nearly all handlooms) — four times as many as the silk industry in Berlin.

Although by the middle of the nineteenth century the establishment of the Zollverein and the building of railways had fostered the expansion of modern manufactures — particularly in the coal, iron, engineering and cotton industries — Germany was still predominantly an agricultural country and in many branches of manufacture the factory had not replaced the workshop and machines driven by steam-engines had not replaced hand-machines. Craftsmen still flourished in town and countryside. There were over 1 million of them — 553,107 masters and 447,502 apprentices and journeymen — in Prussia alone in 1852. It was still possible to travel through many parts of Germany without seeing a factory chimney or hearing the sound of a locomotive. There were pockets of modern industry in the Rhineland, Westphalia, Silesia, Saxony and in the ports of Hamburg and Bremen. Even here the great firms of the future — such as Krupp's steel works at Essen — were operating only on a small scale. But the foundations for future economic growth had been laid and the third quarter of the nineteenth century was to see a great expansion of German industry.

5 *The Role of the State*

The role of the State in Germany in the process of industrialization was very different from what it had been in Britain. The public sector of the British economy in the late eighteenth and early nineteenth centuries had been a very small one. It included a state post-office, a nationalized ordnance factory at Woolwich and several state dockyards. Boards of trustees, appointed by the government, promoted the development of the linen industry in Scotland and Ireland. Mail contracts encouraged certain steamship lines to establish new regular shipping services. And some local authorities operated docks, waterworks and markets. But England's transformation from an agrarian to an industrial country was brought about by private entrepreneurs. The necessary capital came from private investors and not from the government. The turnpike roads, the canals and the railways; coalmines, ironworks, textile mills and shipyards; banks and insurance companies were all founded, financed and operated by private individuals, partners or companies. Institutions of worldwide importance, such as the Bank of England. Lloyd's and the East India Company were also privately-owned. In the climate of public opinion that prevailed at that time, people were satisfied if the State safeguarded the rights of property owners and inventors, maintained a stable currency and protected farmers, industrialists and shipowners from foreign competition. More than this the government was not expected to undertake. The notion that public money should be invested in private enterprise or that the State should run mines or factories was quite foreign to the British way of thinking at that time.

On the other hand in Germany, as W. H. Dawson has observed, industrial progress was 'not hampered by any hard and fast adhesion to a definite line of policy in regard to the limits of public as compared with private enterprise'. The rulers of the German states were expected by their subjects to take an active part in fostering the economic growth of their territories. It was widely held that competent civil servants, dedicated to the public service, could run industrial enterprises in the national interest more efficiently than private entrepreneurs who were in business simply to make a profit.

The policy of the Prussian government with regard to the expansion of the industrial sector of the economy may serve to illustrate how German states promoted the growth of their industries. There was in Prussia a public sector of the economy which represented a substantial investment by the State in mining and manufactures of various kinds. In the coal industry the State owned and operated nearly all the collieries in the Saar as well as two coalmines in Upper Silesia — the *Königsgrube* and the *Königin Luise Grube* — and a mine at Ibbenbüren in Westphalia. These nationalized mines produced over 4,000,000 tons of coal a year in the middle of the nineteenth century — one-fifth of all the coal extracted in Prussia. The Prussian State also owned mines producing iron, lead, silver and zinc, as well as alum works at Freienwalde and Schwemsal. There were royal saltworks at Königsborn in the County of Mark and at Halle-an-der-Saale and Schönbeck in the County of Magdeburg. By 1850 the nationalized saltworks produced over 80 per cent of Prussia's output of salt. The sale of salt was a state monopoly. In the reign of Frederick the Great royal furnaces had been established at Malapane, Kreuzberg, Krascheow, Jedlitz and Dembiohammer. Between 1786 and 1803 von Reden had established two state furnaces in Upper Silesia (at Gleiwitz and Königshütte) and a third in Berlin. In 1850 the nationalized ironworks in Prussia produced 150,000 tons of pig-iron, 80,000 tons of cast-iron, and 90,000 tons of wrought-iron. Other state industrial enterprises included the manufacture of lime in the Mark Brandenburg, the production of porcelain in Berlin, the manufacture of mirrors at Neuhaus, the making of small arms at Spandau and Potsdam and the exploitation of timber from the royal estates.

In addition to mining enterprises there were also a number of nationalized industrial concerns in Prussia in the early nineteenth century, many of them coming under the control of the *Seehandlung* (Overseas Trading Corporation). This privileged state trading and financial institution had had a somewhat chequered career. It had been founded in 1772 after the first partition of Poland. Now in control of the valley of the lower Vistula and the port of Elbing, Frederick the Great proposed to secure the maximum economic advantage from his new possessions. He hoped to divert to Elbing as much overseas trade as possible from Danzig, which was still Polish. When the Seehandlung was set up for this purpose — the king holding nearly all its shares —

it was granted a monopoly of the foreign trade in salt in the eastern provinces of Prussia. It also secured privileges with regard to the timber and linen trades. After surviving initial difficulties caused by the inefficiency and dishonesty of some of its officials the Seehandlung successfully handled numerous business and financial transactions for the government between 1782 and 1804 under the able management of von Streuensee. By the end of the eighteenth century the financial side of the Seehandlung's activities to some extent overshadowed its trading enterprises. The commercial assets of the corporation were being used as security for state loans. When Prussia was defeated by the French at the battle of Jena the Seehandlung defaulted on many of its loans. In 1810 its debts were absorbed in the national debt. In 1820 a royal edict, which reorganized the Seehandlung, declared that in future the corporation was to function as 'a strong organization capable of assisting government departments financially by providing them with credit so that their freedom of action should not be hampered by temporary lack of funds . . . . It should be prepared to assist in raising state loans if this should be necessary in future.' The Seehandlung was allowed to continue its business enterprises as well as acting as a state financial institution. Christian von Rother, the new director of the Seehandlung, believed that the State was just as able to run factories as private entrepreneurs. He declared that he rejected 'the common belief that the State should stand aloof from the natural development of manufactures and commerce and should certainly not itself engage in industrial enterprise. I have shown how false is the familiar cry that a civil servant cannot compare with the private citizen when it comes to running an industry successfully.'

In the 1830s and 1840s Rother extended the work of the Seehandlung to include not only financial transactions and trading activities but also the running of numerous nationalized industrial establishments. In the eighteenth century state workshops had been established in Prussia for a variety of reasons. Sometimes it was felt that only the State possessed the capital and the administrative machinery that was required to set up new industries in particular regions — such as the manufacture of combed woollen cloth at Luckenwalde in the Mark Brandenburg or the opening-up of coalmines in Upper Silesia. Sometimes the duty of the State to maintain the country in a proper state of defence was the major factor in deciding to promote certain industries, such as foundries for casting cannon or workshops to produce gunpowder or small arms. Sometimes the need to improve the balance

of payments in international trade led to the establishment of workshops to manufacture luxury products (largely for export) such as silks
and porcelain. To these traditional reasons for setting up nationalized
factories Rother added new motives. Some of his enterprises were
model factories in which up-to-date machinery was installed. These
were open to inspection and Rother hoped that private entrepreneurs
would follow his example and introduce similar machinery into their
own factories. Sometimes Rother's motive in setting up factories was
to bring work to regions where domestic industries that had once
provided employment were now in decline. This was probably the main
reason for the establishment of various textile mills in his native province of Silesia, where the standard of living of many peasant-weavers
was falling owing to the inability of the linen industry to compete with
more efficient foreign rivals.

The Seehandlung operated several textile factories in the 1840s.
They included a modern mill for spinning combed wool at Breslau, the
first Prussian weaving shed for manufacturing worsted cloth to install
powerlooms at Wüste Giersdorf, flax-heckling and flax-spinning-mills
at Landeshut, Erdmannsdorf, Suchau by Neustädel and Patschkey by
Bernstadt. A cotton-mill was established at Eiersdorf near Glatz. All
these were in Silesia. The metal and engineering plants run by the
Seehandlung were more widely dispersed, for there were zinc-rolling-
mills at Thiergarten by Ohlau in Silesia; an iron-foundry at Burgthal
by Remscheid; and machine-building works at Breslau and Alt-Moabit
(Berlin). There were also chemical works at Oranienburg (in the Mark
Brandenburg), paper factories at Berlin and Hohenofen (by Neustadt)
and a group of factories — a flour-mill, a sawmill, an oil-mill and a
fulling-mill — at Bromberg in Posen. At the Bromberg and Thiergarten flour-mills new American machines were installed. Not all these
factories were entirely owned by the Seehandlung. Some of them were
owned jointly by the Seehandlung and private entrepreneurs. Thus the
Burgthal foundry for the manufacture of cast-steel was run in association with Hasenclever and Burlage and the Seehandlung took one-third
of the profits. The Wüste Giersdorf wool-weaving factory was operated
in partnership first with Grossmann and then with Reichenheim. In
many of the Seehandlung factories the most modern machinery was in
use and skilled foreign workers — such as the Yorkshire powerloom
weavers at Wüste Giersdorf — were employed. The Seehandlung was
also engaged in the transport of freight and passengers. It owned five
merchant ships and ran a small fleet of steamships and tugs on the
Rivers Elbe, Spree and Havel.

The Seehandlung had been involved in wholesale trade since its foundation and Rother expanded this aspect of its work. He tried to assist the sheep farmers by purchasing their wool and by holding it for sale in a warehouse in Berlin and he endeavoured to promote a revival of the linen industry by opening up new overseas markets for its cloths. In 1822 he sent the *Amerika* to Rio de Janeiro with a cargo of linens and soon afterwards William O'Swald twice sailed round the world in an effort to market Prussian textiles in the Far East. These voyages prepared the way for the establishment of a regular trade with North and South America, India and China; this was handled by See-handlung ships sailing from Hamburg. Prussian linens and woollens were exchanged for 'colonial goods', such as coffee and sugar.

In addition to the nationalized undertakings there was a sector of the industrial economy in which private entrepreneurs and the State both played a part. Here the State cooperated with private firms by providing subsidies, credit facilities or machinery, and by guaranteeing the interest on shares. Sometimes public officials supervised the run-ning of private companies or even took full responsibility for their administration. From time to time the Prussian government subsi-dized private entrepreneurs, as when 110,000 thalers were paid to certain spinning-mills in Silesia between 1818 and 1837. Machines were occasionally given to firms on condition that they could be in-spected by other manufacturers. Credit might be given by the State, as when Werner and Mieth received a loan free of interest from the Seehandlung in 1829. But neither this loan — nor a later loan — saved the firm from collapsing. Import duties were sometimes waived to enable firms to buy machines or steam-engines that were not available in Prussia. And by 1851 the Prussian government held shares in five railway companies to the value of over 5,000,000 thalers. In 1850 the directors of the Berg-Mark Railway Company handed over the admini-stration of the line to the State in return for a guarantee of interest on the shares. The railway was now operated by the State, although it remained the property of the shareholders. The private sector of the mining industry was closely supervised by the State. It has been seen that the day-to-day working of collieries and other mining enterprises was regulated by civil servants. Mineowners and their managers could not take decisions on the opening of new seams, the fixing of prices or the marketing of their products without first consulting the local mining officials.

On the whole public opinion approved of Rother's efforts to en-courage economic expansion through the activities of the Seehandlung. But the nationalized factories and workshops were criticized in some quarters in the 1840s. There were those who argued that the State was acting unfairly in relation to private entrepreneurs when it ran nationalized enterprises or when it gave subsidies or machines to one firm and not to another. The critics asked why taxpayers should bear the cost of running some of the nationalized factories at a loss, or why consumers should have to pay higher prices than necessary for wool and alum because the Seehandlung had intervened in these whole-sale trades. In 1845 the king of Prussia ordered that no new industrial undertakings should be established by the Seehandlung and when Rother retired in March 1848 the activities of the Seehandlung were considerably curtailed. By 1854 its ships and most of its factories had been sold. But many nationalized enterprises — the coalmines in the Saar and Silesia, the saltmines and some of the railways, for example — were still run by the State.

While Rother was endeavouring to promote the expansion of the Prussian economy through the Seehandlung, his colleague Peter Beuth, head of the Department of Trade and Industry (Ministry of Finance), was stimulating the progress of manufactures by other means. Beuth considered that technical progress was the key to indus-trialization. In his view it was essential that Prussian manufacturers should instal in their factories the machines and the steam-engines that had turned Britain into the workshop of the world. To familiarize him-self with modern machinery and industrial processes Beuth paid two visits to Britain in 1823 and 1826 and also visited factories and work-shops in France, Belgium, Holland and Saxony. Then he made several tours of the manufacturing districts of Prussia to pass on to manu-facturers the technical information he had obtained in Britain.

In 1819 Beuth was appointed director of the recently reorganized Technical Commission, which was an official organization responsible for administering the patent law and for compiling standard works on scientific and technical subjects. In the following year he played a leading part in establishing the Association for the Promotion of Industrial Knowledge in Prussia, which brought together public officials, army officers, university teachers, industrialists, scientists and artists. The transactions of the association show how thoroughly its members investigated technical progress in foreign countries and in Germany. In 1821 Beuth was largely responsible for the creation of a third institution to foster the development of modern technology in Prussia. This was the Berlin Technical Institute — forerunner of the present Technical University — which provided a two-year course in the basic subjects required by civil engineers and builders. Eventually the length of the course was extended to three years. By 1833 Beuth was able to report that some former students had established firms of their own. August Borsig, who constructed locomotives in Berlin, and Ferdinand Schichau, who built machinery and ships at Elbing, were among Beuth's most famous pupils. Beuth also encouraged the establishment of junior technical institutes in the provinces. When Goethe received a copy of the syllabus of one of these institutes, he wrote: 'We are now assured of the comprehensive care with which the Prussian State is endeavouring to keep pace with the incessant advances in technical methods effected by our neighbours.' The Berlin industrial exhibition of 1844 — supported by over three thousand exhibitors — was a fitting climax to Beuth's career.

In discussing the founding and early history of the Zollverein reference has already been made to the Maassen Tariff of 1818 and to the part played by Motz in securing the removal of many tariff barriers that had formerly restricted trade within Germany. After Motz's death other Prussian civil servants — such as Delbrück, Pommer-Esche and Philipsborn — carried on the work he had begun. The extension of the customs union to include Nassau, Baden and Frankfurt-am-Main, the successful renewal of the Zollverein treaties in 1842 and the conclusion of a navigation treaty with Britain helped to strengthen the economic bonds between the German states and to stimulate industrial expansion.

The State in Prussia not only promoted industrialization directly — by running nationalized undertakings and by assisting private firms in various ways — but it also stimulated the economy in an indirect way by providing a legislative and physical environment favourable to industrial progress. The State was responsible for the provision and maintenance of the main roads, the rivers and the canals. Despite financial difficulties the Prussian government made strenuous efforts to improve the main roads in the period of reconstruction after the Napoleonic Wars. A loan raised in London enabled over 1,000 miles of roads to be built between 1825 and 1828. In Westphalia, Ludwig Vincke (president of the province between 1815 and 1844) showed how an energetic official could improve communications. He succeeded in completing the construction of the great highway running through the province from Wesel to Minden. This road proved to be of great benefit to the coal and iron industries of the Ruhr. Vincke also played an important part in securing the construction of modern harbours at Ruhrort and Duisburg. When the English traveller Banfield visited

Ruhrort not long after Vincke's death he wrote: 'The town lies between the mouth of the Ruhr and an artificial cut, so that it is almost surrounded by water and the traveller on landing, first perceives a statue erected by the inhabitants of Westphalia to the late Baron von Vincke, who, as President of the Province, promoted to the utmost of his power, the commerce of the river and the improvement of its shallow bed.'

Apart from improving communications the State promoted industrial expansion in other ways. The government maintained a stable currency on the silver standard. Strict economy in the administration helped to balance the budget and to reduce the national debt. The Royal Bank of Berlin, heavily in debt after the Napoleonic Wars, was nursed back to solvency and in 1846 — when Rother had been responsible for its management for 9 years—it was transformed into the Bank of Prussia and was authorized to issue notes to the value of 21,000,000 thalers. The Railway Law of 1838 and the Company Law of 1843 helped to provide a legislative framework within which the early industrialization of Prussia could take place. The former regulated the granting of concessions to private railway companies and the way in which railways were to be run, while the latter was concerned with firms operated by partnerships.

It is clear that in the era of the Zollverein and the early railways the State was actively engaged in promoting the industrial revolution in Prussia. A group of able civil servants — Maassen, Motz, Beuth, Nagler, Sello and Vincke — devoted their official careers to operating nationalized industries and to giving encouragement to private entrepreneurs to increase the efficiency of their factories. It might be argued that the Prussian authorities could have achieved more. Thus the Patent Law of 1815 gave inadequate protection to inventors, since most patents were granted for only 5 years. The opposition of leading officials, such as Rother and Nagler, may have delayed the building of railways. Businessmen were demanding a new company law and a fiduciary issue, but these reforms were delayed because some senior civil servants were afraid of a speculative boom such as the railway mania that had occurred in England. And the failure to change the stringent mining laws probably starved the private sector of the coal industry of much needed capital, since investors were reluctant to put money into an industry that was so rigorously controlled by public officials.

Other German states endeavoured to stimulate industrial progress by similar means to those employed by Prussia. Thus Bavaria had two

nationalized coalmines—St Ingbert and Mittelbaxbach—in the Saar
as well as ironmines and furnaces at Amsberg. A third of Bavaria's extensive forests were exploited by the State. Four nationalized saltworks
produced 45,400 tons of salt in 1852. The medicinal baths and waters
of three Bavarian spas—Kissingen was the best known—were state
undertakings. In Munich the Nymphenburg porcelain factory and a popular beer cellar (the Hofbräuhaus) were nationalized establishments,
while in Nürnberg two-thirds of the shares of the Royal Bavarian Bank
were owned by the State. The Bavarian post-office—formerly owned by
the Prince of Thurn and Taxis—had been brought under public control
early in the nineteenth century. The Main-Danube Canal and the
North-South Railway (Hof-Augsburg-Lindau) were owned by the
State. In Hanover there were two state railways and five nationalized
saltworks, while Saxony had a royal porcelain factory at Meissen and a
state cannon foundry at Dresden. Several other German states were
operating nationalized railways in the middle of the nineteenth century.

As modern industries began to grow in Germany in the 1840s industrialists and merchants began to assert their right to manage their
business affairs without any guidance from paternalistic governments.
Private entrepreneurs argued that they could run their factories and
mines without any interference from public officials. At the same time
they began to criticize reactionary governments and to demand liberal
reforms such as the establishment of parliamentary institutions in
states like Prussia where no popular assembly existed. They argued that
press censorship should be abolished and that freedom of speech, freedom of public assembly and trial by jury should be introduced. Friedrich
Engels, writing in 1851, declared that in the 1840s 'the moneyed and
industrial class' of Prussia was no longer prepared 'to continue apathetic
and passive under the pressure of a half-feudal, half-bureaucratic
monarchism'. The liberal manufacturers of the Rhineland — led by
David Hansemann and Ludolf Camphausen — supported the demand for
constitutional reforms and their views were expressed in the Cologne
newspaper, the *Rheinische Zeitung*, which Karl Marx edited for a
short time. Traditional policies—both in politics and in economic
affairs—were being challenged and the way was being prepared for the
attack on the established order that came in 1848.

6   *Revolution and Reaction*

The Revolution of 1848

The main causes for the outbreak of revolution in Germany in 1848 were the urgent need for political reforms and serious economic and social distress. The industrial and professional middle classes considered that they were now entitled to a greater share in the running of the country. Particularly in states such as Prussia and Hanover, which were ruled by autocratic monarchs, the liberals demanded the overthrow of the police state and the granting of a constitution, freedom of the press, the right to form associations and to hold public meetings, as well as trial by jury. The temper of the middle classes in Prussia at this time became evident when the United Diet met in Berlin in February 1847. This was no elected parliament, since its members had been appointed from the eight Prussian provincial assemblies. Frederick William IV hoped that the United Landtag would approve a state loan of 25,000,000 thalers to build the Eastern Railway that would link Berlin with Danzig and Königsberg. But instead of attempting to conciliate the assembly he bluntly declared that he would never allow a written constitution to come between the monarchy and the people. The United Landtag thereupon rejected the proposed railway loan and the king dissolved the assembly.

The reformers demanded not only constitutional changes but German unification as well. They proposed to reduce the powers of the states and to strengthen the power of the central authority. But those who favoured unification failed to agree among themselves on an issue of crucial importance, which would have to be settled before their objectives could be attained. Although at first nearly all Germans favoured the establishment of a united Reich within the frontiers of the existing federation, a time came when there was a sharp division of opinion as to whether a united Germany should be a Germany from which Austria had been excluded (*Kleindeutschland*) or a 'greater Germany', which would include the Habsburg territories that were within the existing federation (*Grossdeutschland*).

The middle-class liberals secured some unexpected allies. Various radical groups had gained some support from peasants, craftsmen and factory operatives. These workers had little interest in political reforms or German unification. But they were interested in bread-and-butter questions. Exploited by great landlords, capitalist merchants or factory owners, they were all too familiar with poverty and unemployment. The peasants in regions as far apart as Silesia and Baden demanded the final abolition of serfdom. Rural domestic workers, like the peasant-weavers in Silesia, wanted higher piecework rates and freedom from the oppression of feudal overlords. The craftsmen in the towns demanded protection against competition from cheap factory products. Many radicals thought that if the liberals could overthrow the reactionary conservatives, who had been the main support of autocratic monarchies, then there might be some hope of alleviating the plight of workers.

Between 1844 and 1848 many German workers both in the towns and in the villages had to face rising prices, food shortages, low wages and unemployment. In June 1844 the wretchedly paid weavers of Silesia rose in revolt and some eighty arrests were made before the troops could restore order. Articles in the *Deutsches Bürgerbuch* for 1845 by the socialists Wilhelm Wolff and Georg Weerth brought home to the German public the miseries of the textile workers in the mountain villages of Silesia and the utter degradation of the lives of the peasants in the Senne district. The failure of the potato crop in 1845 and 1846 and of the grain harvest in 1847 brought distress to almost every part of the country. In northern Germany the price of rye doubled between 1844 and 1847. In Silesia famine conditions prevailed and there was an outbreak of hunger typhus. In south-western Germany the situation was aggravated by the fact that smallholders were losing their right of pasture on the local common and their right to collect wood in the forests.

Domestic workers in the towns and the countryside were finding it difficult to make ends meet owing to competition from newly established factories. The gilds had lost much of their power to regulate manufactures, and were in no position to protect craftsmen faced with a loss of custom and a decline in income. A peasant-weaver could try to make a living from his smallholding if he had no work in industry, but a self-employed artisan in a town who fell upon hard times could choose only between applying for poor relief, seeking a job in a factory or emigrating to America.

To make matters worse, Germany was now sufficiently industrialized to feel the effects of the commercial crisis in England in 1847.

There were business failures in Hamburg, Bremen and many industrial centres. When the finance house of Haber (Frankfurt-am-Main and Karlsruhe) suspended payments, three important factories in Baden— a cotton-mill at Ettlingen, an engineering plant at Karlsruhe and a beet sugar refinery in Waghäusel—found themselves in serious financial difficulties. These firms were rescued by the Baden government, which placated their creditors by guaranteeing the interest on their loans for 15 years.

In 1847 there was serious unrest in many parts of Germany. While in England it had been factory operatives who had been responsible for recent riots—such as the Plug Plot riots in Lancashire—the German disturbances were the work of peasants and craftsmen. In Berlin, which had four thousand unemployed, there were food riots in April 1847. In the spring of 1848 numerous disturbances occurred. At Cologne milit- ant Rhine boatmen forced the steamships, which threatened their livelihood, to cease using the harbour. In Nassau parts of a railway line were destroyed by carters whose trade was declining, while Metter- nich's wine cellar at Johannisberg was confiscated by insurgents. In Württemberg and Baden the peasants attacked mansions and destroyed manorial records of feudal services and dues. In Bavaria the refusal of the king to dismiss his mistress Lola Montez sparked off disturbances in Munich, while in Posen the Poles attacked the local German population.

Political agitators found little difficulty in gaining support from starving peasants and unemployed craftsmen. By 1848 social dis- content had reached such a pitch that a revolution might have occurred without the help of middle-class reformers demanding constitutional reforms. As it was, the political demands of the liberals and the demands of the workers for work and food came (though only briefly) to be united in a single revolutionary movement. Friedrich Engels, writing in an American newspaper in 1851, declared that in 1848 the reactionary German governments had to face 'a heterogeneous mass of opposition springing from various interests, but more or less led on by the bour- geoisie, in the first ranks of which again marched the bourgeoisie of Prussia, and particularly of the Rhine province'.

The revolution in Germany was sparked off by the revolution in France in February 1848, when Louis-Philippe abdicated and the Second Republic was proclaimed. But republicanism had few supporters in Germany and the institution of monarchy survived there. Only two rulers abdicated — Ludwig I of Bavaria in March and the Emperor Ferdinand I of Austria in December. And the Austrian emperor was not dismissed by the revolutionaries but by the reactionary Prince Schwarzenberg. Some unpopular ministers and royal advisers — such as Metternich and Prince William of Prussia — fled from Germany.

The two most important centres of revolutionary activity were Vienna and Berlin, the capitals of the two German great powers, but there were other focal points as well, such as Cologne and Baden. The differences between the revolutionary movements in these places illustrate the complexity of the political situation in 1848. In Vienna, for example, militant university students played an important role in overthrowing Metternich's regime, but their activities had no great significance in Berlin. And while the peasants were the driving-force behind the risings in Baden, it was industrial workers who were the most militant revolutionaries in the Rhineland.

Events in Baden in the spring of 1848 were particularly significant because they showed, at the very start of the revolution, how wide was the gulf between moderate reformers and militant republicans. In Baden the Grand Duke had, as early as 1846, made some concessions to the reformers (led by Karl Mathy and F. D. Bassermann) when he appointed a new and a less reactionary ministry under J. B. Bekk. When news of the rising in Paris reached Baden at the end of February 1848 the radicals organized a mass meeting at Mannheim. The Grand Duke dismissed three unpopular ministers and the government introduced a number of reforms including freedom of the press, trial by jury and the establishment of a people's militia. The extremists, however, were not satisfied. Franz Sigel raised the nucleus of a revolutionary army in Mannheim (the *Sensenkorps*). On 19 March a central revolutionary committee was set up at a demonstration at Offenburg, which was entrusted with the task of organizing popular committees in every province and parish in Baden. This was planned as a shadow administration that was to operate as a rival to the legal administration.

Any hope that the Grand Duke might have had that timely concessions might spare Baden the evils of civil strife was dashed in April 1848, when Friedrich Hecker led a revolt of peasants in favour of the proclamation of a German republic. The poet Georg Herwegh arrived in Baden with a legion recruited from tailors and other craftsmen working in Paris. A student named Langsdorff followed Hecker's example at Freiburg, while Sigel manned the barricades at Mannheim. A little later — in September 1848 — Gustav Struve championed the republican cause by leading a peasant revolt in the Oberland district. Baden troops, with some assistance from Bavaria and Württemberg, put down these risings and restored order. But the armed clashes between those who were satisfied with moderate reforms and extremists who aimed at the overthrow of the princes and the proclamation of a republic showed that — at any rate in Baden — the chances of cooperation between middle-class liberals, peasants and craftsmen were very slim indeed.

Conditions in the Rhineland were very different from those in Baden. While Baden was a rural region where the grievances of the peasants were a dominant factor in local politics, the Rhineland had a great coalfield in the Ruhr, textile industries at Elberfeld-Barmen, Aachen and Krefeld, and cutlery workshops at Remscheid and Solingen. In this province liberalism (supported by many of the manufacturers and merchants) was stronger than anywhere else in Prussia, while extreme radical and socialist views were being championed by the *Triersche Zeitung* and the *Deutsches Bürgerbuch*. The craftsmen, miners and factory operatives of the Rhineland showed a more lively interest in politics than workers in many other parts of Germany.

Cologne and Düsseldorf were the main centres of political activity in the Rhineland. The radical leaders were Roland Daniels, Heinrich Burgers and Andreas Gottschalk in Cologne, and Ferdinand Lassalle and Ludwig Kugelmann in Düsseldorf. In August 1848 three of the radical clubs in Cologne — the Democratic Society, the Workers' Association and the Union of Masters and Men — agreed to cooperate to organize the workers throughout the Rhineland. And it was in Cologne that Karl Marx and his friends published the *Neue Rheinische Zeitung* which — with some six thousand subscribers — was one of the most widely read newspapers in Germany at this time. The weakness of the alliance between the liberals and the workers in the Rhineland became evident a few days after the first number of the paper appeared on the evening of 31 May. When the liberals who had taken shares in the *Neue Rheinische Zeitung* read a fierce attack upon the Frankfurt parliament they hastened to withdraw their financial support. The paper impartially attacked the reactionary German monarchs, the Prussian junkers and the liberal politicians who dominated the Frankfurt parliament and the Prussian national assembly.

Militant revolutionaries in the Rhineland had to act with circumspection, since Cologne was a garrison town and Prussian troops were available to put down any rising that might occur in the province. But in the autumn of 1848 unrest came to a head. On 7 September there was a demonstration in Cologne to denounce Prussia for withdrawing her troops from Schleswig and Holstein by the armistice of Malmö and for failing to free the duchies from Danish rule. On 13 September an open-air demonstration took place in the Frankenplatz in Cologne, presided over by Bürgers. A resolution was passed urging the Prussian national assembly in Berlin to resist by force any attempt to dissolve it. On Sunday 17 September another demonstration was held north of Cologne on the Fühling heath near Worringen, which was attended by deputations of workers from Cologne, Düsseldorf and other towns in the Rhineland. The meeting demanded the establishment of a democratic republic in Germany. The commandant of the garrison in Cologne dealt with the demonstrations by declaring a state of siege in the city on 26 September. He disarmed the civil guard, prohibited public meetings and suspended the publication of the *Neue Rheinische Zeitung*.

Whatever happened in Cologne or Baden — or for that matter in Munich or Dresden — the fate of the revolution in Germany could be settled only in Berlin and Vienna, which were the real centres of effective power. In Berlin the news of the revolution in Paris in February 1848 greatly alarmed Frederick William IV, who declared, in a letter to Queen Victoria, that the French capital was in a state of 'complete anarchy' and that the peace of Europe was threatened. But even after the rising in Vienna and the fall of Metternich on 16 March the king still refused to grant the reforms demanded by the liberals. He agreed to recall the United Diet, but this assembly was not a democratically elected parliament.

On 18 March a crowd assembled in the courtyard of the palace in Berlin in the hope of hearing news of some real concessions to popular demands. Two shots — probably fired by mistake — turned a cheering crowd into an angry mob. Craftsmen, factory workers and unemployed men erected barricades and defied the troops. It was a spontaneous rising rather than a carefully planned revolt by dedicated revolutionaries. Bitter fighting ensued as General Prittwitz's troops systematically cleared the barricades. Early on the following morning (19 March) the king, distressed at the loss of life in the street fighting, issued an address to the citizens of Berlin. He declared that the rising had been fostered by seditious malcontents and foreign agitators, appealed for an immediate removal of all the barricades and promised to withdraw the troops from the streets and squares.

In the afternoon a hostile crowd appeared in the palace courtyard bearing the disfigured corpses of some of the workers who had fallen in the street fighting. When the king appeared on a balcony to pay his tribute to the fallen the crowd insisted that he should come down to the courtyard to inspect the bodies. On 20 March he was forced to proclaim an amnesty for political offences and Mieroslawski, a Pole under sentence of death, was welcomed by a jubilant crowd when he was released from prison. On the same day Frederick William IV's brother, the Prince of Prussia, left Berlin for exile in England. On 21 March the king made a new effort to pacify his unruly subjects in Berlin. He declared his intention of merging Prussia into Germany and of leading the nation to unity and he donned a black, red and gold arm-band when he headed a procession along the Unter den Linden. On the following day (22 March), at the funeral of the citizens who had fallen at the barricades, Frederick William IV had to appear on a balcony of the palace and remove his helmet while the coffins were carried past him. But when the eighteen soldiers who had been killed in the street fighting were buried, the king was not present.

It was not until 28 March that Frederick William IV at last appointed a ministry of reform under Ludolf Camphausen and David Hansemann, two leading liberals from the Rhineland who had led the opposition in the United Diet in the previous year. Camphausen and Hansemann, however, made no attempt to limit the influence of the Prussian army, the feudal aristocracy or the bureaucracy. Not one officer or civil servant was dismissed. Camphausen and Hansemann found themselves in the embarrassing position of having to rely upon their reactionary opponents for support against the militant revolutionaries in the capital. They dreaded the possibility of another popular revolt and they viewed with alarm the activities of the democratic clubs and of men like Stephan Born, who were organizing the artisans and factory workers. The militancy of the workers was seen on 30 May when an unruly crowd of unemployed assembled before the town-hall of Köln (near Berlin) demanding 'the right to work', while in Berlin itself a mob seized a piece of artillery from the royal arsenal.

Despite these difficulties the liberal ministry tried to introduce some measure of parliamentary government into Prussia. In April 1848 the United Diet made arrangements for the calling of a national assembly which, in collaboration with the king, was to frame a constitution.

When the assembly met it proved to be a more radical body than the Frankfurt parliament. But its members, like their colleagues in Frankfurt, spent much of their time in lengthy debates on a draft constitution.

Meanwhile the king and his supporters were preparing for a counter-revolution. Frederick William IV knew that he could count on the loyalty of the junkers, the army, the civil servants and many peasants in Posen and West Prussia who had suffered from the violence of the Poles. In August 1848 the 'Junker Parliament' — a meeting of Prussian nobles and landlords led by Kleist-Retzow and Bismarck — declared that the national assembly must be dissolved, if necessary by force. The inability of either the assembly or the government to maintain order in Berlin was seen on 14 June, when the arsenal was again attacked. Camphausen and Hansemann now resigned.

By the end of October 1848 Frederick William IV was ready to assert his authority again. The fact that the national assembly actually proposed to abolish titles of nobility and to delete the words 'by the grace of God' from the royal title was the last straw. The king replaced the liberal ministry by a conservative ministry under Otto von Manteuffel. On 10 November the national assembly was told to move from Berlin to Brandenburg and on the following day troops under General Wrangel occupied the capital. A state of siege was proclaimed and the civil guard was dissolved. Shortly afterwards the king granted a constitution. It was not a constitution drawn up by (or even approved by) the national assembly — which had been called for that purpose — but was devised (*octroyée*) by the king. By the end of 1848 the king and conservative supporters were firmly in the saddle again.

Meanwhile equally stirring events were taking place in Vienna and in the Habsburg dominions. The forces of reaction, which reformers were determined to overthrow, had long been firmly entrenched in Austria. Metternich—'autocracy's Don Quixote'—had been in office for 39 years and he symbolized everything that the liberals opposed. In the Austrian police state, as in Prussia, power lay in the hands of the army, the nobles and the bureaucracy. There was no constitution, no democratically elected parliament, no freedom of the press, no right of free speech. Louis Kossuth denounced Metternich's administration as a 'gross contradiction of all constitutional principles'. And, as the leading power in the German confederation, Austria had for many years used her influence to support reactionary administrations in the German states. Moreover the Habsburg empire was a multiracial state in which the Magyars, Italians, Poles, Czechs, Croats and Ruthenians were under the domination of the Austrian Germans. Ferdinand I, an epileptic described by Palmerston as 'the next thing to an idiot', was an autocrat whose absolute power was being challenged by the Austrian liberals who were demanding constitutional reforms and by the subject peoples demanding self-government.

In the Habsburg territories there had been unrest even before the revolution broke out in France in February 1848, for there had been rioting in Milan on 2 January. On 3 March Louis Kossuth, champion of Magyar freedom, denounced the detested 'Vienna system' and declared that the Habsburg dominions must in future be bound together by 'the firm cement of a free constitution' and not by 'the evil binding force of bayonets and bureaucratic oppression'. Two days later Count Vitzthum, a secretary at the Saxon legation, wrote from Vienna that 'a troubled sinister mood prevails here in all circles . . . . The suburbs are said to be in a very irritated state . . . . The lower middle class is in manifest fermentation. The most pernicious rumours are being circulated . . . . It is to be foreseen with certainty that we shall wade through streams of blood.'

It was the university students who brought matters to a head in Vienna and it was their demonstrations that sparked off the rising that led to Metternich's downfall. The students' Academic Legion, about four thousand strong, was the first popular militia to gain control over parts of the city and it was more efficient than other revolutionary forces in Vienna. On 12 March two professors presented a petition to the emperor containing the demands of the students, which included freedom of the press, the right of association, a democratic parliament, responsible ministers and trial by jury. When no satisfactory reply was forthcoming the students stormed the Landhaus while the Diet was in session. This started risings throughout Vienna. Metternich resigned and left Vienna on 14 March. On the same day the emperor granted freedom of the press and the establishment of a national guard under the control of a committee of citizens and students.

The Habsburg dominions were now without an effective central government. After Metternich's fall the new ministry could not establish its authority either in the capital or in Hungary, Bohemia and Italy. In Vienna the black, red and gold flag of the revolution flew from St Stephen's tower and the city was controlled by revolutionary committees that were supported by the Academic Legion and the National

Guard. From time to time street demonstrations forced the legal authorities to give way to the democratic clubs, the students and the revolutionary committees. After a rising on 15 May 1848 the government accepted the demands of the revolutionaries and recognized a new Central Committee of popular organizations. For a time this committee virtually ruled Vienna. Two days later the emperor left his turbulent capital and sought refuge among the loyal Tyrolese in Innsbruck. When the government tried to curb the power of the students by closing the university there was a fresh outbreak of violence in Vienna on 26 May. Again the government was unable to assert its authority and climbed down. This time it actually handed over the public treasury to a newly appointed revolutionary Committee of Public Safety. As Engels observed, 'the alliance between the national guard or armed middle class, the students, and the working man, was again cemented for a time'. Meanwhile in the country districts the ministry was powerless to prevent the peasants from refusing to pay manorial dues or feudal services. On 31 August the Austrian national assembly passed a law abolishing feudal services.

The emperor had to give way not only to the demands of his turbulent subjects in Vienna but also to those of the rebellious provinces. In March and April 1848 new constitutions were proclaimed in Galicia, Hungary and Bohemia, while Jellachich was confirmed in office as governor (or *ban*) of Croatia. It seemed as if the Habsburg dominions might dissolve into their component parts. But this did not happen. The armies of the Empire remained loyal to the Habsburgs, whose fate now lay in the hands of Windischgrätz in Bohemia, Radetzky in Italy and Jellachich in Croatia.

Only 3 months after the revolution in Vienna in March 1848 the forces of reaction gained their first success. This was in Bohemia, where the liberals in the towns and the peasants in the country districts had opposed Metternich's oppressive regime. But in this region the rivalry of the Germans and the Czechs complicated matters. The national feelings of the Czechs were aroused. Their leader Palacky decided to boycott the Frankfurt parliament, which he regarded as a purely German institution. In April he declared that he was 'an Austrian of Slav nationality' and he asserted that the Czechs had the right to decide their own future. He envisaged the Czech lands as an autonomous federal territory within the Habsburg Empire. On 2 June a Pan-Slav congress was held in Prague and on 12 June radical Czech workers and students erected barricades in the streets and defied the Austrian authorities.

Windischgrätz withdrew his troops to avoid further fighting in the streets, but on 16 June he brought up his artillery and crushed the insurgents. This first victory of the counter-revolution was soon followed by a second. On 25 July the veteran Radetzky routed Charles Albert at Custozza near Verona and drove the Sardinian army behind the River Mincio. Shortly afterwards Radetzky reoccupied Milan.

In Hungary, on the other hand, the situation was far from satis-factory from the emperor's point of view. In March 1848 he had reluc-tantly agreed to the appointment of a liberal ministry with Batthyanyi as prime minister, Deak as minister of justice and Kossuth as minister of finance. This ministry cordially supported the revolutionaries in Vienna. The efforts of the reformers to translate their radical aims into practice were soon overshadowed by a more pressing problem. Just as the German-speaking Austrians in Bohemia sought to dominate the Czechs, so in Hungary the Magyars treated the Croats, Serbs and Ruthenians in their midst as second-class citizens. The Magyars demanded freedom from Austrian oppression for themselves while denying to the Slavs the right to self-determination. It did not take the emperor's supporters long to appreciate how this situation could be turned to their advantage. Jellachich, the able governor of Croatia, served their purpose admirably. On 11 September 1848, at the head of a Croat army, he crossed the River Drave and invaded Hungary. At the eleventh hour the Austrian government hesitated to plunge Hungary into civil war and sent Count Lamberg to command the rival Magyar and Croat armies. But the Count was brutally murdered by a mob after arriving in Budapest. The Austrian government was stung into action. On 26 September the emperor, in a manifesto, denounced the Hungar-ian ministers as rebels. A revolutionary Committee of National Defence under Kossuth was now in control in Budapest. Jellachich and his Croats were defeated at Velencze on 29 September. He was granted an armistice of 3 days and withdrew in good order in the direction of Vienna.

In October 1848, baulked of a victory in Hungary, the Austrian government determined to assert its authority in Vienna. The revolu-tionaries played into the hands of their enemies. Infuriated by the dec-laration of war upon Hungary, the Vienna mob ran wild on 6 October and a state of anarchy existed in the city. Count Latour, the minister of war, was done to death and his body was hung on a lamp post. The arsenal was stormed. The emperor, who had recently returned to his palace at Schonbrünn, fled for the second time on 7 October and sought refuge in Olmütz. At the same time the majority of the deputies of the new Austrian parliament (*Reichstag*), who had been deliberating on a new constitution, left Vienna for Kremsier.

The Austrian government decided that the time had come to restore order in Vienna. Jellachich marched on Vienna and invested the city. On 30 October he avenged his defeat at Velencze by routing a Hungarian force that had been sent against him. But the Austrian government did not wish Jellachich and his Croats to have all the credit for capturing Vienna and when Windischgrätz announced his intention of marching on the Austrian capital he was appointed commander-in-chief of all the forces investing the city. Windischgrätz and Jellachich began their attack on 28 October.

Joseph Bem, a Polish patriot who had served under Napoleon, tried to organize the defence of the city, but his task was a hopeless one as he was distrusted by those whom he was trying to help and overwhelming forces were ranged against him. Vienna fell on 1 November. A new ministry was appointed under Prince Felix Schwarzenberg and the success of the counter-revolution in Vienna was complete. The capital was placed under martial law and the leaders of the revolutionary regime were shot. The victims of the purge included Julius Becker and Hermann Jellinck, editors of a radical newspaper. The most prominent victim was Robert Blum, who had recently come to Vienna at the head of a mission from the radical party of the German parliament at Frankfurt. His demand for diplomatic immunity was contemptuously rejected and the Austrian government ignored subsequent protests by the Frankfurt parliament. Franz Bodenstedt, in his memoirs recalled that in Vienna in those days 'it was as if the value of life had lessened, like the value of Austrian paper money . . . . Horrible stories were rife of the excesses and atrocities which the Croats were said to have perpetrated in the suburbs.'

By December 1848 it was apparent that the revolution in Germany was failing to achieve its aims and that the reactionary forces in the country were recovering the power they had apparently lost in March. In Berlin, Vienna, Cologne, Prague and Milan the military were firmly in control. In Prussia the army was ready to suppress any risings that might occur in the provinces or in the smaller German states. In the Habsburg dominions Radetzky was poised to deliver a final blow to the Sardinians, while Windischgrätz and Jellachich were ready to invade Hungary. On 31 December 1848 the *Neue Rheinische Zeitung* reviewed the events of the past year and declared that the middle classes had lost their chance of gaining political power by setting up a constitutional monarchy. 'It is now clear that a social-republican revolution is the only practical alternative to a feudal reactionary counter-revolution.'

Meanwhile a German parliament was meeting at the Pauluskirche in Frankfurt-am-Main to draw up a new German constitution. In March 1848 the Federal Diet had adopted the black, red and gold colours and had appointed an advisory committee of seventeen members to draw up a new constitution. Dahlmann, the Prussian representative, quickly produced a draft constitution that provided for a hereditary sovereign head of state and increased powers for the central authority. His scheme gave the central authority control over the army, foreign affairs and the tariff, leaving other matters to the federal states. But events were moving too fast for Dahlmann and his plan proved to be stillborn.

The initiative for the calling of a popularly elected assembly to draw up a new constitution came not from the Federal Diet but from the liberals in south-western Germany and the Rhineland. In October 1847 a meeting had been held in Heppenheim between a group of leading liberals from Württemberg, Baden and Hesse-Darmstadt and David Hansemann and Gustav Mevissen from the Rhineland. They discussed plans for future cooperation to secure a reform of the constitution.

The liberals took their next step on 5 March 1848, when Heinrich von Gagern of Hesse-Darmstadt called a conference at Heidelberg of fifty-one representatives from the diets of several German states. This meeting was not a representative gathering since so many of the deputies came from south-western Germany — twenty-one from Baden alone — while the historic provinces of Prussia and Bavaria were not represented. Only one representative came from Austria. This self-appointed conference decided that a new constitution should be drafted by a democratically elected parliament. Even at this early stage of the revolution there was a rift between the moderate reformers and the militant republicans. While Heinrich von Gagern warned the conference of the dangers of mob rule, Hecker declared that he was a social democrat and that he stood for 'complete freedom for all by whatever form of government it is to be attained'.

On 12 March 1848 the Heidelberg conference appointed a committee of seventeen to issue invitations to members of the various diets in Germany to attend a Preliminary Parliament (*Vorparlament*) to

organize elections for an assembly that would draw up a new constitution. No invitations were sent to members of the Prussian United Diet,
since they were in session in Berlin and would presumably not be free
to come to Frankfurt. Instead invitations were sent to members of the
municipal councils of Prussian cities. In addition a certain number of
prominent liberals were invited by name to attend the Preliminary
Parliament. Meanwhile, on the day before this assembly met, the
Federal Diet invited the federal governments to arrange for the election
of 'a national representative assembly whose task should be to bring
into being a German constitution by acting between Governments and
people'.

The Preliminary Parliament met in Frankfurt on 31 March and
decided that the national assembly, which was to draft a new constitution, should consist of deputies each representing fifty thousand
citizens. They should be elected by universal manhood suffrage.
Whether direct or indirect election took place would depend upon the
electoral law in each German state. The Preliminary Parliament submitted these plans to the Federal Diet, which gave its approval. So
although the Heidelberg conference had been a self-appointed assembly
that had no legal standing, the recommendations of the Preliminary
Parliament were given official sanction by the Federal Diet. In the
circumstances it may be argued that when the Frankfurt parliament
met it was not a revolutionary assembly but an official body elected by
a procedure sanctioned by the Federal Diet. Most of the deputies —
those from Austria, Prussia and Bavaria for example — secured their
seats by indirect and not by direct election. In Prussia all men over
24 voted for delegates to attend regional electoral colleges, which
chose the deputy to represent that constituency.

The Frankfurt parliament had 605 members, though 831 deputies
sat in it at one time or another. It was a predominantly middle-class
assembly, being dominated by state officials, professional men and
representatives of industry and commerce. No working man was elected
and only one peasant sat in the assembly. Most of the members had
served on state or provincial assemblies and had had some experience
of the working of parliamentary institutions. The fact that the Prussian
national assembly was meeting in Berlin at the same time that the
German assembly was meeting in Frankfurt deprived the national
parliament of the services of some able men who might have represented
Prussian constituencies.

Heinrich von Gagern presided over the Frankfurt parliament and in his inaugural address declared that two tasks lay before the deputies. They had been elected to frame a new constitution and to secure the cooperation of all German governments to promote national unity. The parliament appointed committees to deal with various aspects of its work. The most important was the constitutional committee of thirty members, which was charged with the duty of drawing up a constitution. But the committee — and later the full assembly — spent much time debating the fundamental rights of the German people. It was not until January 1849 that the Frankfurt parliament at last embodied these fundamental principles in a law, and by that time the reaction had made sufficient progress in Austria and Prussia for these states to reject it.

Meanwhile a draft constitution had been drawn up by the constitutional committee and had been submitted to the full assembly. It was not, however, finally approved until March 1849. The constitution was stillborn. Frederick William IV rejected the offer of the imperial title from the Frankfurt parliament, saying that such an offer would have to be confirmed by the governments of the various states before he could accept it. Neither the Austrian nor the Prussian government was prepared to agree to the establishment of a new German federation with a constitutional monarch and a liberal constitution that would involve the surrender of powers now wielded by the separate states. Moreover the inability of the Frankfurt parliament to agree upon an issue of such fundamental importance as the frontiers of the new Germany contributed to the failure of the liberals and the radicals to secure the establishment of a new constitution. There were armed risings in the Bavarian Palatinate and in Baden in the summer of 1849 in support of the constitution, but they were easily put down by Prussian troops.

From the point of view of the future industrial and commercial development of Germany the work of the Economic Committee of the Frankfurt parliament was of some importance. It was significant that, for the first time, popularly elected representatives from all over Germany and Austria should meet to discuss such vital issues as protection and free trade, the extension of the customs union to include the whole of the country, the reform of the mining laws, the problem of the entailing of large estates and the grievances of peasants, craftsmen and factory workers. The Economic Committee included some very able men, such as von Rönne (head of the Prussian Board of

Trade), Bruck (the Austrian Minister of Commerce in Schwarzenberg's cabinet), Mevissen (a prominent Cologne banker), Moritz Mohl (a leading Württemberg liberal), the economist Bruno Hildebrand, the Saxon industrialist Eisenstück and the Hamburg merchant Merck. The committee was assisted in its deliberations in August 1848 by a team of commissioners from the various German states.

The protectionists on the committee outnumbered the free-traders, so that the committee was in favour of high tariffs to safeguard Germany's industries. The Economic Committee set up seven sub-committees to deal with various aspects of Germany's economic life. The reports of the Economic Committee show that it was strongly in favour of establishing a unified Germany from an economic point of view. This was reflected in the economic clauses of the draft German constitution of March 1849. It was proposed that Germany should be united for purposes of commerce and tariffs and that all internal duties should be abolished, though certain places and districts might be excluded from the customs union. The federal authority might admit foreign countries into the German customs system. The administration of the tariff and the collection of import duties and common taxes and excises were to be in the hands of the central authority and not of the separate states. It was laid down that a fixed proportion of the customs revenue should be used to defray the normal expenses of the German federal administration, while the remainder should be divided among the states. Individual states would be allowed to levy excise duties only in accordance with federal laws. Had this constitution come into force the Zollverein would have been absorbed in a wider German customs union. The draft constitution also provided for the abolition of transit dues on German rivers. Charges levied at harbours and locks should not exceed the cost of the services rendered to shippers.

Although the draft constitution of 1849 never came into effect the debates of the Economic Committee were not without results. Some of the reforms it had discussed were later passed into law in most — if not all — German states. In the 20 years after the revolution of 1848 the peasants were freed from feudal obligations, the mining laws were reformed, the transit dues on the rivers were abolished and an industrial code was established.

The members of the Frankfurt parliament, however, were not content to devote their energies to the task of framing a new German constitution. Leading liberals — who had overthrown reactionary ministers in their home states — now imagined that they could rule all Germany from Frankfurt. But this was an idle dream since the Frankfurt parliament did not possess the resources that a government needs to enforce its decisions. In June 1848 the assembly passed a law establishing a provisional Central Authority in Germany and in July the Federal Diet handed over its functions to this body. But although the new Central Authority had a Regent (*Reichsverweser*) — the Archduke John of Austria — and a cabinet, it never exercised any real power. It had no civil service, no financial resources, no army, no police force, no judiciary. All that the Frankfurt parliament could do was to pass laws and to hope that the various states would enforce them. The German states, however, were not prepared to accept laws passed by the Frankfurt parliament as binding upon themselves. Nor were they ready to accept orders from the regent or his ministers. In the second half of 1848 neither of the two German great powers was either willing or able to impose the will of the Frankfurt parliament and its Central Authority upon the whole of Germany.

Before long the liberal politicians at Frankfurt received a rude awakening. It was the crisis in Schleswig and Holstein that revealed the impotence of the Frankfurt parliament. The problem of these two duchies was a complicated one. Their duke was the king of Denmark. Holstein, with a German population, had been included in the German Confederation in 1815 but Schleswig — with a mixed German and Danish population — had been left outside. Despite the existence of a Danish minority in Schleswig the liberal members of the Frankfurt parliament regarded the two duchies as an integral part of Germany — just as they regarded Posen (with its Polish population) and Bohemia (with its Czech majority) as parts of Germany. The claims of Danish, Polish and Czech nationality were brushed aside.

In February 1848 Frederick VII, the new king of Denmark, issued a new constitution giving legislative powers to a joint parliament for the three parts of his dominions — Denmark, Schleswig and Holstein. Neither German nor Danish nationalists cared much for this. Then in March, under popular pressure in Copenhagen, King Frederick formed a new ministry, including four nationalists who supported a policy of integrating Schleswig and Holstein in the Danish state. It was announced that Holstein could have a separate constitution as a member of the German Confederation but that Schleswig — being an integral part of the Danish State — would share in a common constitution with Denmark. Upon receipt of this news the German nationalists in Holstein, already in a state of excitement following the events in Paris in February, set up a provisional government in Kiel. Danish troops entered Schleswig, while the Federal Diet—with the enthusiastic approval of the Frankfurt parliament — recognized the Kiel administration and authorized Prussia to occupy the duchies. In April 1848 Prussia and other German forces carried out this 'federal execution' and occupied the two duchies. Denmark replied by blockading the Elbe estuary. This action inflicted considerable damage on the trade of Prussia and Hamburg. Russia and Britain warned Prussia against upsetting the existing balance of power in the Baltic. In the circumstances Prussia negotiated an armistice with Denmark at Malmö in August 1848. The Frankfurt parliament indignantly rejected the armistice but eventually the liberals realized that they were powerless in the matter and agreed to accept the armistice. On 18 September 1848 a great mass meeting in Frankfurt denounced the assembly for accepting the withdrawal of Prussian troops from the duchies and the Central Authority called in Austrian and Prussian troops to defend the Pauluskirche from angry demonstrators. On this occasion two conservative members of the Frankfurt parliament—Prince Lichnowsky and General von Auerswald—were brutally murdered by a mob in a village just outside Frankfurt. Shortly afterwards—in November 1848—the execution of Robert Blum in Vienna showed that the Frankfurt parliament was not even able to protect the persons of its own members. By this action the Austrian government plainly showed its contempt for the Frankfurt parliament.

The Zollverein Crisis of 1849-52

The economic clauses of the draft German constitution, approved by the Frankfurt parliament, aimed at securing the economic unification of the country. Provision was made for the establishment of a customs union that would embrace the whole of Germany. There could be little doubt that public opinion supported this proposal. But Prussia feared that if such a customs union were set up she would lose the dominant position she enjoyed as the leading state in the Zollverein. The danger seemed to have passed when it became clear that the draft constitution would never come into force. But in October 1849 the proposal for an enlarged German customs union was revived in an unexpected quarter. An article in the *Wiener Zeitung*, inspired by the Austrian government, suggested that all the German states, including the Habsburg dominions, should be united in a customs union that would have a home market of seventy million consumers. It was a favourable moment to put forward such a suggestion since the Zollverein treaties were due to expire at the end of 1853 and new agreements would have to be negotiated if the union were to continue.

The collapse of the revolution in Vienna in October 1848 had been followed by the appointment of Prince Felix Schwarzenberg as head of a new ministry. His cabinet included some very able men, such as Franz von Stadion, Alexander von Bach and Karl Ludwig von Bruck. Schwarzenberg and his colleagues were determined to reassert Habsburg authority not only over the Italians, the Magyars and the Czechs but also in Germany. And in Germany this involved resisting any attempt on the part of Prussia to take advantage of the revolutionary situation to challenge Austria's old-established supremacy. On the political front Schwarzenberg was successful. By the convention of Olmütz (29 November 1850) Prussia in effect recognized the re-establishment of the Federal Diet of 1815 as the only legal central authority in Germany and gave up her attempts to dominate a 'little Germany' through a parliament attended by representatives of Prussia and some of the smaller states that met at Erfurt in March and April 1850. Prussia, on the other hand, eventually succeeded in preventing the Zollverein from being absorbed in a wider Austro-German customs union dominated by Austria.

The article in the official Austrian newspaper the *Wiener Zeitung* (26 October 1849), which first put forward the plan for a central European customs union, had been written by Gustav von Höfken, who was on the staff of the recently established Ministry of Commerce. It represented the views of Karl Ludwig von Bruck, who had been appointed Minister of Commerce in November 1848. Bruck was a native of Elberfeld who had settled in Trieste, where he had realized the significance to Austria of the increasing popularity of the new overland route to India by way of Egypt. He saw that the increased use of this route enhanced the opportunities of expanding the trade and shipping of Trieste. Bruck played a leading part in establishing the Austrian Lloyd shipping company, which competed with rival foreign firms to secure the new traffic using the overland route. In 1847 the English economist J. R. McCulloch observed that the Austrian mercantile marine had secured 'a very large share of the trade of the Mediterranean and Black Sea'.

Bruck was influenced by List's views on fiscal policy. He considered

that the future economic growth of Germany and the Habsburg dominions could be secured only by the establishment of a central European
customs union surrounded by a high tariff wall. As a member of the
Economic Committee of the Frankfurt parliament he had realized that
he could almost certainly count upon considerable support in Germany
for such a proposal.

Bruck appreciated that if Austria were to take the initiative in
establishing an Austro-German customs union she must first set her
own house in order. Soon after Schwarzenberg's ministry took office
it began to plan a series of economic reforms, which the Austrian
historian Friedjung has described as an achievement 'almost equal to
the founding of the German Zollverein'. These reforms included the
abolition of the customs frontier between Austria and Hungary (June
1850), the introduction of a new tariff that put an end to prohibitions
and greatly reduced export duties, transit dues, bounties and drawbacks (February 1852), the speeding up of railway construction and
the reorganization of the postal system. But these reforms did not go
far enough. They did not balance the budget, reduce the national
debt or solve the problem of Austria's depreciated paper currency. It
would have strengthened Bruck's position if the reforms that were
achieved could have been put into operation before negotiations were
opened with Prussia for the establishment of an Austro-German
customs union. The Austrian administrative machine moved slowly
and Bruck pushed forward with his plan while schemes for economic
reforms were still under discussion and had not yet been brought into
effect. This placed Bruck at a disadvantage when he tried to persuade
German states to support his plan for an enlarged customs union. The
Zollverein had been in operation since 1834 and its members knew what
revenues to expect from it. But the reorganized economic structure of
Austria—upon which the proposed new customs union would have to
be built—existed only on paper during most of the negotiations.

The article in the *Wiener Zeitung*, which gave an outline of Bruck's
plan, observed that Germany had so far failed to attain economic unity.
There were still four separate tariff regions—Austria, the Zollverein,
the Tax Union and some small states in the north (such as Hamburg
and Bremen), which were not members of any customs union. Very
different tariffs existed in the four regions. It was suggested that many
advantages would be gained by setting up a central European customs
union to include the Habsburg dominions and all the German states.
The expected reduction in smuggling would increase the revenues

from the tariff. Manufacturers would find new opportunities by supplying a greatly extended home market. The new union would be a powerful economic unit capable of fostering overseas trade by securing favourable terms in commercial treaties with foreign countries. The article recognized that practical difficulties prevented the immediate establishment of an Austro-German customs union and suggested that unification should be achieved in four stages over a period of years.

Rudolph von Delbrück, a young official in the Prussian Ministry of Commerce, saw the threat to the Zollverein implicit in the article in the *Wiener Zeitung* and he promptly wrote a reply in the official *Preussischer Staatsanzeiger*. Delbrück welcomed suggestions for future cooperation between Austria and other German states on such matters as monetary reform, railways and postal arrangements. But in his view the establishment of a central European customs union was out of the question. He argued that the economies of the Zollverein, the northern German states and the Habsburg dominions were so different that it would not be possible to reconcile their conflicting interests and different fiscal policies. Despite these objections to the very idea of a central European customs union, the Prussian government expressed itself willing to discuss with Austria the matter raised in the article in the *Wiener Zeitung*.

This move by the Prussian government forced Bruck to formulate his plans more precisely. In a memorandum of 30 December 1849 he enumerated the benefits that the existing tariff regions would secure from the establishment of an Austro-German customs union. The Zollverein manufacturers would gain a larger home market and one that would be adequately protected from foreign competition by higher import duties than those levied under the existing Zollverein tariff. Hamburg, Bremen and Hanover, in return for giving up their very low import duties, would also enjoy free access to a much enlarged home market. And they would find that their commerce would enjoy the support of a powerful union of states that would be capable of protecting their interests overseas. Austrian manufacturers were promised adequate tariff protection against foreign imports. Competition within the new union would stimulate Austrian manufacturers to improve methods of production and to take full advantage of a larger home market.

In his memorandum of December 1849 Bruck assumed that the proposed central European customs union would levy higher import duties than those imposed by the Zollverein. He criticized the Zollverein tariff for sacrificing the protection of German industry in favour of a simple system for collecting duties, while he praised the protectionist draft tariff recently drawn up by the General German Union for Safeguarding Home Industries. But Prussia was not prepared to adopt the high import duties that Bruck and the protectionists desired. Delbrück and other Prussian officials responsible for Zollverein affairs believed that the existing tariff suited the needs both of Prussia and of the Zollverein as a whole. So long as Bruck advocated a high tariff for his proposed customs union it was inevitable that his scheme would be opposed by the Prussian government.

The Prussian government replied to the Austrian memorandum in a note of 28 February 1850. Prussia declined to enter into negotiations for the establishment of an Austro-German customs union, but expressed her willingness to discuss other ways of improving economic relations between Austria and the Zollverein. In the following month Delbrück visited Vienna to discuss the problem informally with Austrian ministers and officials. Prince Schwarzenberg told him that he intended to start conversations with the governments of the German states with a view to establishing an Austro-German customs union on the basis of Article 19 of the federal constitution. Schwarzenberg apparently proposed to ignore the existence of the Zollverein and seemed to think that its members would be prepared to negotiate separately with Austria to establish a new and a wider customs union when the existing Zollverein treaties lapsed in 1853.

In a second memorandum — dated 30 May 1850 — Bruck explained his proposals at greater length. He elaborated many of the arguments that he had advanced in previous accounts of his plan, but on this occasion he went into more detail concerning the administrative machinery that was to operate the proposed Austro-German customs union. In the past Bruck had avoided this issue and had given the impression that what he had in mind was the establishment of a federation of existing customs regions — the Habsburg dominions, the Zollverein, the Tax Union and the northern German coastal states — which would retain their own identities. Now Bruck described new administrative organs to run the proposed customs union that would be closely linked with those of the revived German Confederation. He suggested the establishment of a central authority with far wider powers than those wielded by the Zollverein congress, since it would not only be responsible for fixing the tariff, negotiating commercial treaties and appointing consuls abroad, but it would also exercise some supervision over transport, postal and telegraph services as well. These proposals were not acceptable to Prussia. The high tariff advocated by Bruck was bad enough but the suggestion that the Zollverein should be merged into a new union controlled by the Confederation was even worse.

Bruck's plan was widely discussed in Austria and Germany. In the Habsburg dominions it was supported by industrialists and craftsmen who did not fear German competition but was opposed by those who considered that they would be ruined if cheap German manufactured goods appeared on the Austrian market. Support also came from land-owners and farmers in Hungary, who welcomed an opportunity to sell agricultural produce in the German market. In Germany Bruck's plan was supported by the protectionists and denounced by the free-traders. Both in Austria and Germany the advocates of the establishment of a 'Greater Germany' regarded Bruck's scheme as a step in the right direction.

It has been seen that the Prussian government was so opposed to Bruck's scheme that it was not prepared to negotiate with Austria on the matter. Other German states adopted an equivocal attitude. Some of them welcomed certain features of Bruck's plan — particularly the proposed high tariff and the participation of Austria, which might be expected to curtail Prussia's influence over German economic affairs. But all thought primarily of their own financial interests. They were drawing substantial revenues every year from the Zollverein and they were not prepared to join an enlarged union unless Austria would give them a firm guarantee that they would not suffer financially by doing so.

Bruck resigned as minister of commerce in May 1851 and resumed his business career as a director of the Austrian Lloyd. He was disappointed at the failure to start negotiations for the establishment of an Austro-German customs union and he differed from some of his colleagues on financial and railway questions. Delbrück took advantage of Bruck's resignation to strengthen Prussia's position in the Zollverein by securing the adhesion of Hanover. In June 1851 Bismarck wrote to Leopold von Gerlach:

> I should very much like to know if the negotiations between the Zollverein and Hanover are still in being and are making progress. The consolidation of the healthy northern German elements by

means of the bond of material interests — even if it involved the Zollverein in the loss of its southern German members — would not fail to advance the conservative cause in our own internal politics and would justify us in regarding Federal political developments with greater composure.

Klenze, who represented Hanover in the negotiations, realized that Prussia urgently needed to include all northern Germany in the Zollverein in case the three southern German states should decide to join the Austrian customs system. Consequently he was able to secure very favourable terms for Hanover in a treaty with Prussia that was signed in September 1851. Hanover gained excellent financial terms — a guaranteed revenue of 75 per cent more than that to which she would be entitled on a basis of population. Prussia agreed that the rails needed for the completion of Hanover's railway system should be admitted free of duty and that in 1854 the Zollverein import duties on coffee, tea, tobacco, syrup and cognac should be reduced. At some financial sacrifice Prussia had gained economic control over virtually all northern Germany — except Hamburg and Bremen — and had firmly linked Westphalia and the Rhineland with her eastern provinces. Germany's major industries, mining regions and lines of communication lay to the north of the River Main and now came under Prussian influence. Even if the southern states left the Zollverein the major states in the north — Prussia, Saxony and Hanover — could operate a viable customs union of their own. In November 1851 the Prussian government invited members of the Zollverein to a conference in Berlin to discuss the future of the customs union when the Zollverein treaties expired at the end of 1853. Prussia stated that the terms of the recent agreement that she had made with Hanover would be embodied in the new treaties.

Prince Schwarzenberg now attempted to seize the initiative in the struggle for economic supremacy in Germany. He published the revised Austrian tariff — which was to come into force early in 1852 — and he issued invitations to a conference to be held in Vienna to consider the establishment of a customs union between Austria and the German states. Prussia declined the invitation but proposed that negotiations for a commercial treaty with Austria should take place after the Zollverein treaties had been renewed.

The conference called by the Austrian government met in Vienna on 4 January 1852. No representative from Prussia attended. Three draft agreements were drawn up between Austria and the major German states other than Prussia. The first was a commercial treaty and the second envisaged the establishment of a customs union in 1859. The third was a secret convention that would come into force if Prussia continued to oppose the establishment of an Austro-German customs union. It provided for the establishment of a customs union between Austria, Bavaria, Württemberg, Baden, Saxony, Nassau, Hesse-Cassel and Hesse-Darmstadt. In April 1852 representatives of the German states, which had agreed to the proposals recently discussed in Vienna, met at Darmstadt. They decided to set up a little customs union among themselves that would negotiate with the Austrian government for the establishment of an Austro-German customs union — if necessary without Prussia. It was hoped to keep these conventions secret, but they were published in the *Vossische Zeitung* on 24 April.

While the discussions in Darmstadt were taking place, news was received of the death of Prince Schwarzenberg at the age of fifty-two. Since the collapse of the revolution he had been the driving force behind the political and economic reorganization of Austria and the attempt to establish a central European customs union. Delbrück paid tribute to his 'creative power and ruthless energy'. Now that Schwarzenberg was dead and Bruck was out of office, the Austrian government was not able to press forward with the same vigour with its plans for the economic domination of Germany.

The negotiations at Darmstadt were followed by a meeting of the members of the Zollverein in Berlin. Here the supporters of the plan to establish an Austro-German customs union urged Prussia to enter into negotiations with Austria. But Prussia repeated both her refusal to negotiate and her offer to discuss a commercial treaty with Austria after the renewal of the Zollverein treaties. Shortly afterwards the Czar of Russia and his foreign minister Nesselrode visited Vienna and Berlin and urged the Austrian and Prussian governments to settle their differences over the future economic organization of Germany. But their efforts were unsuccessful and a complete deadlock was reached in September 1852, when Prussia told members of the Zollverein that in future she would negotiate separately with each state concerning the renewal of its Zollverein treaty.

The deadlock was broken when Bruck decided to return to active politics. At his suggestion Buol, the new Austrian foreign minister, wrote to Manteuffel, the Prussian minister president, urging the opening of direct negotiations between Austria and Prussia. At last Prussia agreed to enter into discussions with Austria before (and not after) the Zollverein treaties had been renewed. Bruck was appointed the Austrian representative in these discussions, while Delbrück and Pommer-Esche were the Prussian representatives. Agreement was reached surprisingly quickly and an Austro-Prussian commercial treaty was signed on 19 February 1853. The treaty provided for a system of differential import duties so that many goods exchanged between Austria and the Zollverein would in future pay lower duties than those levied on imports from other countries. In the past the Zollverein had granted preferences only in exceptional circumstances. Now the trade between Austria and the Zollverein was placed on an entirely different footing from trade between either Austria or the Zollverein and other states.

Bruck regarded the February treaty as a great success for Austria since, in his view, it could be regarded as a first step towards the establishment of an Austro-German customs union. Indeed the treaty actually provided for negotiations in 1860 to set up such a union. But Hock, an official in the Austrian Ministry of Finance, took a more realistic view when he admitted that for Austria the February treaty was only 'a not very advantageous armistice'. Delbrück was well satisfied with the treaty because it paved the way for the renewal of the Zollverein treaties (including the agreement between Prussia and Hanover) for another 12 years. Nothing had come of Bruck's dream of an Austro-German customs union and the chances of the revival of the plan in the immediate future were very slim indeed.

7   *Germany at the Crystal Palace, 1851*

The struggle between Austria and Prussia for economic leadership in Germany had followed hard upon a revolution, a commercial crisis and harvest failures, which had slowed down industrial expansion, consumer demand, investment and railway building. Nevertheless Germany was well represented at the 'Great Exhibition of the Works of Industry of all Nations', which was held in London at the Crystal Palace in 1851. The number of German entries did not fall far short of the French entries. When Scott Russell, secretary of the Society of Arts, visited Berlin in the autumn of 1849 to give the Prussian authorities information concerning the proposed exhibition, he was warmly welcomed by ministers like August von der Heydt and by officials like von Pommer-Esche and J. W. Wedding. At first each German state made its own arrangements for sending exhibits to London. In Prussia, for example, an official commission of fifteen members — headed by G. W. von Viehbahn and Rudolph von Delbrück — was set up for this purpose. Prussia urged members of the Zollverein to cooperate so that all the German entries to the exhibition might be shown together. But it was not until February 1851 that a Zollverein commission was established to do this and it was only at the end of March that Saxony and Württemberg fell into line with other Zollverein states in this matter. Hamburg, Mecklenburg-Strelitz and Mecklenburg-Schwerin, although not members of the Zollverein, were represented on this commission. But the exhibits of Bremen, Lübeck, Hanover and Oldenburg were shown separately from the rest of the German entries.

The exhibits sent to the Crystal Palace made it possible to assess the progress made by German manufacturers in recent years. The traditional skills of German craftsmen were shown in the exhibits of porcelain from Meissen and Nymphenburg; toys from the Black Forest; furniture from Hamburg; pencils from Stein (Nürnberg); cutlery from Solingen and Remscheid; and books from Leipzig. These were mainly the products of small-scale industries and many of them were declining in importance when compared with the products of large-scale factory industries. It was woollen and cotton cloths and the products of the iron, steel and engineering industries that showed that Germany was moving into the modern industrial age.

There were 1,720 German exhibitors at the Crystal Palace and most of them came from Prussia, while next in importance were those from Saxony, Württemberg and Bavaria. Some large undertakings held aloof from the exhibition. They included the Prussian Overseas Trading Corporation (Seehandlung) and the well-known engineering firms of Borsig, Henschel, Mannhardt and Maffei. Suspicion of foreign competitors — the fear that products shown at the exhibition might be copied by unscrupulous rivals — may account for the failure of these firms to send any exhibits to London.

The German iron and steel industry was well represented at the Crystal Palace by exhibits from the Prussian state foundries in Silesia, from the metalworks in the Siegerland and from undertakings in the Ruhr such as those of Krupp, Stinnes, Mannesmann and Haniel. It proved to be a turning-point in his career when Alfred Krupp showed his 4,300-pound block of steel and a 6-pounder field gun with a cast-steel barrel. Friedrich Harkort, who had played a leading part in fostering the industrialization of Westphalia and the Rhineland, wrote that Krupp's steel ingot was 'one of the most remarkable monuments in the history of the industrial development of Germany'. The subsequent expansion of Krupp's output of steel and armaments proved to be a striking feature of the growth of the Ruhr industrial region. Equally significant was the electric telegraph shown by the recently-established firm of Siemens & Halske, for this represented a new industry in which German inventors and entrepreneurs were to excel in later years. On the other hand Germany's exhibits of textiles were, on the whole, disappointing. In an attempt to compete in mass markets with rival industries more advanced than their own, textile manufacturers were often turning out cloths of only moderate quality. Their designs lacked originality and indeed were sometimes simply copied from those of foreign competitors.

Several German visitors to the Crystal Palace were disappointed at the failure of the Zollverein to show its exhibits to the best advantage. Doubtless the main reason for this was that each German state had made its own arrangements and the decision of members of the Zollverein to collaborate had come too late to be effective. A writer in the *Vereinsblatt für deutsche Arbeit* complained of 'the contempt with which visitors generally look down upon the German entries at the exhi-

bition . . . . In conversation with foreigners one hardly ever hears
Germany mentioned. One might almost suppose that as far as the
English, Americans, French and Russians are concerned, Germany
does not exist.' The journal also complained that German exhibitors
had not gone to the Crystal Palace determined to win as many medals
as possible.

In his first report on the exhibition the London correspondent of
the influential Augsburg *Allgemeine Zeitung* observed that while the
exhibits from England and France were unmistakably English and
French in character, the German exhibits lacked any specifically
national characteristics. The writer argued that too many German
manufactured articles were mere copies of foreign products. But a
report from the official Zollverein Commission struck a more opti-
mistic note and expressed satisfaction at the high standard attained
by the German exhibits. They had shown to the world 'the great
significance of our German Fatherland' in the production of manufactured goods and of craftwork of artistic merit. Other German
commentators argued that while England and the United States concentrated on the manufacture of mass-produced articles and France
was famed for her high-quality luxury goods, Germany had achieved
a happy mean between these extremes and was able to make both
popular cheap goods and more expensive products.

Whatever their views concerning the Zollverein goods displayed
at the Great Exhibition, German visitors could not fail to be impressed
by the evidence of England's dominant position at that time as the
leading manufacturing country in the world. And they saw that
England's industrial power was reflected in her political power in
international affairs. They realized that if German industry continued
to expand, political unity might become a reality and not merely a
dream. Twenty years after the Great Exhibition this had come about.
By 1871 Germany had become the leading industrial country on the
Continent and at the same time she had achieved the unity that had
eluded the Frankfurt parliament in 1848.

II

The Rise of the Great Industries
1851-1873

8   Boom and Slump, 1851-57

The years 1851 to 1873 have been described as 'a period of specially intensive growth' for the German economy. It was a period of rising prices, expanding demand, growth in productive capacity, and rising exports.

Industry and agriculture on the Continent had been depressed between 1847 and 1849. During the revolution industrial output had declined, prices had fallen, unemployment had risen, the value of shares had sunk and gold and silver had been hoarded. There had been a flight of capital from the Continent to the United States, where railways were being built and new regions in the west were being opened up. German investments in the United States amounted to at least 150 million dollars in the 1850s. The collapse of the revolution was followed by a period of economic recovery. In Germany—indeed in all the countries on the Continent that were being industrialized—there was a boom in industry and agriculture between 1851 and 1857.

Various factors promoted an economic revival in the 1850s. One was the establishment of authoritarian governments on the Continent that re-established law and order. In 1848 many middle-class liberals had supported revolutionary movements but their attitude had soon changed when they realized that a successful revolution might leave extremists in control. There was a fear of anarchy. So they dropped most of their demands for constitutional reforms and accepted the establishment of authoritarian regimes. Before long Louis Napoleon, the Habsburgs and the Hohenzollerns were in power, supported by the army, the police, the clergy and the civil service. The leaders of the revolution were in prison or in exile. Press censorship was revived; workers' associations were forbidden; public meetings and demonstrations were severely restricted. That reactionary governments enjoyed a wide measure of public support at this time—as guardians of law and order—could be seen by the large majorities gained by Louis Napoleon in the plebiscites of 1848 and 1850.

The reactionary regimes realized, however, that some concessions would have to be made not only to the middle classes but also to the peasants and to the urban workers. It is something of a paradox that on the one hand the authoritarian rulers halted any advance towards democracy and suppressed freedom of expression, while on the other hand they were responsible for far-reaching economic and social reforms. Thus in Prussia the peasants were at last freed from manorial dues and obligations. The mining industry was liberated from the shackles of rigid government control and its burden of taxation was reduced. The railway network—essential to industrial progress—was rapidly expanded and a number of lines were nationalized. A factory law prohibited the employment of children under the age of 12 and reduced the labour of those aged between 12 and 14 years to 6 hours a day. Factory children were not allowed to work at night and provision was made for their part-time education. In Austria, as in Prussia, the feudal obligations of the peasants disappeared. Prince Schwarzenberg, like Manteuffel, introduced a number of reforms which stimulated the economic development of the country. Württemberg led the way in Germany by abolishing restrictions on entry into trades. By the 1860s most German workers were free to move from one part of the country to another and they could emigrate if they wished to do so. About 2 million people left the country between 1850 and 1870 to settle overseas.

The authoritarian governments on the Continent also fostered industrial and agricultural progress by reducing tariffs and by establishing larger economic units. When Britain adopted a free-trade policy she hoped that other countries would follow her example, but only a few of the smaller states on the Continent, such as Belgium, did so. The larger countries considered that their industries had not yet developed sufficiently to warrant dropping protective duties. But some progress was made in abolishing internal tariff barriers. In Germany, although Bruck failed to establish a central European customs union, the Zollverein absorbed the Tax Union, while Austria abolished her customs frontier with Hungary. The Austro-Prussian commercial treaty of February 1853 introduced a system of preferential duties which—in the view of Tooke and Newmarch—was 'almost equivalent in its effects to a free trade measure of the most absolute character'. Russia abolished her customs frontier with Poland, while her tariffs of 1851 and 1857 were more liberal than previous tariffs. In Switzerland the tariff barriers between the cantons disappeared. In France Napoleon III at first hesitated to reduce import duties, since public opinion strongly favoured the traditional prohibitive tariff, but in 1860 the Anglo-French treaty of commerce provided for a substantial reduction in the level of many French import duties. These reforms enabled goods to be exchanged more freely in many parts of Europe and fostered the economic expansion of the 1850s.

Another factor that helped to stimulate economic progress at this time was the expansion of European influence in various parts of the world. The French extended their possessions in Algiers, the Russians in Amur and the English in India, while in 1854 Japan emerged from her isolation and came into commercial contact with the western world. The opening up of new regions overseas provided Europe with raw materials and foodstuffs in return for manufactured products. Although the lion's share of this trade was in English hands, German merchants began to open up commerce between Hamburg and Africa and the Pacific. William O'Swald in Zanzibar, Carl Woermann in the Cameroons and J.C. Godeffroy in Samoa were active in regions formerly neglected by European traders or dominated by English and American merchants.

The boom of 1851-7 was not halted by the Crimean War. Neither Germany nor Austria took part in the war. Both gained some advantage from their neutrality by supplying belligerents with foodstuffs, textiles, armaments and shipping facilities. Prussian merchants handled some of Russia's foreign trade that normally went by sea. In 1855 the Hull Chamber of Commerce reported that 'the frontiers of Prussia being open to the transport of goods to and from Russia, it appears that the articles of flax, hemp, tallow, and linseed to some extent, have been able to bear the heavy land-carriage charges for shipment at Memel and Königsberg, so that the importation of these articles (linseed excepted) has been kept fully adequate to the consumption of this district'. Moreover, the presence of French and English troops in Turkey paved the way for a revival of trade in the eastern Mediterranean when the war was over.

More important than the factors discussed so far was the increased output of gold in the 1850s. The sudden influx of gold to Europe from the United States and Australia had consequences as significant as those that had followed the Spanish exploitation of the Potosí silver-mines in the sixteenth century. Tooke and Newmarch estimated that between 1848 and 1856 California, Victoria, New South Wales and Russia produced gold to the value of £174,425,000. This rapid increase in the world's stock of gold has been described as 'a Currency Extension

Act of Nature'. It led to a general rise in prices, which gave industrialists and businessmen confidence in the future. The gold discoveries,
as *The Times* put it, gave 'an electric impulse to our entire business
world'.

The new gold—coupled with the export of foodstuffs and raw materials—enabled Americans and Australians to buy more manufactured
goods from Europe. And the lure of gold was one factor that stimulated
the flow of new settlers to the United States and Australia. About
1.5 million Germans — mainly from the south-west of the country —
emigrated to the United States between 1846 and 1857. These settlers
became purchasers of European manufactured goods and this too
encouraged business activity in Britain and on the Continent and
helped to maintain employment at a high level.

The increased supply of gold strengthened both the currencies and
the banking systems of many European states. While Britain was on the
gold standard, the states on the Continent were on the silver standard.
In the 1850s central banks increased their holdings of gold. In 1849,
for example, the Bank of France held virtually only silver reserves, but
5 years later rather more than half the reserves were in gold.

Moreover the new gold enabled central and other banks to secure
greater cover for their note issues and to extend more credit to businessmen. In the early 1850s the Bank of England charged only 2.5 per
cent for loans, but then an ever-increasing demand for credit forced
the rate up to nearly 6 per cent in 1856. In Prussia the increase at this
time was less spectacular—from 4 per cent to 5 per cent.

At the same time changes of a more radical nature were taking
place in continental banking. The 'banking revolution' was yet another factor that stimulated economic progress in the 1850s. In 1848
the *Comptoir National d'Escompte* was founded in Paris and the
Schaaffhausen Bank of Cologne was reorganized. This heralded the
establishment of a new type of credit bank on the Continent. The
Crédit mobilier of Paris was the most famous of these credit banks,
which acted as agents in placing the shares of new firms on the market.
The credit banks purchased shares in new firms and their representatives often became directors of the companies that they had helped
to float. This close association between business and banking became
an important feature of the financial organization of industry in
Germany. Some of the new banks were authorized to issue notes.
In 1851 only 9 German banks had the right to issue notes, but in
1857 there were 29. The Prussian authorities became alarmed at the

number of small notes issued by these banks that were in circulation and in 1855 Prussia forbade the circulation of non-Prussian banknotes under 10 thalers in value.

The State soon followed the example of the credit banks and joint-stock companies in attracting the savings of small investors. Hitherto state loans had been floated by groups of private banks that specialized in this kind of business. During the Crimean War Austria and France floated loans of a new type. They were offered to the general public in small shares that could be purchased in instalments. They proved to be very popular with small investors. Three French loans issued in 1854 and 1855 raised £60,000,000. A little later another French state loan attracted nearly 700,000 subscribers.

In 1856 the French consul in Leipzig wrote that in Germany 'every town and every state—however small it may be—wants its bank and its Crédit mobilier . . . . It seems that as much energy is being put into covering Germany with a network of credit banks as has been put into creating a railway network'. His English colleague reported in the same year:

> New railways are everywhere projected, and numerous mining and other industrial companies are being formed . . . . In Saxony alone, above 30 new coal-mining associations have lately been established for working newly discovered beds of coal, chiefly in the district of which Zwickau is the centre. But the favourite enterprises of the day are credit institutions, or banks, upon the plan of the French Crédit mobilier.

The economic boom of the 1850s owed much to the gold discoveries, the new credit banks, the new joint-stock companies and the activities of the State. But its effects might have been delayed had not transport facilities been expanded to meet the need to move more people and more freight than before. Germans could hardly have crossed the Atlantic in their tens of thousands if Bremen had not developed as a major port for emigrants. And the extension of the railway network speeded up the movement of raw materials to the factories and of manufactured goods to the consumers. The length of railway lines in operation in Germany was over 11,000 kilometres in 1860 as compared with 5,856 kilometres ten years before. In Prussia the capital invested in railways rose from 158.5 million thalers in 1848 to 362.5 million thalers in 1857.

The industrial expansion in Germany in 1851-7 was also stimulated by the introduction of foreign capital and skill. The activities of French and English entrepreneurs may serve as an example. There was a substantial investment of French capital in collieries in the Ruhr and Silesia and some French iron companies owned coalmines in Germany. The general manager of the Phoenix Mining and Metal-lurgical Company — one of the largest firms in the Ruhr in the 1850s — was Charles Detillieux, a French engineer. The firm operated 11 blast furnaces, 2 coalmines and several iron-ore mines. Detillieux also established the Gelsenkirchen Mining Company. French capital and mining skill promoted the expansion of Germany's zinc, lead, copper and silver industries. André Koechlin of Mulhouse and the Marquis de Sassenay reorganized the Stolberg and Westphalian Mining, Lead and Zinc Manufacturing Company in 1852. The *Société de la Vieille-Montagne* exploited zinc and other non-ferrous metals in the Rhineland and Silesia. The Rhenish Copper Mining and Foundry Company was dominated by French capital and had a French general manager and a French chief engineer. In the glass industry French entrepreneurs established the Glass Company of Aachen in 1852-3. André Koechlin was the first chairman of the board of directors, while the Marquis de Sassenay was the general manager. After the Crimean War *The Economist* wrote: 'Frenchmen have invested immense sums in the railways, banks, Crédits mobilier [*sic*], and enterprises of all kinds which have been started in Germany since the peace.'

English entrepreneurs were also active in Germany in the 1850s. Their enterprises in the Ruhr included the Ruhrort Coalmining Com-pany (Westende mine), the New Scotland Mining and Ironworking Company, the Anglo-Belgian Mining Company and the Hibernia and Shamrock Mining Company (founded by the Irish entrepreneur W.T. Mulvany). An English firm—the Imperial Gas Association—supplied many German towns with gas.

At the start of the boom the Cologne banker Gustav Mevissen warned his countrymen of the danger of allowing German industry to fall under foreign domination. He wrote:

> Owing to our failure to participate in so productive an activity as the exploitation of our mines — a source of national wealth hitherto inadequately tapped owing to a lack both of a spirit of enterprise and of capital—there has, in recent years, been an ever-increasing danger that this will fall into the hands of foreign speculators. It

is well known that for some time in the Rhineland a number of coal measures have been acquired on behalf of French and English capitalists who will profit by exploiting them. The treasures beneath the soil of our Fatherland thus help to increase the preponderance which foreign capital already possesses elsewhere and the produce of German labour will benefit foreign shareholders. It is obviously in the supreme interests of our economy that we should retain not only these earnings but also the capital itself.

All these factors promoted an expansion of industry in the early 1850s that Germany had never known before. Between 1851 and 1857 the output of coal in the Zollverein rose from 5.8 million tons to 14.8 million tons and that of pig-iron rose from 225,000 tons to 535,000 tons. The value of textile manufactures rose from £ 31.8 millions a year in the 1840s to nearly £40 millions a year in the 1850s. The expansion of the coalfields, such as the Ruhr, was particularly striking. New mines and ironworks were established and the production of coal, pig-iron, steel and textiles rapidly increased. New railways were built, new banks of the traditional kind and new credit banks were founded, and new joint-stock companies were set up to operate all kinds of manufacturing enterprises. As Max Wirth put it, 'tall chimneys grew like mushrooms' in this period.

Germany's industrial expansion was briefly halted in 1857 by an economic depression that began in the United States and had worldwide repercussions. Although Germany was not so seriously affected as the United States or Britain, the crisis checked economic growth and exposed the weaknesses of some of the recently established joint-stock companies and credit banks. Some German manufacturers and bankers received a salutary lesson on the folly of over-expansion. The prosperity of the early 1850s had led to a spirit of over-optimism in the business world. While many of the new industrial undertakings and banks had conducted their affairs in an efficient manner, some had tried to expand their operations too quickly and had declared larger dividends than was prudent.

The fate of the Phoenix Mining and Metallurgical Company may serve as an example. In 1854 it was reported that this iron and coal firm 'exceeds all previous enterprises in splendour and size; its fine premises are rapidly approaching completion; two furnaces at Dilldorf and two in Ruhrort are in full blast . . . . The company has already erected . . . 40 puddling hearths . . . . The company has a capital of three million thalers and wants to increase this to six million'. But in 1858 the company was short of funds and was unable to persuade investors to buy any new shares. In 1860 no dividend was paid. A year later an anonymous critic denounced the management for the way in which a promising enterprise had been allowed 'to meander on leisurely . . . without a care for the future, or the money and fate of the shareholders'. Eventually nine-tenths of the capital had to be written off.

At the same time some of the new credit banks came in for severe criticism. The Magdeburg Chamber of Commerce, in its report for 1860, declared that such banks had been

. . . established in places lacking all the opportunities which lead to successful business. They recklessly unloaded their notes onto the public. Their statutes allowed them to embark upon transactions which no note-issue bank ought to be allowed to undertake and, in doing so, they placed themselves on a level with the Paris Crédit mobilier. By their loans to industry and by their policy of discounting bills they wantonly encouraged over-speculation and the wildest business activities. They misled people into setting up factories and other establishments by persuading them that the credit they were offering was of a permanent nature. But they soon had to withdraw their support when their own credit was shattered and when their own notes—by which the newly-established firms were forcibly fed—no longer sufficed to support the original over-optimistic credit. It is usually believed that here in Germany ruinous bank crashes — such as have occurred in Great Britain and in the United States—are not possible or at any rate are unlikely. People think that in Germany they are reasonably protected from folly and incompetence by the supervision which the state exercises over the banks and by the regular publication of bank returns. That the first precaution—government supervision—is a protection of doubtful value, particularly in the smaller states, is proved by the financial returns of various banks that lie before us. In these financial returns and in the enterprises promoted by German banks of issue we find plenty of evidence to support our assertion that a bank can be ruined as quickly and as suddenly with government supervision as without it. When we see that a bank with an acknowledged deficit equal to a quarter of its original capital, is nevertheless allowed to pay a dividend to its shareholders, and when dubious and half-lost sums are included in bank balances and bank statements as if they were assets, we doubt whether we are so very far off from the road that will lead us to a state of affairs similar to that of the United States.

The depression of 1857 began in the United States. A bumper grain harvest led to a fall in wheat prices, which placed some farmers in the western states in financial difficulties. Unable to pay interest on existing loans, they tried to borrow more money from the local banks. The difficulties of these banks in turn had repercussions in the eastern states. In August 1857 the failure of the Ohio Life Insurance Trust led to a panic and in September there were many bank failures in states as far apart as Pennsylvania and Virginia. In October there was a run on the New York banks and eighteen closed their doors. When news reached England of the collapse of the Ohio bank some firms engaged in American trade ran into difficulties since they had sent goods to the United States on credit and feared that these debts would never be paid. In October four Glasgow firms that made sewed muslin fabrics and traded in the American market failed. They owed over £1,600,000 to the Western Bank of Scotland, which had to suspend payments. Friedrich Engels wrote that 'in Glasgow in addition to the 30 failures mentioned in the press, numerous medium-sized and small firms have gone to the wall without comment from anybody'. In Liverpool the Borough Bank and Messrs Dennistoun failed, while in London two firms of bill-brokers could not meet their obligations. The Northumberland and Durham District Bank and the Wolverhampton and Staffordshire Bank suffered a similar fate.

The crisis soon spread from England to the Continent. In cities such as Hamburg the merchants who were engaged in various branches of import-export trade found themselves in serious difficulties. It has been seen that in Germany some banks and industrial undertakings were vulnerable to any shock to public confidence. The failures in New York, London and Hamburg led to panic selling of shares and to runs on banks. The tempo of business slowed down and the growth of the economy was checked.

Moreover the situation was aggravated on the Continent by a 'silver drain'. In the 1850s there had been an expansion in the trade between Europe and the United States on the one hand and India and China on the other hand. Eastern exports to the West — silk, tea, cotton and rice—were larger than western exports to the East and the balance had to be paid in silver. At first this posed no problems, since the influx of new gold to Europe freed some silver for the eastern trade. In 1856-7, however, there was an abnormal increase in the 'silver drain' owing to unusually high silk imports from the Far East and to an exceptional flow of silver to the East at the time of the Indian Mutiny and the second China War. So at the very time that banks, bill-brokers, merchants and industrialists faced a world depression, central and other note-issuing banks on the Continent experienced difficulties in maintaining adequate silver supplies for their requirements.

In Germany it was the export and import mercantile and finance houses of Hamburg that were most severely hit by the commercial crisis. The English failures and the rise of the bank rate in London led to a panic in Hamburg that was a focal point for financing the trade of northern Germany and the Baltic. The outstanding acceptances of the merchants of Hamburg had risen sharply during the boom and amounted to £30 million in 1857. The British consul-general reported on 23 November that 'commercial confidence is entirely at an end among the merchants and moneyed capitalists of Hamburg; and that only bills on *three* or *four* of the first houses are negotiable at the highest rate of interest'. A week later he wrote that 'the embarrassments of ᵗhe mercantile community here still continue undiminished'.

One hundred and fifty Hamburg firms with liabilities of £15 million failed and they included some of the oldest and most reputable merchant houses, such as that of Christian Matthias Schröder. Various attempts were made to restore confidence. A Discount Guarantee Association was set up but its funds were quickly exhausted. Then an official Loan Institute was set up to make advances to merchants on the security of their goods. Administrators were appointed to manage the affairs of firms that could not at the moment meet their liabilities but had a good chance of doing so in the future. By 10 December 1857, 65 out of 135 bankrupt firms had been placed in charge of administrators. Next the senate set up another discount fund and sought financial aid from outside Hamburg. The Prussian government, having financial problems of its own, turned down Hamburg's request, but then help came from an unexpected quarter. The Austrian government arranged for the National Bank to send £750,000 in silver by special train to Hamburg. Finally the Hamburg Union Bank (*Vereinsbank*) and the Bank of North Germany were persuaded to guarantee 40 per cent of the acceptances of five leading Hamburg firms, on the understanding that the senate guaranteed the other 60 per cent. These measures restored confidence to some extent and by the end of 1857 the worst of the crisis was over; although early in 1858 there were still 34 million pounds of coffee unsold in Hamburg warehouses, while considerable quantities of butter could not be sold as food but had to be disposed of cheaply to carters who used it to grease the wheels of their waggons.

The crisis in Hamburg was soon followed by failures in other parts of Germany. In Berlin several firms collapsed, including Palmié Brothers—with debts of over 1,500,000 thalers—and the woollen manufacturer Julius Cohen, who shot himself. The major ports, such as Stettin and Danzig, suffered severely, though Bremen had only fourteen failures. The reason for this, according to Max Wirth, was that—unlike their neighbours in Hamburg—the merchants of Bremen did not indulge in luxurious living, and did not engage in risky speculative enterprises. There were also bankruptcies in several inland commercial centres such as Cologne, Magdeburg, Leipzig and Stuttgart. In Austria one of the most spectacular failures was that of the firm of Boskowitz, which had burned its fingers by speculating in grain. Industrial undertakings in Germany were less affected than commercial firms engaged in export-import trade. But the textile regions suffered from a decline in orders. The government of each German state tried to alleviate the effects of the crisis in its own way. In Prussia, for example, the law limiting the rate of interest was suspended for three months, and the Bank of Prussia was authorized to give credit to merchants and manufacturers on the security of goods.

Recovery was slow. The foreign trade of the Zollverein declined from 994 million thalers in 1857 to 886 million thalers in 1859. An association of Berlin merchants reported in 1858 that

. . . confidence, once greatly encouraged by speculation, suddenly vanished. Expensive goods which had been stored in warehouses were disposed of quite slowly and at considerable sacrifice by merchants. Markets vanished, for consumers believed that they could —indeed must—wait for yet a further fall in prices. They bought with the greatest hesitation and caution. Goods were thrown onto the market at bargain prices. There was also a great reluctance to give credit. Many orders were cancelled owing to lack of confidence. This state of affairs was fairly common in all places of business.

Everywhere months passed before industry and commerce showed signs of recovery from the calamitous events which continued into the early months of 1858.

The boom of 1851-7 had enabled Germany to develop as an industrial power to such a degree that she could not hope to avoid involvement in a world economic crisis. Some of her merchants, bankers and manufacturers learned by bitter experience that over-trading and over-production could lead to disaster. By the 1860s the German economy had shed some of its inefficient firms. Larger companies were being established and banks were adopting a more cautious policy in financing new industrial enterprises.

9   The Banking Revolution

In 1848, when Germany was in the throes of a political revolution, an event occurred in Cologne that inaugurated a very different kind of revolution. This was the reorganization of the Schaaffhausen Bank. Few people realized at the time that this was a new type of financial institution and that it heralded a new era in the history of banking. While English bankers considered long-term involvement in industry to be unsound banking practice, those responsible for running the new credit banks in Germany were directly concerned with promoting the establishment of new manufacturing enterprises. They were prepared to risk their depositors' money in a way that English bankers would have considered irresponsible. Consequently — although they incurred losses from injudicious investments from time to time — the new credit banks in Germany played a vitally important role in fostering the forward march of the industrial sector of the economy.

When the old-established private bank of Abraham Schaaffhausen ran into financial difficulties in 1848 its creditors agreed to its reorganization as a joint-stock company. The policy of Gustav Mevissen, the driving force behind the new venture, was to buy shares in recently established industrial and commercial undertakings and so encourage the economic expansion of Cologne and the Rhineland. At first the resources of the bank were limited, since it had to pay off the debts of its predecessor. Even so it was able to assist some new companies in its early days. These included mining companies — such as the Hörder Verein, which exploited blackband-ore near Dortmund — local railways, insurance companies, a cotton-mill and an engineering plant. In 1852 the directors of the Schaaffhausen Bank declared that they did not propose to call new firms into being by making large investments in their shares. They proposed to give limited financial aid to promising new companies in the Rhineland and so encourage private investors to buy shares in these undertakings.

The business handled by the Schaaffhausen Bank was at first too small to attract much attention. It was the initial spectacular success of a new credit bank — a 'company-promoting bank' — in France that gave an impetus to the creation of such institutions all over the Continent. The Crédit mobilier of Paris was founded by Emile and Isaac Pereire, who had already made their reputation as promoters of railway companies. With them were associated the brothers Achille and Benoît Fould. The former was a minister of state, while the latter was a partner in the banking house of B. L. Fould & Fould-Oppenheim. The Pereire brothers had been influenced by the doctrines of Saint-Simon and by the activities of the *Caisse Laffitte* in France and the *Société générale* in Belgium. They believed that the financial needs of the State and the promotion of public utilities and industrial undertakings should not depend solely upon the goodwill of a small group of powerful Paris banks. The Pereires proposed that a new credit bank should be established in Paris through which the savings of small investors could be used to promote the establishment of public works and manufacturing enterprises. By purchasing shares in new companies they hoped to encourage other investors to follow their example.

It is hardly surprising that this grandiose scheme should have been opposed by conservative financiers, who feared that they would have to face serious competition from the new bank. James Rothschild denounced the proposed new bank. He declared that it would give the Pereires 'exorbitant financial power' and that it would 'excite speculation' and flood the country with 'an ever-increasing mass of paper'. The new bank would grow into an irresponsible monopoly. Rothschild foresaw for France a gloomy future 'full of storms and calamities' if Louis Napoleon agreed to the establishment of the new bank.

But Louis Napoleon did authorize the setting-up of the Crédit mobilier. He was not impressed by the warnings of James Rothschild, who had been a staunch supporter of the Orleanist regime. The memorandum that officially established the Crédit mobilier appeared in the *Moniteur* on 20 November 1852. The new credit bank had an initial capital of 60 million francs — 120,000 shares at 500 francs a share.

In their first report the directors of the Crédit mobilier explained why the new bank had been set up and what it proposed to do:

The idea of the Crédit mobilier is born of the insufficient credit available for the organisation of business on a large scale in this country, of the isolation in which the forces of finance are placed, of the lack of a centre strong enough to draw them together.

It is born of the need to bring upon the market the regular support of new capital designed to aid in the development of public and industrial credit.

It is born of the exorbitant conditions under which loans are made upon the public funds and the difficulties which arise therefrom for the definitive placement of even the best securities.

It is born moreover of the need to centralize the financial and administrative activities of the great companies, especially railway companies, and so to utilize for the greatest advantage of all, the capital which each in turn has on hand. . . .

It is born, finally, of the necessity of introducing into circulation a new agent, a new fiduciary currency, carrying with it its daily interest, and enabling the humblest savings to fructify as well as ample fortunes.

The Pereires, however, had even more ambitious schemes than this. They hoped that the Crédit mobilier would stimulate not merely the industrialization of France but the industrialization of neighbouring countries as well. When the Crédit mobilier was set up its shareholders included foreign bankers such as Abraham Oppenheim of Cologne and Solomon Heine of Hamburg. Through the Crédit mobilier French capital could exploit the dominant resources of underdeveloped countries such as Austria, Russia, Spain, Italy and Portugal. The interest on French investments abroad would be a valuable source of income in the future.

In the 1850s the Pereires ran what appeared to be a remarkably successful enterprise. The Crédit mobilier paid high dividends — over 40 per cent in 1855 — and at the height of its fortunes it handled nearly one-third of the new securities launched in Paris. It played a leading role in promoting the railway amalgamations that gave France one of the best-organized railway systems in Europe. The Crédit mobilier reorganized the collieries in the Loire coalfield, united the omnibus companies in Paris, founded insurance and gas companies and established a great shipping company (*Compagnie générale transatlantique*) and an equally important construction company (*Compagnie immobilière*). It also invested funds in many undertakings abroad, either directly or through the subsidiary credit banks. In Austria, Russia and Spain it set up companies that operated public utilities, railways, mines and industrial enterprises. It had a substantial stake (40 million francs) in a new French land bank — the *Crédit foncier* — and it subscribed to French state loans. Although the Crédit mobilier had only a short life — it crashed in 1867 — its brilliant achievements in the 1850s inspired the establishment of many credit banks in France and elsewhere. Clapham writes that it was 'a forerunner of all later "industrial banking", and in particular of the close associations with industry of the great banks of imperial Germany'.

One was the Bank of Commerce and Industry that was set up in Darmstadt in April 1853. Its promoter was Moritz von Haber, a banker from Karlsruhe, and his financial backers were the Cologne bankers Abraham Oppenheim, Gustav Mevissen, W. L. Deichmann and W. Wendelstadt. They had to surmount various obstacles before their credit bank could open its doors. It was not easy to find a suitable city in which the authorities would allow a new bank to be established. In Frankfurt-am-Main the opposition of the Rothschilds was sufficient to ensure the opposition of the Frankfurt senate to the proposed bank. And the Prussian authorities were reluctant to see another credit bank set up in Cologne where one was already in existence. But the Grand Duke of Hesse-Darmstadt was glad to welcome a new bank to his capital and Oppenheim and his associates established the bank there. Darmstadt was close to Frankfurt, so much of the business of the bank could be transacted on the Frankfurt stock exchange. Next came the problem of raising the initial capital. Owing to the opposition of established banks there was little likelihood of selling shares of the new bank in Frankfurt, Cologne or Berlin. So Oppenheim turned to the Pereires for help. The promoters of the Darmstadt Bank formed a syndicate with the Crédit mobilier to raise the necessary money. It was arranged that the Crédit mobilier should buy a block of shares and that ten thousand shares (at par) should be allocated to shareholders of the Crédit mobilier who wished to invest in the Darmstadt Bank. The efforts of the syndicate were nearly thwarted by the wrecking tactics of a rival group of German bankers, but in the end the Darmstadt Bank was successfully launched. Rondo Cameron observes: 'Although the initiative for the bank came from Germany, the inspiration, the idea, most of the capital and a large part of the practical experience both in promoting it and in organizing its operations came from the Crédit mobilier.'

At first progress was slow, since the Darmstadt Bank had many enemies among the established banks. But initial disappointments were followed by a period of expansion. Between 1854 and 1859 the Darmstadt Bank invested in the Austrian state railways, helped to finance five German railway companies and handled three German state loans. Like the Crédit mobilier, it invested in new manufacturing enterprises — textiles, mining, engineering and shipping. These included the North German Lloyd Shipping Company of Bremen and the Concordia Spinning and Weaving Company (formerly S. Woller) of Bunzlau and Marklissa. In 1855, however, the board of directors of the Darmstadt Bank warned their shareholders not to expect too much from investments in industrial undertakings. The Darmstadt Bank also set up a subsidiary bank — the Bank of South Germany — which had the right to issue notes. And the bank established branches in several German cities, as well as an agency in New York. Moreover it extended its activities abroad. In 1858, for example, it helped to float a state loan in Sweden. In the previous year — at the time of the commercial crisis — it had been able to make loans to the hard-pressed Hamburg senate and to several banks that were in difficulties. Early successes, however, led to over-confidence. The Darmstadt Bank declared dividends that were too high — 16.6 per cent in 1855 and 15 per cent in 1856 — and it paid the penalty for its mistakes in later years, when the shareholders had to be content with much lower dividends.

In 1856 David Hansemann reorganized the Discount Company of Berlin as a credit bank and it eventually became one of the leading banks in Germany. It had been established as a small private discount bank in 1851 and its activities had been purely local in character. Now it was turned into a limited liability partnership (*Kommanditgesellschaft*). Hansemann chose this form of organization because he could not obtain a charter from the Prussian government to establish a joint-stock company. To secure the initial capital of 10 million thalers he secured the collaboration of Gerson Bleichröder, who had recently succeeded his father as head of the private Bleichröder Bank. Bleichröder raised some of the money on the Paris money market. The Discount Company — like the Darmstadt Bank — supported the development of railways at home and abroad and subscribed to state and municipal loans. In 1859 Hansemann played a leading part in forming what later became known as the 'Prussian Consortium'. This was a group of banks that joined together to raise a loan for the Prussian government. The money was needed to defray the cost of mobilizing the army at the time of the war of Italian unification. The Discount Company also gave financial support to industrial undertakings as far apart as the Eschweiler coalfield in the west and the collieries of Upper Silesia in the east.

The year 1856 also saw the founding of another credit bank in Berlin. This was the Berlin Commercial Company, which had a capital of 15 million thalers, of which at first only 3,740,150 thalers were paid up. This company was a joint venture of bankers established in Berlin and the Rhineland. Thus Bleichröder and Mendelssohn were Berlin bankers, while Mevissen and Oppenheim were Cologne bankers. In the past German banks had generally been local banks operating in a particular region such as the Rhineland, but the Berlin Commercial Company provided a link between the financial operations of two of the most important economic regions in Germany. Like other recently established credit banks, the Berlin Commercial Company invested in German and foreign railway companies, in state and municipal loans and in industrial undertakings. In 1857 it took over the private bank of Breest & Gelpcke in Berlin. The Berlin Commercial Company did not establish any branches but conducted all its business from one office.

The refusal of Prussia to grant charters to new joint-stock banks encouraged the rulers of some of her small neighbours to authorize the founding of such banks in their territories. One of them was the *Mitteldeutsche Kreditbank*, which was established in the tiny duchy of Sachsen-Meiningen in 1856. Unlike other credit banks set up at this time, it had the right to issue notes. It soon appointed the firm of August Siebel to act as its agent in Frankfurt-am-Main. It invested in state loans — such as the Swedish loan of 1857 — and also in mining and manufacturing enterprises. Like other local banks, such as the Dessau Credit Bank, the *Mitteldeutsche Kreditbank* played an important part in promoting the expansion of the lignite industry in central Germany. It was also instrumental in founding the German Mortgage Bank in Meiningen.

Numerous other banks were established in Germany in the 1850s that followed a policy similar to that pursued by the Darmstadt Bank and the Discount Company. They were, for the most part, regional banks operating in a particular district. The Bank of Silesia (Breslau), promoted by local bankers, merchants and great landowners, fostered the expansion of mining and textiles in Silesia. The Commercial Company of Magdeburg invested money in the shares of firms operating in the province of Saxony, while the General German Credit Institute of Leipzig did much of its business in the kingdom of Saxony. The North German Bank (Hamburg) was able to come to the assistance of local firms that were in difficulties during the commercial crisis of 1857.

In Austria two important credit banks were set up in 1855, largely on the initiative of Karl Bruck, who had been appointed Minister of Finance in that year. One was the Credit Institute for Commerce and

Industry (*Kreditanstalt*), which was promoted by Anselm Rothschild of Vienna, though some of the initial capital was raised by James Rothschild in Paris. The other credit bank was a mortgage institute (*Hypothekenbank*), a subsidiary of the Austrian National Bank, with a capital of 100 million florins.

Most of the credit banks established in the 1850s were located in northern and central Germany and served the main industrial and commercial regions of the country. South of the River Main, on the other hand, different types of banking institutions developed, such as the craftsmen's banks in Württemberg.

The credit banks undoubtedly fostered Germany's industrial expansion. It was with their help that money was raised for state and municipal loans, for the completion of the railway network, for the construction of public works, for the establishment of new mining and manufacturing enterprises and for the promotion of shipping and overseas trade. While the meteoric career of the Crédit mobilier came to an abrupt and inglorious end, the Darmstadt Bank, the Discount Company and the Berlin Commercial Company eventually became three of the great German banks. Their achievements were similar to those of the Crédit lyonnais and the Société générale in France and the Kreditanstalt in Austria. But the significance of the banking revolution should not be exaggerated. Other German banks—both note-issuing banks and others—continued to work on traditional lines. They too fostered industrial expansion, but they did so by discounting bills of exchange and by making loans to manufacturing concerns rather than by promoting new industrial enterprises, by performing the functions of a stockbroker or by purchasing blocks of shares.

In the 1850s another type of bank was established in Germany. This was the Schulze-Delitzsch cooperative credit bank. Hermann Schulze-Delitzsch realized that craftsmen and shopkeepers might need credit just as much as mineowners or industrialists. In 1850 he brought together ten artisans to found his first society in Eilenburg in the Prussian province of Saxony. It began as an organization for the cooperative purchase of raw materials and developed into a cooperative credit bank. By 1859 there were over a hundred such cooperative associations in Germany and the movement had developed sufficiently for Schulze-Delitzsch to call a conference at Weimar to set up an association of cooperative banks. F. W. Raiffeisen's rural cooperative banks to provide credit to small farmers came a little later. One of the first was established in Anhausen, on the edge of the Westerwald, in 1862.

10   *The Great Industries*

The industrialization of Germany made rapid progress in the 1850s and 1860s. The demand for consumer and capital goods increased with the expansion of the population and the growth of towns. Industrial efficiency was improved by the extension and reform of the Zollverein; by removing state control from mining; by exploiting hitherto neglected natural resources such as lignite and potash; by encouraging investment through joint-stock companies and credit banks; by establishing larger units of production; and by improving transport facilities. In the 1850s the rise of prices in Europe that followed the arrival of new gold from California and Australia stimulated economic expansion, while in the 1860s tariffs were lowered by commercial agreements such as the Anglo-French (1860) and the Franco-Prussian (1862) commercial treaties. This encouraged the expansion of industry in Germany and the extension of her trade to new markets in Europe and overseas. At the same time German manufacturers were able to take advantage of new inventions and processes — the discovery of coal-tar dyes and the ammonia process for making soda; the invention of the electric dynamo, the steel converter and the open-hearth process. And this was the era in which some of the great pioneers of Germany's industrial expansion — Krupp and Stumm for example — were at the height of their powers.

The 1860s saw the climax of the struggle between Austria and Prussia for control over Germany. Bismarck, who became minister president of Prussia in 1862, succeeded in driving Austria out of Germany. In 1865 Prussia was able to renew the Zollverein on her own terms and to put an end to the privileges that Austria had enjoyed under the February commercial treaty of 1853. In 1866 Prussia defeated Austria at Königgrätz and dissolved the Confederation of 1815. In the new North German Federation, Prussia dominated Germany north of the River Main.

By 1871 Germany was producing 30 million tons of coal a year, 8.5 million tons of lignite, and 1.4 million tons of pig-iron. Her output of coal and pig-iron now exceeded that of France and Belgium, though it was still far behind that of England. The textile industries also expanded. Germany's consumption of raw cotton rose from 46 million pounds in 1850 to 147 million pounds in 1869, and her production of woollen manufactures rose from 555,000 hundredweights in 1852 to 1,072,000 in 1870. At the same time foreign trade doubled in value from £105 millions (1850) to £212 millions (1870). Over 270 joint-stock companies were set up in the 1850s. In 1854 Gustav Mevissen declared: 'At the present time it is becoming more and more evident that an all-important factor in stimulating industry is the uniting of capital and knowledge through the founding of joint-stock companies.' Visitors to the industrial exhibition in Paris in 1867 could see how German manufacturers had been making progress in recent years. Krupp's huge cannon barrel, the Hörder Verein's steel plates and Borsig's steam-engines for locomotives were examples of the high standard of Germany's industrial products.

Coal and Lignite

Germany had ample deposits of coal and lignite, but they had not been fully exploited in the first half of the nineteenth century. In many parts of the country there was still enough timber for fuel and for smelting purposes. Some coalfields, such as Upper Silesia and the Saar, were in remote regions and their output could expand only when railways had been built. The mining laws of Prussia—in which most of the coalfields were located—discouraged private enterprise. The powers of mining inspectors were so extensive that private owners could not operate mines as they thought fit.

After 1850 Germany's timber resources declined and the country became more industrialized. There was an increased demand for coal and lignite from ironworks, railways, gasworks, factories, workshops and domestic consumers. New railways linked the coalfields with great centres of population. By the Joint-Ownership Law of 1851 the Prussian State relinquished its control over mining exploitation, finance, sales, the engagement of workers and the fixing of wages. Owners and managers of collieries were placed in the same position as those who ran other industrial enterprises and were virtually free from state supervision. Only the employment of juveniles, safety regulations and the qualifications of mining engineers continued to be the responsibility of the State. The tax on the gross output of mines was now reduced from 10 per cent to 5 per cent, which was the same as the tax that had been levied in the territories on the left bank of the River Rhine since 1810.

Ten years later the last privileges of the miners' gilds were abolished in Prussia. Members of gilds lost their right to secure employment in mines in preference to non-members. Miners could now move freely from one part of the country to another and the Ruhr was able to expand its labour force by attracting migrants from beyond the River Elbe. In 1863 the miners' friendly societies were reformed. They ceased to be organizations recognized and protected by the State and became purely voluntary associations, financed and operated jointly by the owners and the workers. In 1865 a law was passed that created a single mining administration for the whole of Prussia. Gustav Schmoller complained that these reforms in the mining laws were 'an offence against all the traditions of the Prussian State because of their exaggerated Manchesterdom'. It may be doubted whether this criticism was justified. The coal industry expanded rapidly under private enterprise and this, in turn, stimulated the growth of other industries. And the Prussian State continued to have an important stake in the coal industry, since the collieries in the Saar and three mines in Upper Silesia continued to be owned and operated by the State.

The growth in demand for coal and coke, the rise in prices, the extension of railways and the reform of the Prussian mining laws enabled the coal industry to share in the general prosperity of the early 1850s. Prospectors searched for deposits of coal and new colliery companies were set up with the help of credit banks. There was a rush on the part of Germans and foreigners to exploit the wealth that lay beneath the soil in the coalfields. Mushroom towns sprang up near the new mines; land prices rose; and high wages were paid to miners. But within a few years the commercial crisis of 1857 brought the coal boom to an end. Sales fell and prices declined. Coal stocks began to accumulate at the pithead. Some collieries closed down and there was unemployment in the coalfields.

A period of reconstruction followed in the 1860s. Unprofitable mines were closed, colliery companies were amalgamated and links were formed between coal and iron firms. Coal-owners began to cooperate for various purposes. The Ruhr Mineowners Association, for example, was formed in 1858. German coal was now competing successfully with English coal in northern Germany and with Belgian coal in the Rhineland, while coal and lignite were gradually replacing wood in central and southern Germany. The coal industry was becoming more efficient. Some shafts were lined with iron casings and steam-engines were installed to haul coal to the surface. The production of coal—and the output per man-shift—increased. Germany was both an importer and an exporter of coal—importing from England and exporting to France and Holland. By 1870 Germany's coal exports amounted to nearly 4 million tons a year. Between 1860 and 1871 coal output rose from 12.3 million tons to nearly 30 million tons and Germany became—a long way behind Britain—the second coal-producing country in the world.

The expansion of the German coal industry was not matched by improvements in the condition of the miners. In 1867 the miners in the Ruhr complained to the king of Prussia that the mineowners now had a free hand in fixing the hours of work and the rate of wages. And in 1869 — in a report on the condition of the coalminers in Saxony — Friedrich Engels declared that they worked in 12-hour shifts and earned only from 2 thalers to a little over 3 thalers a week.

At this time the Ruhr replaced Upper Silesia as Germany's most important coalfield. In 1850 Upper Silesia produced twice as much coal as the Ruhr. Twenty years later the position had been reversed and the output of the Ruhr was nearly double that of Upper Silesia. In the first half of the nineteenth century the mineral wealth of the Ruhr had not been adequately exploited. After 1850 there was a dramatic change and the district sprang suddenly to life as a great industrial complex. In the 1840s mines had been opened at Mülheim, Essen and Bochum, which lay on the main highway running through the Ruhr district. Here many types of coal were mined, such as steam-coal, gas-coal and coking-coal. The availability of coke encouraged the establishment of iron-foundries in the Essen-Bochum region so that eventually the Ruhr became as famous for its ironworks and engineering plants as for its coalmines. In the 1850s and 1860s new — and much deeper — deposits were worked further north at Gelsenkirchen, Werne and Dortmund. Here—in the Emscher and Lippe basins—the sinking of deep shafts made it possible to mine a great variety of types of coal. The completion of the local railway network stimulated the expansion of the Ruhr at this time. The main lines were the Cologne-Minden, the Berg-Mark and the Rhenish Railway and all three acted as magnets to mining prospectors and promoters of new colliery companies. Equally important was the improvement of transport facilities on the River Rhine, where coal was now being moved in 500 ton barges, drawn by steam-tugs. Shares in mining companies were eagerly snapped up by German and foreign investors, who realized that the abolition of government controls had given entrepreneurs opportunities they had never enjoyed before. Between 1850 and 1857 nearly a hundred new mines were opened in the Ruhr, and output rose from 1.6 million tons to 3.6 million tons. The output per miner rose from 700 tons in 1855 to 986 tons in 1864. Two of the largest enterprises established at this time were the Hibernia mine near Gelsenkirchen (which was promoted by a group of Irish capitalists) and the Harpen Mining Company (which operated the Heinrich Gustav mine at Werne and the Prinz von Preussen mine at Bochum).

The promoters and speculators overreached themselves and, as in Silesia, the boom in the Ruhr came to an end in 1857, when the price of coal began to fall. Despite the completion of the railway network, transport facilities proved to be inadequate. There were not enough waggons to carry the increased output of coal, so that stocks began to accumulate at the pithead. There was a crisis in the industry and some of the less efficient collieries had to close down. A period of reconstruction followed. Coalmines were amalgamated into larger units of production and further technical improvements were introduced, so that by 1862 the eleven largest mines in the district each produced over 100,000 tons of coal a year. In the 1860s the Ruhr had become a great conglomeration of mining and industrial centres with a dense population. Old medieval towns and villages had become factory towns where mines, ironworks, engineering plants and workshops were surrounded by workers' houses. The output of coal in the Ruhr rose to 9.2 million tons in 1865 and 11.8 million tons in 1870.

Two coalfields lay to the west of the Rhine—the Eschweiler and the Saar. The Eschweiler coal measures were situated near Aachen in the valleys of the Rivers Inde and Wurm. They were difficult to work owing to the irregularity of the seams. The exploitation of the coalfield had been stimulated in the 1840s by the opening of the railway from Cologne to Aachen and Liège. Much of the coal was sold locally and provided fuel and power for the textile-mills and metal workshops of Aachen, Eschweiler, Stolberg and Burtscheid. The coalfield prospered during the boom of 1852-7 and output increased from 424,000 tons to 690,000 tons. At this time most of the mines in the valley of the Inde were operated by the Eschweiler Mining Company, run by the

Englerth family, while most of the mines in the valley of the Wurm were in the hands of the United Wurm Collieries. After the commercial crisis of 1857 both companies were faced with increased competition from the Ruhr and from Belgium. Their reaction was to increase productivity by taking over small neighbouring coalmines. The United Wurm Collieries took over the *Pannesheider Verein*, while the Eschweiler Mining Company took over the Anna and the Maria coalmines. After these amalgamations the Eschweiler Mining Company — with an output of 540,000 tons in 1863 — was in a dominant position in the district. Its largest colliery was the Centrum mine, which at that time had the largest output of any coalmine in private hands in Germany.

The Saar coalfield lay near the French frontier in the south-western corner of the Prussian province of the Rhineland. A few mines were in the neighbouring Bavarian province of the Rhenish Palatinate. The coal lay much nearer the surface than in the mines that were being opened up in the Ruhr in the 1850s. But the quality of Saar coal was poor. Because of its remote location and poor transport facilities in the first half of the nineteenth century most of the coal produced in the Saar was used by local industries, particularly by the iron-foundries and engineering plants. Only the coming of the railways enabled coal from the Saar to reach more distant markets.

The collieries in the Prussian part of the Saar were owned and operated by the State. Two collieries in the Rhenish Palatinate were nationalized Bavarian mines. On the other hand the production of pig-iron and coke in the Saar was in the hands of private entrepreneurs. Two of the region's most important ironmasters at this time were Karl Stumm and Karl Roechling.

The expansion of the Saar industrial district in the 1850s was stimulated by the construction of railways. The short Saarbrücken-Forbach line — Prussia's first nationalized railway — linked the Saar with the French railway network. Saarbrücken was also linked with the Rhine port of Ludwigshafen by the Bavarian Ludwig Railway. During the boom of 1850-7 Leopold Sello, who had been in charge of the Mining Office at Saarbrücken since 1816, crowned his life's work by opening up new mines in the valley of the Saar and along the railways. Coal output rose from 700,000 tons to 2.4 million tons. In the 1860s further progress was made. Communications were improved by the opening of the Saar Coal Canal — linking the coalfield with the Rhine-Marne Canal — and the construction of the Rhine-Nahe Railway. Technical improvements included the installation of many steam-engines in the mines. In the Prussian state mines their number increased from 78 in 1863 to 160 in 1871.

At this time the Prussian State dominated the economy of the Saar, since it owned nearly all the collieries and railways and was the largest employer of labour in the district. The Saarbrücken chamber of commerce, founded in 1863, complained that the State was selling coal to French customers at a lower price than to German customers and that freight charges on the Saar coal canal were unduly favourable to French industrialists.

In 1866 the Cologne banker Abraham Oppenheim tried to interest Count Itzenplitz, the Minister of Commerce, in a plan to transfer the nationalized coalmines in the Saar to a joint-stock company in which the government would hold a majority of the shares. When the Prussian government was short of money at the time of the outbreak of the war against Austria, Oppenheim suggested that not only the state coalmines but also the state railways and forests in the Saar should be run by a joint-stock company. Karl Stumm, the Neunkirchen ironmaster, protested to Bismarck against these proposals and they were rejected by the government.

Upper Silesia was rich in coal and other mineral deposits such as iron-ore and zinc. The largest coal measures lay between Gleiwitz, Beuthen and Kattowitz. Two smaller coalfields lay further south at Rybnik and Nokolai. The resources of this mineral region could not be fully exploited in the first half of the nineteenth century since they lay in a remote province on the frontiers of Russian Poland and Austria, far away from a port or from any large centres of population. Transport by road was very difficult, particularly in the winter, and only small quantities of coal could be shipped from Gleiwitz to Kosel on the River Oder by the Klodnitz Canal. And even as late as the 1860s there was little demand for coke from the local furnaces, since adequate supplies of charcoal could still easily be obtained from the great forests of the region. On the other hand the coalfield of Upper Silesia had certain advantages over other coalfields since the deposits lay near the surface, the seams were level and thick and coal and iron-ore were found close together.

The coalfield had been opened up in the last quarter of the eighteenth century first by the Prussian State then by some of the wealthy local magnates, who owned great estates and provided the capital to exploit the deposits of coal, iron and zinc that lay on their own properties. The collieries, foundries and zinc works were generally larger than those in the Ruhr, and they were often worked together as mixed enterprise. The State owned and exploited the *Friedrichs-grube*, the *Königsgrube*, and the *Königin Luise Grube*, while the noble families Henckel-Donnersmarck (two branches), Ballestrem, Pless, Tiele-Winckler, Renard, Hohenlohe and Schaffgotsch operated numerous mines and foundries. The families of Pless and Tiele-Winckler were in a privileged position, since they had the sole right to develop mines on their vast estates. But other great landowners were subject to the Prussian mining code and — until 1850 — had to accept the fact that the state's mining officials wielded wide powers over the administration of their collieries. As early as 1842 a German writer boasted that the industrial development of Upper Silesia was 'the equal of England and foremost on the continent of Europe'.

In the 1850s the output of the coalfield expanded. The Upper Silesian Railway, which ran from Breslau to Myslowitz, was opened in 1846 and was soon carrying large quantities of coal and iron and zinc products. From Breslau the coal and iron were sent to Berlin by the Lower Silesia-Mark Railway. To foster the development of the coalfield, von der Heydt, the Minister of Commerce, decided that the State must control these two lines so that it could fix freight charges at a level that would enable the mineowners and ironmasters of Upper Silesia to make full use of the new means of transport. The Lower Silesia-Mark Railway was purchased by the State in 1852, while the administration of the private Upper Silesian Railway was taken over by the State in 1857. Another factor that stimulated the industrial development of Upper Silesia at this time was the conclusion of the Austro-Prussian commercial treaty of February 1853, which opened the Austrian market to Silesian coal.

During the boom of 1850-7 some joint-stock companies were established in Upper Silesia. Industrialists and financiers from Breslau and Berlin began to invest in Silesian coal, iron and zinc enterprises. Sometimes the undertakings passed into new ownership, but sometimes the noble proprietors continued to hold a substantial interest in the mines and ironworks founded by their ancestors. The commercial crisis of 1857 was followed by a period of reconstruction that saw the amalgamation of various mining enterprises, so that by the 1860s two-thirds of Upper Silesia's coal came from six undertakings. In 1859-60 the firm of Borsig, which built locomotives in Berlin, erected a great industrial complex at Biskupitz by Zabrze, which included a colliery. The 1860s saw the increased use of steam-power in the coalfield. In 1863 only 9 steam-engines were in operation: in 1871 there were 318. The production of coal in Upper Silesia rose from 3.8 million tons in 1850 to 6.5 million tons in 1871. The character of the region was rapidly changing. Set among vast forests and stretches of heath were pockets of industrial urbanization in which old market towns, such as Gleiwitz and Beuthen, were growing into large towns and completely new industrial centres — such as Königs-hütte — had appeared on the map.

There were also three small mining regions in Lower Silesia on the foothills of the Sudeten Mountains — Waldenburg, Neurode and Kupferberg. The seams were irregular and the coal was of poor quality. But as early as 1819 the French mining expert Héron de Villefosse had praised the efficiency of the working of the *Fuchsgrube* near Waldenburg. It was the opening of the Silesian Mountain Railway in 1844 that heralded the expansion of the coalfields of Lower Silesia. The output of coal rose from 400,000 tons in 1851 to over 1 million tons in 1871.

The only coalfields of any importance outside Prussia were three small basins in the kingdom of Saxony. These deposits, lying at the foot of the Erzgebirge, were neither extensive nor of high quality. Little of the coal was suitable for coking. In the second half of the eighteenth century the government had rewarded prospectors who found new coal deposits, and had subsidized the opening-up of new mines, but without much success. In the nineteenth century, however, Saxony produced enough coal to provide the power needed by her expanding industries.

The Zwickau coalfield was the largest in the kingdom of Saxony. It had been worked in the Middle Ages and the mines had been described in 1530 in a report by Agricola. In modern times regular production had begun in the 1820s and by 1850 the output of fifty-seven collieries amounted to 336,000 tons. To the east of Zwickau lay the Lugau-Ölsnitz deposits, which had been worked for a brief period in the 1830s and had then been abandoned. Work was resumed in the 1850s but by 1862 only about 180,000 tons of coal a year were being produced. The small Döhlen coalfield lay to the south-west of Dresden and was important for the industrial development of the capital of Saxony. As in other German mining regions, it was the building of railways that enabled the production of coal to be expanded in Saxony. The opening of the Zwickau-Leipzig line in 1845 and the Lugau-Chemnitz line in 1859 were landmarks in the history of the growth of the coal industry in Saxony. By 1863 Saxony was producing nearly 2 million tons of coal a year.

In addition to its vast reserves of bituminous coal Germany also possessed large deposits of lignite (brown coal), which is a fuel inter-mediate between bituminous coal and peat. Nine tons of lignite is equal to about 2 tons of coal in heat value. Lignite was either mined underground or quarried in surface workings. Since lignite had a high content of water and crumbled when dry it was not usually transported but was used locally or converted into briquettes near the workings. Some mines were nationalized while others were in private hands. In 1851 the Prussian State owned three lignite mines in the Halberstadt region and four in the Eisleben basin, which produced 150,000 tons a year. By the middle of the nineteenth century, as timber resources declined, lignite was used as a substitute for wood, particularly in those parts of the country that were distant from coalfields. Lignite could be used in factories, workshops and foundries and also—in the form of briquettes—in the home. Mineral oils could be extracted from lignite.

Scattered lignite deposits lay in central and western Germany. In central Germany there were lignite basins in the Harz Mountains (Hal-berstadt), in the Prussian province of Saxony (Halle-an-der-Saale—Merseburg—Eisleben), in the kingdom of Saxony (Borna), in the Nieder Lausitz (Senftenberg), in Lower Silesia (Görlitz) and in Posen (Brom-berg). It was not until the 1840s that lignite was exploited on a com-mercial scale in these districts. By the 1850s lignite had become a fuel of some importance in the province and kingdom of Saxony and nine-tenths of Germany's lignite came from those territories. The new fuel stimulated the industrial expansion of central Germany, especially the development of the beet sugar, salt, potash and chemical industries. The revival of the saltworks of Halle-an-der-Saale, Dürrenberg, and Kösen in the 1850s was due largely to the availability of lignite. One of the most important entrepreneurs was Adolf Riebneck, a miner from the Harz, who established a plant near Weissenfels-an-der-Saale in 1858 in which lignite was distilled to produce tar. Three years later he erected a large factory which produced mineral oils, such as paraffin, from lignite.

In western Germany the Ville lignite basin lay 50 kilometres west of the Rhine between Cologne, Bonn and Düren and covered an area 72 kilometres long and 6.25 kilometres wide. The thick beds—of rather inferior quality—could be exploited by open workings. In 1851 this region produced 112,000 tons of lignite. There were also lignite deposits east of the Rhine in the Haar hills and in the Sauerland. Further south lignite was mined in the grand duchy of Nassau, where it was used by local craftsmen and industrialists such as their iron-masters. In southern Germany lignite was mined in Bavaria near Regensburg, while in the foothills of the Alps a superior type of lignite called *Pechkohlen* was found. The production of lignite in Germany rose from 1.5 million tons in 1850 to 3.7 million tons in 1861 and 8.5 million tons in 1871. The lignite produced in 1871 was equal in heat value to about 1.9 million tons of bituminous coal.

Iron and Steel

In the 1860s Germany produced about 1 million tons of iron a year in various forms, such as pig-iron, bar-iron, cast-iron, wire and steel. By 1870 she was turning out 1.4 million tons of pig-iron and 170,000 tons of steel. This output was greater than that of France or Belgium, although France possessed in Lorraine the largest ironfield in western Europe. Most of Germany's iron-ore deposits were low grade and lay in the Prussian districts of Upper Silesia, the Saar and the Siegerland. In the Siegerland a type of pig-iron called *Spiegeleisen* — particularly well suited to the manufacture of steel — was made from local iron-ore that contained some manganese. In the Ruhr deposits of blackband (coal with iron-ore) were found in 1849. Next in import-ance were the *minette* deposits of Luxembourg and the ironfields of Nassau in the valleys of the Dill and Lahn. Deposits of iron-ore were also worked in Hanover (Ilsede-Peine and Salzgitter), Thuringia and the southern states. Germany produced 1.4 million tons of iron-ore in 1864. These supplies were supplemented by imports from Lorraine that were smelted in the furnaces of the Saar.

It was, however, Germany's resources of charcoal and timber rather than her deposits of iron-ore that enabled her to become the leading producer of iron and steel on the Continent. In the early nineteenth century she still had adequate reserves of timber from which to make the charcoal that her numerous small furnaces con-sumed. These ironworks were generally located in hilly wooded districts adjacent to iron-ore deposits. When Germany's charcoal supplies declined and when some of her ironfields were worked out, many of the small old-established furnaces were closed, while large new modern furnaces were erected on the coalfields.

As Germany's main coalfields lay in Prussia it was in that state that the new iron and steel industry — based upon coke — was established. The Ruhr, Upper Silesia and the Saar became as well known for their furnaces, foundries and steelworks as for their coalmines. Blast furnaces, puddling and rolling-mills and engineering and machine-building plants were set up at Essen, Bochum, Dortmund, Aachen, Gleiwitz and Kattowitz. In the early 1860s about two-thirds of Germany's ironworks lay in Prussia and they produced over half a million tons of pig-iron a year. Over three-quarters of this was produced in coke furnaces.

Although the first German coke blast furnace had been installed at Gleiwitz as early as 1796, Germany had been very slow to adopt a process that had long been used in Britain. In 1846 only 17 out of 69 blast furnaces in Upper Silesia used coke. Western Germany was even more backward in this respect, since only 5 coke furnaces were in operation in 1850. In that year the first coke blast furnace was fired in the Ruhr at the Friedrich Wilhelm Hütte near Mülheim.

In the 1850s, however, as less timber — and therefore less charcoal — was available, more coke was made in Germany and more iron-ore was smelted with coke. The leading coalfield for coke production at this time was the Saar. In the Ruhr, coke was made at the Sälzer-Neuack, the Franzisca and some other collieries. Between 1852 and 1861, 75 iron companies were set up in Germany, while during the boom of 1851-7, 27 coke furnaces were erected in the Ruhr.

In other parts of Germany a few large modern iron and steelworks were set up — Borsig's works at Biskupitz in Upper Silesia, the Ilseder Hütte in Hanover, the Kraemer furnaces at St Ingbert in the Bavarian Saar, for example — but on the whole progress was slow in the less important iron districts. In Nassau, in the Eifel and in Saxony old-established ironworks in relatively remote districts continued to use charcoal in the 1860s. Modernization was delayed by the existence of numerous tiny units of production. Thus Nassau had 459 iron-ore mines in 1860. In Luxembourg the breakthrough came in 1859, when the capital of the little duchy was linked by rail with the iron-ore basin of Esch-an-der-Alzette.

For many years after Neilson had replaced the cold blast in the furnace with a hot blast, few changes occurred in the methods by which iron and steel were made. But in the 1850s the manufacture of steel was revolutionized by two inventions that reduced the price of steel, so that what had virtually been a precious metal became a metal in everyday use. The first new process was that invented by

Henry Bessemer, while the second was the Siemens-Martin process. The Bessemer converter produced steel by passing a blast of air through molten cast-iron. It was a speedy process and could make as much steel in 20 minutes as the furnaces that it replaced had produced in 1½ days. The Siemens-Martin process raised the temperature in an open-hearth furnace by using the outgoing hot gas to heat the incoming gaseous fuel.

Bessemer converters were quickly introduced on to the Continent. In Germany Alfred Krupp had early information concerning Bessemer's invention because Alfred Longsdon, his trusted agent in London, was the brother of Bessemer's partner Robert Longsdon. In 1862 a Bessemer converter—supervised by the chemist Karl Uhlenhant—was set up at Krupp's works and in the following year another was erected by the Hörder Verein. If phosphoric ores were used in this converter brittle steel was produced. Since many German ores were phosphoric, Bessemer converters did not spread so quickly in Germany as in England. Those that were installed used imported non-phosphoric ores from England, Elba and the Basque provinces of Spain.

The other new method of making steel at this time was the Siemens-Martin process, which was first used in steelworks at Sireuil in France in 1865. It was introduced into Germany by the firm of Borsig in 1868. The open hearth had certain advantages over the Bessemer converter and these eventually proved to be decisive. It could produce steel of higher quality than Bessemer steel, and scrap-iron as well as pig-iron could be fed into the furnace. On the other hand, the open-hearth furnace was slower and more expensive to operate than the Bessemer converter. And those who used open-hearth furnaces, like those who installed Bessemer converters, had to wait until the invention of the Gilchrist-Thomas process in 1878-9 before they could use phosphoric ores, such as the *minette* ore of Lorraine.

The establishment of bigger iron and steel undertakings was a feature of the period 1850-70, since modern methods of production required considerable capital investment and large units of production. In the Saar about half of the ironworks were in the hands of the Stumm family, while in the Ruhr, Krupp's steelworks expanded. Mixed iron and coalworks were established. A number of firms making iron and steel products acquired coalmines to secure a regular supply of coke. The Prussian State, which owned nearly all the coalmines in the Saar, also operated some ironworks. In the Ruhr the Phoenix

Company, the Vulcan Company and Krupp all bought or leased collieries. In Upper Silesia coal and iron-ore deposits sometimes lay so close together that it was natural for their owners—whether great landlords or joint-stock companies—to work them together. Heymann observes 'This development was quite natural for the territorial magnates possessed the iron and coal as well as the land itself'. They had skilled mining engineers and they alone had the necessary capital. A company from outside the province—the locomotive-builder Borsig — acquired both coalmines and ironworks in Upper Silesia in the 1860s. This was an early example of an engineering undertaking securing control over supplies of both coal and iron.

It may be added that the most important non-ferrous metals to be produced in Germany at this time were zinc, lead and copper. In the 1860s Germany produced more zinc than she needed from her mines in Upper Silesia and the Rhineland and she became the largest exporter of this metal in the world. The price of zinc in Breslau determined the world price. Lead, too, was produced in considerable quantities— mainly in Upper Silesia, the Siegerland and the Eifel (Bleiberg) — and her exports (particularly to the United States) were greater than her imports. Copper production from mines at Eisleben and Stadtberger expanded considerably but was not sufficient to meet the whole of the home demand.

Textiles

From the point of view of units of production, manpower employed and exports, the textile industries were—apart from agriculture—the most important economic activity in Germany in the middle of the nineteenth century. In 1861 there were in these branches of manufacture three-quarters of a million workers in full-time employment and some thousands of part-time handloom weavers. In Prussia there were more large factories (each employing over five hundred workers) in the textile industries than in all other industries put together. The value of the net exports of textile goods in 1860 was 67,200,000 thalers—at a time when the Prussian state budget amounted to 130,000,000 thalers. The various textile industries were making very unequal progress towards technical efficiency and large-scale factory production. The old-established linen industry was changing slowly and with much difficulty. Wool and silk were making rather greater advances though some antiquated methods survived. But the cotton industry was forging rapidly ahead towards large-scale capitalist production. The textile industries were located in many parts of the country. While Prussia was in a dominant position as far as coal and iron were concerned, there were important centres of cotton spinning in Saxony, in Hanover and in the southern German states.

Cotton

In 1861 the cotton industry was the largest of the textile industries in Germany. The spinning branch had 310 mills, running 2,250,000 spindles, while the weaving branch had 940 establishments. The 1850s had seen a considerable expansion in the cotton industry, the net imports of the raw material having risen from 342,345 hundredweight in 1850 to 1,533,256 hundredweight in 1861. Some large cotton factories with up-to-date machinery had been established in Gladbach, Augsburg and Chemnitz. The *Gladbacher Spinnerei und Weberei* had 15,000 spindles and 250 looms. Despite a substantial expansion in their output of yarn — 1,226,000 hundredweight in 1861 — the spinning-mills could not supply the weaving factories with all the yarn they required. Between 1856 and 1861 well over a third (37.5 per cent) of the yarn woven in Germany came from abroad. The weaving branch of the industry made rather less progress in introducing new machines than the spinning branch. In Saxony, for example, over half the looms were handlooms in 1861, though in Bavaria cotton weaving had been fully mechanized. The output of cotton cloth was not sufficient to supply the home market and Germany was still importing the finer fabrics from Lancashire. Between 1860 and 1870 the amount of yarn consumed in Germany and the quantity of cotton goods exported remained almost stationary.

To some extent this was due to the shortage of the raw material during the American Civil War of 1861-5. The German cotton industry was, to a considerable extent, dependent upon the southern states of the United States for its raw cotton and when the southern states were blockaded the price of cotton rose sharply. In Saxony, Silesia, Berlin and the Rhineland many cotton-mills and finishing works closed or worked on short time and there was serious distress among the operatives. But in Bavaria and Württemberg the dislocation suffered by the cotton industry was not so severe. The cotton spinners of southern Germany were already accustomed to use some cotton from India and they were able to increase their supplies from this source. And cotton centres such as Augsburg, that were a long distance from a port, normally maintained larger stocks of the raw material than textile towns that were close to a port.

One result of the crisis was that, particularly in southern Germany, the mills spun more Indian and Egyptian cotton than before. By 1867 only one-third of the raw material used in southern Germany came from the United States. The cotton famine saw the collapse of a number of small inefficient firms. In Saxony the number of spindles declined from 707,000 in 1861 to 472,000 in 1874 owing to the disappearance of many small factories using out-of-date machinery. German manufacturers were able to buy modern spinning-machines and powerlooms from Lancashire engineering firms, which were in difficulties at this time and were prepared to cut their prices. On the whole the efficiency of the German cotton industry was improved during the cotton famine.

Wool

Although the woollen industry was not modernized as quickly as the cotton industry, the output of woollen cloth grew at a steady, if not very spectacular, rate between 1850 and 1870. But what was spectacular was the fact that sales abroad, particularly in the United States, grew more rapidly than sales at home, and that the woollen manufacturers took the place once held by the linen manufacturers as Germany's most successful exporters of textile goods. By 1864 the value of net exports of woollen goods — finished cloths and stockings — was greater than the value of net imports of raw wool and woollen yarn by nearly 13,000,000 thalers.

At one time the home clip had been large enough to supply the wool-mills at home and also to export some wool abroad. In the middle of the nineteenth century Germany continued to export a certain amount of high-quality native wool — particularly that produced in Saxony — but now considerable quantities of raw wool were imported from Australia, Cape Colony, Russia and Austria. As late as 1870, however, the home clip still accounted for three-fifths of Germany's consumption of raw wool. As Clapham observes, this was 'a very creditable proportion in the then conditions of international trade'.

In the preparatory process of the manufacture of cloth, the raw material was either carded (for woollens) or combed (for worsteds). The spinning of carded wool was a much older process than the production of yarn from fine combed wool. The spinning of carded wool was located in well-established centres in Prussia (the Rhineland,

Brandenburg and Silesia) and in Saxony (Chemnitz). The combing and spinning of fine wool was being mechanized at this time. Heilmann's comb and Roberts' self-actor were the two major innovations in the combing and spinning of fine wool. But there were obstacles to the rapid development of this branch of the woollen industry. It was more expensive to set up combing and spinning factories for fine wool than to establish factories for carding and spinning coarser wools. Moreover the German wool combers could not supply the worsted-mills with anything like the combed wool that they required, so that in the 1860s the manufacture of worsteds depended, to a considerable extent, upon the importation of suitable yarn from abroad. And the worsted industry had to face severe competition from English and French rivals in rich overseas markets and had to be content to send its exports at cut prices to the underdeveloped countries of the Continent.

Meanwhile the weaving branch of the woollen industry was being modernized by the widespread introduction of powerlooms, although large numbers of handloom weavers were still at work in the 1860s. The best-quality German woollens and worsteds were as good as those produced elsewhere. An official report on the Paris industrial exhibition of 1855 praised the German clothmakers for having 'taken the first place among all the nations'. But the report criticized German woollen manufacturers for their lack of originality, and for imitating designs from other countries.

Linen

Linen was the lame duck of the German textile industries in the nineteenth century. It has been seen that in the eighteenth century the export of linens had been a very important item in Germany's international trade. At one time linen had accounted for a quarter of Prussia's exports. Frederick the Great had declared that Silesia — the centre of Prussia's linen industry — was as important to him as Peru was to the king of Spain. After the Napoleonic Wars the linen industry never recovered its former position as a leading export industry and even lost ground at home. Central and South America, once a major market for German linens, were now supplied with Irish linens by English merchants. An expanding industry may have little difficulty in finding the capital to introduce improved methods of production. But in a declining industry it is a different story. In 1850 a report by a commission appointed by the Prussian Landtag summarized the difficulties to be overcome in establishing up-to-date linen spinning-mills in Silesia. The cost of erecting such a factory was 40 per cent higher than in England, while the cost of running it was 20 per cent higher. This was because coal, iron, machinery and factory equipment were all more expensive in Silesia than in England.

A social factor also deserves mention. Many linen workers in Silesia — women spinners and male handloom weavers — spent only part of their time on industrial work. The rest of their time was spent in cultivating their smallholdings. Despite great distress — culminating in the weavers' riots of 1844 — the Silesian peasant-weavers generally refused to leave the land to become full-time factory workers. Consequently very few factories for mechanical flax spinning and powerloom linen weaving were established in Silesia. But in Hanover, Westphalia and the Rhineland the production of linen cloth by machinery made some progress. In 1851, for example, Carl Bozi, who had gained experience in the linen industry in Belfast, established a successful flax spinning-mill in Bielefeld. In 1861 Germany still had only 136,000 mechanical flax spindles and 350 linen powerlooms, at a time when Britain had 1,780,000 linen spindles, and France had 600,000.

In the 1850s and 1860s the weaving branch of the linen industry enjoyed a period of relative prosperity owing to several favourable — but temporary — factors. By the Austro-Prussian commercial treaty of February 1853 the Zollverein placed hand-made Austrian linen yarn on the free list while Austrian machine-made yarn paid only a low import duty. Shortly afterwards, during the Crimean War, the frontier between Russian Poland and Silesia was not strictly guarded, so linen goods could easily be smuggled from Silesia into Russia. And then in the early 1860s, during the cotton famine, the temporary shortage of certain cotton goods forced people to use linen goods instead. In the circumstances there was some improvement in the state of the German linen industry between 1853 and 1865 and the level of exports was maintained. But after 1865 the industry began to decline again.

Silk

The German silk industry was of relatively minor importance. It was more concentrated from a geographical point of view than other textile industries. The main centres of production were Brandenburg and the Rhineland (Krefeld). Exports from Brandenburg went to Russia and the Balkans while those from Krefeld were sent to England, Scandinavia and South America. In the 1850s the number of factories, looms and workers declined but the consumption of raw materials and the output of finished silks increased. In 1870, however, the raw silk consumed by the German industry was less than one-seventh of the silk consumed in France. A number of small workshops employing handloom weavers disappeared and some large factories using power-driven machinery were established. In 1858, for example, there were 8 silkworks in the Rhineland each employing over 500 workers. Three of them employed over 1,000 workers. The German silk manufacturers depended upon the French silk industry for new machines and new ideas.

11   The Struggle between Prussia and Austria for Economic Supremacy, 1862-65

The commercial treaty of February 1853 was no more than an armistice in the struggle between Prussia and Austria for economic supremacy in Germany. Austria had secured the adoption of preferential duties on trade between the Habsburg dominions and the Zollverein and also an undertaking from Prussia to reopen negotiations in 1860 for the establishment of an Austro-German customs union. By 1860 Schwarzenberg and Bruck were dead but their ideas lived on and the Austrian government still hoped to persuade Prussia to agree to the admission of Austria into an enlarged Zollverein. But the Prussian government — and the civil servants responsible for economic affairs — were just as determined that Austria should continue to be excluded from the Zollverein.

Economic developments between 1853 and 1860 favoured the Prussians and not the Austrians. The Zollverein, despite temporary setbacks — such as the commercial crisis of 1857 — advanced rapidly towards industrialization, while Austria remained a predominantly agrarian region. There were districts in Austria in which modern manufactures made progress but, for the most part, the country remained relatively underdeveloped. Moreover she had serious currency problems and her public finances were in disorder, especially after the war against France in 1859. As Prussia forged ahead from an economic point of view, it became less likely that the Habsburgs would ever be able to force their way into the Zollverein. Again, the Zollverein had a tariff that gave manufacturers only a very moderate degree of protection against foreign competition. Now Prussia was moving towards the adoption of free trade. Austria on the other hand remained faithful to a policy of high protection. This situation made it virtually impossible for Austria to entertain serious hopes of entering the Zollverein.

The early German free-trade agitation of the 1840s led by Prince Smith, had petered out during the revolution of 1848 and the subsequent reaction. It was revived in the 1850s as part of a wider movement in favour of economic liberalism. Those who attended the meetings of the influential Congress of German Economists — the first was at Gotha in 1858 — demanded not merely the introduction of free trade but many other reforms as well, such as the ending of the privileges of the gilds, the abolition of state and municipal controls over industry, the removal of restrictions on the issue of bank notes, the establishment of private railways and the ending of transit dues and tolls on roads and rivers. These proposals were supported by Schulze-Delitzsch (one of the founders of the cooperative movement), Prince Smith (the leading free-trader), Otto Michaelis (editor of the *National-zeitung*) and Julius Faucher (editor of the *Vierteljahrschrift für Volkswirtschaft*). Several senior Prussian civil servants, such as Delbrück, sympathized with the aspirations of the liberal economists. And Bismarck, once a supporter of state and gild regulations, had come to realize some of the drawbacks of these restrictions. When he had represented Prussia at the Federal Diet he had lived in the Free City of Frankfurt and had seen for himself at first hand how the local craftsmen had abused their privileges. In 1853 he wrote:

> Here the gild system has so far remained intact, and we are spared none of the disadvantages that it brings — that is, excessive prices for manufactured articles, indifference to customers and therefore careless workmanship, long delays in orders, late beginning, early stopping, and protracted lunch hours when work is done at home, little choice in ready-made wares, backwardness in technical training, and many other deficiencies.

Bismarck went on to accuse the Frankfurt gilds of 'successfully exploiting the public and excluding competition'.

The importance of the Congress of German Economists at this time has been summed up as follows:

> Whoever hoped to be regarded in wide circles of the population as an expert economist and a progressive thinker on economic problems joined the Congress and sought to make himself heard at its meetings. The majority of the members were deputies in parliamentary bodies (who influenced new legislation) and their appearance at the Congress gained them the support of electors. The wealthy middle class saw that its interests were being furthered by the Congress and therefore gave it every support. The Federal Governments and both senior and junior civil servants could not

disregard the decisions of the Congress. Even opponents of the principles for which the Congress stood, were often forced to take part in its deliberations in the hope of having some attention paid to their point of view.

The movement in favour of economic liberalism achieved numerous successes at this time. In Austria a decree of December 1859 swept away many restrictions on private enterprise. Within the next few years Saxony, Württemberg and Baden had followed suit. In Prussia laws passed in the early 1860s freed the mining industry from almost all state and gild restrictions. The economist Gustav Schmoller complained of the 'exaggerated Manchesterdom' of the Mining Law of 1865 which, in his view, was 'an offence against all the traditions of the Prussian State'. In 1868 the North German Federation issued a decree which put an end to the last of the privileges of the gilds. 'It enabled the employer to hire as many workers as he wanted, the handicraftsman to practise his calling in defiance of gild regulations, the buyer to purchase his wares in any market and from any dealer'. The construction of new railways was now left to private enterprise to a much greater extent than before. In Prussia Count Itzenplitz, the minister of commerce from 1862 to 1873, declared that it was of no consequence who built railways, so long as someone built them. Several lines—Berlin to Görlitz and Tilsit to Insterburg, for example — were constructed by private companies, and during the Seven Weeks War the Prussian government raised over 17 million thalers by selling railway shares in its possession. At the same time the movement of goods was being eased by the reduction or removal of various taxes and tolls. The Zollverein transit dues on goods crossing Germany were abolished in 1861. Between 1861 and 1863 shipping dues on the Rhine, the Elbe and other important rivers were reduced. The vexatious tolls, levied by Denmark on the Sound (1857), by Hanover on the Elbe (1861), and by Holland on the Scheldt (1863) were abolished by international agreements.

While the movement in favour of economic liberalism was advancing in various fields, little progress towards the achievement of free trade was made in the Zollverein in the 1850s. Since a single state could veto any proposal at the Zollverein General Congress it was a simple matter for the protectionists to block all attempts to reduce import duties. In 1856 the king of Prussia appointed a commission to recommend reductions in the import duties imposed by Zollverein and observed that it was 'a political necessity to proceed with such a reduction of the Zollverein tariff, so that Austria cannot follow suit too soon'. Shortly afterwards Bismarck complained that Prussia 'was being hindered by the veto of individual German states, from improving her internal financial legislation' and that, if necessary, Prussia should 'denounce the whole Zollverein as soon as we are legally entitled to do so'.

In 1860 an opportunity occurred to reopen the whole question. By signing the Anglo-French (Cobden-Chevalier) treaty of commerce Napoleon III abandoned the traditional French fiscal policy of high protection and agreed to a substantial reduction of the French tariff on a wide range of British manufactured products. France now had two tariffs — the new low tariff for imports from Britain and the old high tariff for imports from all other countries. The Prussian government was determined to secure for German exporters the same low duties as those that had been granted to British exporters. Napoleon III regarded the Cobden Treaty as the first step in the establishment of a low-tariff bloc in western Europe and he was eager to open negotiations with other states on the Continent in order to achieve this object. In the circumstances both the French and the Prussian governments were prepared to open discussions for a commercial treaty.

The negotiations, which took place in Berlin, were opened in January 1861 and were eventually brought to a successful conclusion on 29 March 1862, when a commercial treaty between France and Prussia was initialled. The treaty was signed on 2 August 1862. De Clercq, the French representative, began by making three proposals, two of which the Prussian negotiators (Delbrück, Pommer-Esche and Philipsborn) had no difficulty in accepting. The first was that the Zollverein transit dues should be abolished. This was done almost immediately. The second was that the Franco-Prussian treaty—like the Cobden Treaty—should include an unconditional most-favoured-nation clause by which any future tariff concession made by France to a third country should be automatically passed on to Prussia and any concession made by Prussia should similarly be enjoyed by France. Again the Prussian representatives agreed. And they agreed knowing that by doing so they were making it impossible for the Austro-Prussian commercial treaty of February 1853 to be renewed in its existing form, since the preferences enjoyed by Austria under that agreement were not compatible with the most-favoured-nation clause granted to France. De Clercq's third suggestion was more difficult to accept. He proposed a 'levelling of tariffs' by which those Zollverein import duties that were higher than those of France should (except for wines and silks) be reduced to the French level. And de Clercq also asked the Zollverein to adopt the French classification of goods for tariff purposes and should levy *ad valorem* instead of specific duties. Delbrück and his colleagues could not agree to a fundamental change in the existing method of classifying and levying Zollverein import duties or to reducing virtually all duties to the level of French duties as fixed under the Cobden Treaty. Eventually a compromise was reached. The French agreed that the Zollverein should continue to levy specific and not *ad valorem* import duties, while the Prussian negotiators made concessions with regard to the reductions to be made in Zollverein import duties on French goods. France reduced most of her duties on Zollverein goods to the same level as those charged on British goods under the Cobden Treaty. German manufacturers of iron products and textile fabrics welcomed new opportunities of exporting to the French market.

Austria was strongly opposed to the Franco-Prussian commercial treaty of 1862. In a memorandum of 7 May 1862 the Austrian government made known its displeasure in no uncertain terms. The Austrian government observed that, by granting France unconditional most-favoured-nation treatment, Prussia had made it impossible to continue to give Austria preferential treatment when the Austro-Prussian treaty of February 1853 expired. Austria complained that the Franco-Prussian treaty would lead to 'the economic severance of Austria from the rest of Germany'. Count Bernstorff, the Prussian foreign minister, replied that a reform of the Zollverein tariff had become a matter of urgency. Germany could not lag behind 'when Great Britain and France went before us on the path of great economic reform'. He scoffed at the idea that Prussia had made a bad bargain for the Zollverein and he curtly rejected the cool assumption that Austria was entitled to interfere in Prussia's commercial negotiations with a foreign country. He wrote: 'I must, with the utmost decision, claim for the Zollverein the full right to act in this respect as they themselves think proper.' Rechberg, the Austrian foreign minister, thereupon revived Bruck's plan for the establishment of an Austro-German customs union that would absorb the existing Zollverein. Prussia promptly rejected the proposal, explaining that Rechberg's scheme was incompatible with the new Franco-Prussian commercial treaty.

Rechberg realized that Austria was in no position to force Prussia to abandon her commercial treaty with France and to enter into negotiations for the establishment of an Austro-German customs union. His only hope lay in securing sufficient support for his policy from members of the Zollverein who were opposed to the liberal tariff embodied in the Franco-Prussian treaty, either because they objected to the introduction of what was virtually a free-trade tariff or because they feared Prussia's growing political power in Germany. At first Bavaria, Württemberg, Hesse-Cassel and Hanover firmly rejected the commercial treaty with France. Bismarck, on taking office as minister president of Prussia, soon made it clear that he would stand no nonsense from members of the Zollverein who refused to accept the Franco-Prussian commercial treaty. He told the upper house of the Prussian parliament that

> ... the government would be glad to be able to renew the Zollverein after the expiration of its present term. Such a boon, however, must be made dependent upon the fulfilment of the programme to which it has adhered in agreeing to the treaty of 2 August and, in so far as her fellow states do not feel themselves in a position to follow this programme, Prussia could not renew the Zollverein with them.

The states opposed to the liberal tariff agreed upon in the Franco-Prussian commercial treaty — Bavaria, Württemberg, Hesse-Cassel, Hanover and some smaller states — discussed among themselves the possibility of forming a united front against Prussia. But little progress was made in 1863. Then in the summer of 1864 they held a conference in Munich at which agreement was reached on 'heads of proposals' for the gradual assimilation of the tariffs of Austria and the Zollverein. But this was little more than an academic exercise. Prussia remained firm and time was running out for those who opposed her policy. In May 1864 Saxony agreed to renew her Zollverein treaty on the basis of the Franco-Prussian commercial treaty. Hanover followed suit in July. And in October all members of the Zollverein accepted the renewal of the customs union on Prussia's terms.

The Zollverein was renewed for 12 years by a treaty signed in May 1865, which included the tariff reductions agreed upon in the Franco-Prussian commercial treaty. Prussia had at last been able to reform the Zollverein tariff on free-trade lines. She had also secured a substantial reduction in the financial privileges enjoyed by Hanover and Oldenburg since 1854. But Prussia had been unable to get rid of the Zollverein General Congress with its *liberum veto* or to secure the establishment of an elected Customs Parliament. Neither Austria nor the southern German states that favoured protection had been able to prevent Prussia from introducing a liberal Zollverein tariff. Austria had to accept the situation and in April 1865 she signed a new commercial treaty with Prussia. She lost the privileged position in the German market that her exporters had enjoyed since 1854 and had to be content with most-favoured-nation treatment. Delbrück and his colleagues could be well satisfied with the way in which they had conducted the prolonged negotiations that had eventually led to the conclusion of the Franco-Prussian commercial treaty and the renewal of the Zollverein.

12   Bismarck and Economic Unification, 1867-73

The final struggle between Austria and Prussia for political and
military domination in Germany came only 6 months after Prussia
had defeated Austria in the struggle for economic supremacy. The
treaty renewing the Zollverein on terms advantageous to Prussia
came into force in January 1866 and then in the following June civil
war broke out in Germany. Prussia faced the armies not only of
Austria but of all members of the German Confederation, except
for a few small states such as the two Mecklenburgs. The Zollverein
treaties automatically lapsed when hostilities began and legally the
customs union was dissolved. But in practice the Zollverein survived.
It was an astonishing case of 'business as usual' during a civil war.
Military operations did little to hamper the movement of goods from
one part of the country to another. Customs duties continued to be
collected and the revenues were sent to Berlin, where the officials
divided the proceeds among the member states as if profound peace
reigned throughout the land. The Zollverein revenues declined by
only 11 per cent in 1866. The fears expressed before the outbreak of
hostilities that a civil war would have disastrous consequences on
the German economy were proved to be groundless.

One reason for this was the speed with which the Prussians defeated their enemies. Prussian forces occupied Holstein on 27 June and
defeated the Hanoverians at Langensalza on 27 June and the Austrians
and Saxons at Königgrätz on 3 July. Within a month peace had been
concluded by the Treaty of Prague. Austria agreed to the dissolution
of the German Confederation and to the reorganization of Germany
without Austrian participation. The humiliation of Olmütz (1850)
had been amply avenged. Austria also accepted that Prussia could
make any territorial changes she pleased north of the River Main,
except that Saxony's independence and territorial integrity were to
be preserved.

Prussia annexed Hanover, Hesse-Cassel, Nassau, Schleswig-
Holstein and Frankfurt-am-Main. She had at last linked her eastern
and western provinces and dominated northern Germany from Aachen

to Memel. The old German Confederation, which had included Austria, was replaced by a new North German Federation composed only of the states north of the River Main. The three southern states — Bavaria, Württemberg and Baden — were left in isolation but were soon linked to Prussia by military conventions and by membership of the Zollverein.

Prussia's triumph enabled Bismarck not only to change the political structure of Germany but also to reform the Zollverein. The North German Federation was itself a customs union and negotiations were soon undertaken to establish a new Zollverein, which would include this federation and the three southern German states. (Hamburg and Bremen were in an anomalous position, since they were members of the North German Federation but were not members of the Zollverein.) The new Zollverein treaties, signed in July 1867, came into force on 1 January of the following year. The old discredited General Council (and its *liberum veto*) disappeared. Its place was taken by a Customs Council and a Customs Parliament. The Council was composed of members of the upper house (*Bundesrat*) of the North German Parliament, sitting with plenipotentiaries appointed by the governments of the southern German states. The members of the Council were all appointed by the governments concerned and one delegate could cast all the votes of the state that he represented. The new Customs Parliament, on the other hand, was composed of elected representatives. They were members of the lower house (*Reichstag*) of the North German Parliament, and southern German members were elected in the same way as their colleagues from northern Germany. For the first time popularly elected representatives had a voice in the affairs of the Zollverein. Decisions in the Customs Council and the Customs Parliament were taken by majority vote. Prussia's position in the new Zollverein was stronger than in the old Zollverein. Prussia summoned and dissolved the Customs Council and the Customs Parliament. Nearly one-third of the votes of the Customs Council were held by Prussia and her representative submitted the decisions of the Customs Council to the Customs Parliament for approval. Prussia signed commercial treaties with foreign countries on behalf of the Zollverein. This legal preponderance reflected Prussia's economic strength, particularly in the mining, engineering and textile industries. As Benaerts observes, 'such an industrial preponderance was bound to prepare the way for political hegemony'.

At elections for the Customs Parliament held in the southern

German states in the spring of 1868 the main issue put before the electors was whether this assembly should be expanded into a German Reichstag with the power to legislate on a wider range of subjects than the tariff and commercial treaties. Bismarck hoped that an extension of the law-making powers of the Customs Parliament might be possible, so as to pave the way for the political unification of Germany in a peaceful manner. But the electors in southern Germany voted by a decisive majority in favour of strictly limiting the powers of the Customs Parliament to those laid down in the recently concluded Zollverein treaty. In view of the recent civil war in Germany this decision was hardly surprising.

On 27 April 1868 the king of Prussia opened the Customs Parliament, which was Germany's first popularly elected assembly since the dissolution of the Frankfurt parliament nearly 20 years before. In an early debate Bismarck made it clear that he had given up his plan to enlarge the functions of the Customs Parliament. He declared that he had no intention of pressing the southern German states to enter the North German Federation. If ever the states south of the River Main adhered to the North German Federation they would do so voluntarily. For the moment the particularists in Bavaria and Württemberg had got their way. But soon the danger from France was to cause them to change their minds.

Between 1868 and 1870 the Customs Parliament continued the process of liberalizing the Zollverein tariff that had been begun with the conclusion of the Franco-Prussian commercial treaty of 1862. When the Zollverein was absorbed by the new united Reich in 1871 Germany had a free-trade tariff, similar to that of Britain. Most raw materials, manufactured goods and foodstuffs were on the free list, though some pig-iron products continued to pay an import duty until 1877. Revenue duties were imposed upon tobacco and coffee. And by signing commercial treaties with most of her neighbours the Zollverein had become part of a low-tariff bloc, in which goods moved more freely than before or since.

Meanwhile the North German Federation was pressing forward with various economic reforms. Shipping dues on the Rhine, Main and Ruhr were abolished. Restrictions on the rate of interest that a lender could charge were removed. The introduction of the metric system ended the use of a bewildering variety of weights and measures in various German states. A post-office that served all the states in the North German Federation was established under Heinrich

Stephan, who was soon to play a leading part in the establishment of the World Postal Union. The post-office run by the Prince of Thurn and Taxis in several states was taken over by Prussia in return for compensation amounting to 3 million thalers. The Industrial Code (*Gewerbeordnung*) and the Code on Bills of Exchange (*Wechselordnung*) were adopted in 1869. A new Company Law, passed by the North German Reichstag in 1870, greatly simplified the method of setting up joint-stock companies, but unfortunately it did not give adequate protection to investors.

The victory of Prussia and her German allies over France in 1870 was followed by the adhesion of Bavaria, Württemberg and Baden to the North German Federation to form a united Reich in 1871. The annexation of Alsace and Lorraine at this time secured for Germany the largest iron-ore field in western Europe as well as large iron and steelworks, engineering establishments and textile-mills. The constitution of the new Reich gave extensive powers to the central authority, which was made responsible for the tariff, excise duties, the currency, industrial relations, weights and measures and the appointment of consuls abroad. On the other hand the Federal States retained control over direct taxes, technical education and all forms of transport. Bavaria and Württemberg kept their own post-offices and telegraph services, while Hamburg and Bremen remained outside the customs area of the Reich. While there can be little doubt that political unification fostered future economic progress in Germany it is also true that unification was not an essential condition of industrial expansion. As Knut Borchardt has observed: 'Politically and economically Prussia on her own had been strong enough since 1866 for sustained growth; the foundation of the empire may rather be seen as a result of Prussian growth than as a condition of growth in Germany.'

The unification of the country was quickly followed by several economic reforms that were designed to cement Germany's newly-found political unity. The Currency Law of May 1873 established a uniform metric currency — the mark — in place of the thaler, gulden and other coins. The new currency was based upon the gold (instead of the silver) standard and the 273 million francs that France had paid in gold as part of the war indemnity helped Germany to build up a gold reserve. In the same year the Reich Railway Office was set up to administer the railways of Alsace-Lorraine (now the property of the Reich), to ensure that all railway administrations carried out their legal duties and to prepare draft laws for the consideration of the Reichstag. In 1875 the Reichsbank, which absorbed the Bank of Prussia, was established as a national central bank with an initial capital of 182 million thalers. Thirteen banks gave up their right to issue notes and before long the only banks — other than the Reichsbank — to have their own notes were the state banks of Saxony and the three southern states.

By 1873 Germany had at last secured both economic and political unity but this had been achieved at the cost of expelling Austria from Germany. Many of the factors that had for so long hampered the expansion of industrial progress had now disappeared. The restrictions formerly imposed by craft gilds and by municipal authorities had been swept aside. A legal framework had been established within which entrepreneurs were free to set up factories, craftsmen were at liberty to open workshops and workers could take jobs where they pleased. Germany had great resources of coal, iron-ore and chemicals. She had a network of railways and inland waterways. Her major ports were developing overseas commerce on a large scale. Germany had numerous credit banks which fostered the founding of new industrial enterprises. Her system of technical education ensured the supply of well-trained men who would become the industrial leaders of the future. On the land the disappearance of serfdom and the progress of scientific farming enabled agricultural output to be increased to meet the needs of a growing population. It soon became evident that the industrial progress that had been made in the 1850s and 1860s had been but the prelude to still greater industrial expansion in the last quarter of the nineteenth century.

13   The Speculation Mania of 1872-73

In Western Europe and in the United States the period 1850 to 1870 had been one of economic expansion, which had been fostered by the new gold from California and Australia, by the establishment of credit banks and joint-stock companies and by the building of railways and steamships. There had been setbacks owing to wars and slumps but every recession had been followed by a period of recovery. Economic growth reached a climax in the early 1870s. Railway building expanded rapidly in many parts of the world and international trade expanded after the opening of the Suez Canal in 1869. The boom was particularly marked in the iron and steel industry and in the construction of railways. Britain experienced what Disraeli called 'a convulsion of prosperity'. In 1871 *The Times* surveyed the economic scene with 'undisturbed satisfaction' and declared that 'our commerce is extending and multiplying its world-wide ramifications'. In 1873 British exports amounted to £256,000,000 as compared with £190,000,000 in 1869. The export of iron and steel products more than doubled between 1868 and 1873 while coal exports rose even faster. In the same period in the United States 150 new furnaces were built and 23,500 miles of railways were opened.

In Germany the boom had certain special characteristics. The victory over France, the establishment of a united Reich, and the receipt of a huge indemnity coupled with the newly-gained freedom from government restrictions on the establishment of joint-stock companies engendered a feeling of self-confidence throughout the country. There were no limits to the optimism of businessmen who imagined that continued economic growth was a law of nature. By September 1873 France had paid Germany an indemnity of 5,000 million francs. In April of that year in the *Preussische Jahrbücher*, Ludwig Bamberger — a prosperous banker and a leading member of the National Liberal Party — urged that, in the interest of economic stability, the last instalment of the indemnity should not be accepted before the 5 years stipulated by the Treaty of Frankfurt. But his warning was ignored. France succeeded in raising loans at home and abroad and she paid the indemnity fully 2 years before the date originally fixed. As Bamberger had foreseen the sudden expansion of the currency in circulation in Germany led to inflation. Both prices and wages rose quickly. To make matters worse the reform of the currency was badly bungled, since the old thalers and gulden were not withdrawn immediately the new marks were issued. For a time too many new and old coins — and notes too for that matter — were in circulation. This aggravated the inflation. Berlin, where the new gold coins first appeared, became the most expensive city in the world.

The German government kept only a small part of the indemnity out of circulation. A mere 120 million marks were deposited in the war chest in Spandau in readiness for the next war. Most of the indemnity was soon allowed to find its way into the pockets of consumers, whose increased expenditure contributed to the ever-increasing cost of living. Generous gifts were made to generals and senior civil servants. Delbrück, for example, received 600,000 marks (20 marks = £1). Government agencies were set up to distribute money from the indemnity to war pensioners, to provincial authorities in Prussia and to contractors working on the new Reichstag building and on various military installations. Some of the money paid to building contractors soon found its way into the pockets of workers as wages. The government also used some of the proceeds of the indemnity to pay off loans raised by the North German Federation and by various German states. Those who received this money seldom reinvested it in gilt-edged securities but preferred to buy shares of a more speculative character. Many invested their savings in railways at home and abroad — particularly in Austria-Hungary and the United States.

During the Franco-Prussian War the German economy had been geared to the war effort and the absence of men on active service had depleted the labour force. When peace came there was a demand for more consumer goods, which was stimulated by the availability of money from the French indemnity that had been pumped by the authorities — directly or indirectly — into the economy. At the same time there was a virtually worldwide demand for certain capital goods, such as iron and other materials for building railways. Before 1870 official approval had been required to establish a joint-stock company but after a new Company Law had been passed by the North German Reichstag in June 1870 — and passed in 4 days after only a brief debate — no such approval was needed. There was an immediate boom in the promotion of new companies. In Germany over 120 new credit banks were established in 1869-72. In Prussia nearly 1,000 companies were set up between the middle of 1870 and the middle of 1873. In a single year (1872) 21 construction companies, 49 banks and 12 railway companies were established. The nominal capital of all the companies founded in Prussia in that year was over 1,500 million marks. In the first half of 1873 another 196 companies were set up. Some companies were new undertakings, some were mergers of existing firms and some were family businesses that were converted into joint-stock companies. Some companies were perfectly sound undertakings. The Gelsen-kirchen Mining Company, for example, founded in 1873 with financial support from Adolph Hansemann's Discount Company, became — under the able leadership of Friedrich Grillo and Emil Kirdorf — one of the largest coalmining enterprises in Germany. But other companies were ephemeral projects from which only the promoters made money. The boom was not confined to any particular sector of the economy. It affected capital and consumer interests alike. New banks were established such as the Deutsche Bank and the Dresden Bank, which developed into two of the most important banks in the country. A number of finance houses called 'building banks' were set up to exploit the housing shortage by speculating in building land. New collieries, ironworks and engineering plants were established and new railways were built. There was hectic activity in the construction industry as office blocks, public buildings, fortifications, barracks, and expensive private residences were erected. One of the most ostentatious private mansions to be built at this time was Krupp's Villa Hügel at Essen, which had 200 rooms. But not enough houses for the workers were being built in Germany. It was estimated that Berlin had 10,000 homeless in 1871. No wonder that in the following year there were serious disturbances in the city on the part of workers without a roof over their heads.

Austria-Hungary experienced a similar boom without the injection into the economy of additional purchasing power from an indemnity. Industry and agriculture revived after the setback caused by defeat in the Seven Weeks War. The establishment of the Dual Monarchy in 1868 brought new confidence to the business community. A good harvest coupled with recent extensions of the railway network stimulated exports of grain and improved the balance of payments. There was a boom in railway construction and in banking. The output of coal, iron, beet sugar and beer expanded. In Austria alone some 900 companies were set up between 1867 and 1873, including 604 industrial enterprises, 175 banks, 34 railway companies, 39 insurance companies and 23 mining undertakings, as well as some construction companies and 'building banks'.

Before long the boom in Germany and in Austria-Hungry degenerated into a wild orgy of speculation. Treitschke observed that 'during the speculation mania it really seemed as if the limits of human folly had been immeasurably extended'. There was a frantic rush to buy shares, land and houses, in the hope of making a quick profit from a rise in price. Gambling on the stock exchange and the property market became a national pastime. Bankers, who should have known better, stoked the fires of speculation. An American observer wrote in 1873: 'Bankers, large and small, have had no scruple against burdening the public with shares in all sorts of enterprises, selling the same at par and at a premium, when the intrinsic value was never more than 50 or 60 per cent.' He criticized 'those German bankers, who, from a desire to make large gains, were influenced to wink at the flimsy nature of many of the securities which they assisted to float in the market'.

Friedrich Engels drew attention to one aspect of the speculation mania when he wrote:

> The rapid development of industry and in particular of stock exchange swindling has dragged all the ruling classes into the whirlpool of speculation . . . . Ministers, generals, princes and counts deal in shares in competition with the cunningest stock exchange Jews, and the state recognises their equality by conferring titles wholesale upon these stock exchange Jews. The rural aristocracy, who have been industrialists for a long time as producers of beet sugar and as distillers, had long ago left the old and respectable days behind and now swell the lists of directors of all sorts of sound and unsound joint-stock companies. The bureaucracy is beginning more and more to despise embezzlement as the sole means of improving its income; it is turning its back on the state and is beginning to hunt after the far more lucrative posts on the administration of industrial enterprises. Those who still remain in office follow the example of their superiors and speculate in shares, or 'participate' in railways etc. . . .

Engels recommended his fellow socialists to read a book by Rudolf Meyer on the speculation mania of 1871. Meyer drew attention to the activities of the bankers Gerson Bleichröder and Adolph Hansemann as company promoters. Bleichröder was the Berlin agent of the Paris Rothschilds and he was Bismarck's personal banker. He was summoned to Versailles in 1871 to discuss with Alphonse Rothschild the methods by which the international money market could cope with the transfer of large numbers of bills of exchange from their French owners to the German government. The need to raise a large foreign loan was also discussed. Adolph Hansemann ran the Discount Company, which was one of the leading credit banks in Germany. He had access to government circles through a senior civil servant named Wehrmann, whom he rewarded with 'a well-paid sinecure' in his bank. Both Bleichröder and Hansemann could rely upon certain deputies to support their interests in the Reichstag and in the Prussian parliament.

During the boom of 1871-3 the two bankers expanded their industrial empires. Though often rivals they were prepared to cooperate when it suited them to do so. Together they took over the state railways of Mecklenburg and Brunswick and a number of private lines. Bleichröder — in association with the Berlin Commercial Company — established the Prussian Mining Ironworks Company, which took over the Hibernia and Shamrock coalmines in the Ruhr. Adolph Hansemann was also active in the Ruhr, where his Discount Company had substantial financial interests in both the Gelsenkirchen Mining Company and the Dortmund Union Company, which was a merger of several collieries, the most important of which was the *Neue Schottland* mine. And Bleichröder and Hansemann also founded or secured financial control over many other undertakings including railways, local banks, insurance companies and breweries.

One reason why these bankers were able to take over industrial undertakings and to promote new manufacturing enterprises was that both of them could rely upon certain state financial institutions for loans. The Discount Company borrowed from the Overseas Trading Corporation (Seehandlung), an old-established banking concern, which raised state loans and made short-term advances to government departments. And Bleichröder appears to have been allowed a measure of control over the Guelph Fund, which administered properties and financial assets belonging to the deposed king of Hanover and elector of Hesse-Cassel. Towards the end of 1872 Bleichröder and Hansemann each received a loan of 15 million thalers from the government. These financial favours helped the two bankers to expand their industrial interests in the early 1870s.

Responsible businessmen, bankers, parliamentarians and government officials must have been aware of the activities of unscrupulous promoters and of corruption in high places and in the press. Throughout the year 1872 there seemed to be a conspiracy of silence on the part of men who should have spoken out. It was not until 14 January 1873 that the Liberal deputy Eduard Lasker told the lower house of the Prussian parliament that certain newly-formed railway companies were paying highly placed individuals to use their influence to obtain concessions from the Prussian Ministry of Commerce. On 7 February, in a speech that took three hours to deliver, Lasker exposed in detail some of the railway scandals of recent years. The speech was quickly printed as a pamphlet and large numbers were sold. For the first time the public in Germany had an inkling of how small investors were being swindled by some of the promoters of joint-stock companies.

Lasker attacked three men who were all influential members of the conservative party. Hermann Wagener was the senior civil servant in the office of the minister president of Prussia and had direct access to the king. He had been one of Bismarck's most trusted advisers for many years. He had edited the well-known *Neue Preussische Zeitung* (or *Kreuzzeitung*). Prince Biron of Courland and Prince zu Putbus were members of the Prussian aristocracy and had seats in the upper house of the Prussian parliament. Wagener and two associates had formed a joint-stock company to build the Pomeranian Railway. A dispute between the promoters led to a civil action in the law courts and during the hearing some dubious transactions came to light. Lasker alleged that the company had deliberately misled government officials concerning its true financial position. Prince Biron of Courland had been the leading promoter of a railway to link Breslau and Warsaw. The directors had failed to tell the shareholders that, although they had secured a concession to build the section of the line that lay in Prussia, they had not obtained permission from the Russian authorities to extend the railway to Warsaw. When the line stopped at the frontier the value of the company's shares fell. Meanwhile the promoters were drawing very satisfactory profits from the construction company that was building the line. Prince zu Putbus has been described as 'a professional though not very experienced promoter'. He was concerned with a number of railway companies in which irregularities had occurred. Lasker blamed Count Itzenplitz, the minister of commerce, for failing to deal with promoters who were engaged in very dubious practices. He suggested that Count Itzenplitz was so anxious to get railways built in Prussia that he — and his officials — would turn a blind eye to clear breaches of the law.

A royal commission was promptly set up to investigate Lasker's allegations. It held fifty-six sessions and examined the affairs of twenty-six railway companies. Its report brought to light many irregularities in the management of the companies concerned. For example, it was apparently common practice for directors to falsify their accounts so as to inflate the cash in hand from partly paid-up shares. Although the commission examined the affairs of the Pomeranian Central Railway in particular detail it did not unearth sufficient evidence to warrant bringing any charges against Wagener. But the consequences of the scandal were very serious for Wagener. He had to retire from the civil service; he gave up his seat in the Reichstag; and he faced financial ruin when the Pomeranian Central Railway collapsed. By contrast Prince zu Putbus and Prince Biron escaped scot-free. They continued to sit in the upper house of the Prussian parliament and they continued to be received at court. Prince zu Putbus, an army officer, was cleared by a military 'court of honour'. Count Itzenplitz, however, resigned as minister of commerce. Although the promoters whom Lasker had attacked suffered little more than some adverse publicity, the report of the commission and Itzenplitz's resignation fully vindicated his action in exposing some of the scandals associated with the promotion of railways in Prussia at this time. But the purity of Lasker's motives may be questioned. It is significant that he attacked only companies promoted by his political opponents. Putbus, Biron and Wagener were all Conservatives. Lasker was silent concerning the financial activities of members of his own party.

Lasker's revelations, however, were only the tip of the iceberg. Bismarck was apparently satisfied with the enquiry into the affairs of twenty-six railway companies and with the resignations of Wagener and Itzenplitz. He hoped that the Reich Railway Office, established in June 1873, would be able to prevent any fresh scandals in the future. But the government undertook no further enquiries into other joint-stock companies established by promoters of dubious integrity. The press was strangely silent. It was not any leading national newspaper but a popular illustrated family magazine (*Die Gartenlaube*) that brought fresh scandals to light at the end of 1874. The writer was Otto Glagau and his attack upon 'stock exchange and company promotion swindles' was later expanded into a book in two volumes.

Glagau showed how the railway promoter Dr Strousberg had made money at the expense of investors. Only a few years before Strousberg had been regarded as a brilliant entrepreneur who had performed a great public service by raising capital to complete Germany's network of railways. He was called the 'railway king' and the 'doctor who works miracles'. Little is known of his early career. He was born in East Prussia and went to school in Königsberg. He spent some 20 years in London, where he edited two trade journals. In his memoirs he stated that when he returned to Germany he entered the life insurance business and that it was purely by accident that he became involved in the building of railways.

Strousberg's first venture was a line from Tilsit to Insterburg in his native province of East Prussia. He began by acting as the agent of English financiers who had secured a concession in 1862 to construct the railway. Before long he was in control of the undertaking. He went on to build other lines, mainly in the eastern provinces of Prussia — the Oder (right bank) Railway, the Mark-Posen Railway, and the Halle-an-der-Saale-Sorau-Guben Railway.

To promote his railways Strousberg did not seek financial support from the banks or wealthy investors but sold shares to small savers. To gain their confidence he placed articles in local newspapers that confidently predicted that the proposed railway would make large profits in a short time. The editors of the newspapers were bribed by cash payments, by gifts of railway shares or by additional revenues from advertisements. Next Strousberg would persuade a few noblemen, local dignitaries and senior civil servants to accept seats on the board of directors in return for handsome fees. They might have little knowledge of railways but their titles — duke, count or privy councillor — dazzled the more gullible investors. A further inducement to investors was an initial issue of preference shares. Next Strousberg would set up subsidiary finance and construction companies that were nominally independent firms but were in fact controlled by the railway company. Considerable profits might be made from the subsidiary companies, even though the railway company itself was not a financial success. The sub-contractors engaged by the construction company were paid partly in railway shares. But the contractors needed cash and they quickly sold their shares. By doing so they often caused the price of the shares to fall on the stock exchange. Strousberg's critics argued that this method of building a railway greatly inflated the cost of construction. These high costs were later recovered from the public through high fares and high freight charges.

From his modest beginnings in East Prussia and Posen Strousberg
went from strength to strength and became a very wealthy man. In a
few years he built up a vast business empire that included an estate in
Bohemia, railways in Germany, Hungary, Rumania and Russia, an
engineering plant in Hanover, ironworks at Dortmund and Neustadt,
a cattle market and slaughter house in Berlin and land for a housing
estate in Antwerp. He sat as a Conservative in the North German
Reichstag. In September 1869 Engels, having recently visited Germany, wrote: 'Strousberg is without doubt the greatest man in Germany. He will soon be made Emperor! . . . His guiding principle is
to swindle investors, while acting fairly towards his suppliers and
other industrialists.' As an industrialist he was always alive to new
ideas and he was one of the first to introduce the Bessemer process
into Germany. But when the Franco-Prussian War broke out the
shares of many of his companies fell and he soon found himself in
financial difficulties. It was in vain that he sold some of his industrial
properties in the hope of saving something from the wreck of his
fortunes. Lack of funds forced him to give up some of his railway concessions, with the result that he lost large sums that he had deposited
as caution money. He went bankrupt and found himself in a debtors'
prison in Moscow. When his creditors met in Berlin in 1876 they
were told that his assets were in several different countries and that
it was unlikely that they would ever recover more than a fraction of
the money owing to them. Strousberg became the scapegoat for all
the dishonest company promoters who had grown rich at the expense
of small savers during the speculation mania and he died in poverty
in Berlin in 1884. Men like Strousberg could never have flourished
if there had not been thousands of gullible Germans who were willing
to gamble their savings on schemes that promised quick returns.

The speculation mania came to a dramatic end in 1873. In Vienna
the day of reckoning came on 8 May, when the city was full of visitors
who had arrived for the international industrial exhibition. On that
day shares tumbled on the stock exchange and fortunes were lost. In
a few days three hundred bankruptcies were announced and there was
an epidemic of suicides. The government proclaimed a moratorium
on financial transactions until 28 May and Article 14 of the Bank Act
of 1862 (as amended in March 1872) was suspended, so the National
Bank of Austria was no longer obliged to exchange its notes for gold
or silver on demand. An American official declared that the calamity
'involved not merely stock-gamblers, but representatives of every

class who had trusted them, and the wild frenzy of the miserable crowd which assembled when their bubbles burst, threatened tumult and riot, and forcing the bearers of the greatest financial names in the Empire to fly for their lives, compelled the house temporarily to close its doors'.

Within a few months the financial crisis in Austria had spread to Germany. In June 1873 Werner Siemens wrote to his brother William: 'The storm over Vienna is more threatening than ever and here too the lightning will soon strike.' The lightning struck on 28 October 1873, when the Quistrop Bank failed. Shortly afterwards twenty-seven other banks suspended payments — fourteen of them for ever. In the following two months one bankruptcy followed another. Hans Blum wrote:

> Railway companies, banks, construction companies, large factories, joint-stock companies, as well as companies with unlimited liability were ruined . . . . At the same time countless unfortunate private individuals were horrified to discover that they had lost their capital or savings, or that — as shareholders in companies with unlimited liability — they faced the prospect of losing everything that they possessed to satisfy the companies' creditors.

All over Germany firms collapsed, credit was unobtainable and business was stagnant. Never before had a financial crisis been followed by so many suicides. Never before did so many dishonest cashiers and bank clerks flee the country. The financial crisis and the fall in the value of shares was followed by a decline in industrial output. By the end of 1874 the revenue of the railways had fallen sharply. In that year Krupp had to pledge all his vast undertakings to a group of banks led by the Seehandlung to secure a loan of 30 million thalers and it took the firm 13 years to pay off the debt. In 1875 mining companies were in difficulties. Throughout the country prices fell, sales dropped, wages were reduced and unemployment rose. It was not until 1876 that Germany's industrial output had recovered to the level of 1872.

III

The Industrial Giant
1873-1914

14   *Introduction*

Between 1873 and 1914 Germany became the leading industrial state on the Continent and challenged Britain's supremacy in the markets of the world. A book by F. E. Williams, entitled *Made in Germany* (1890), showed how alarmed some observers were becoming at Germany's invasion of Britain's traditional overseas markets. Germany's prosperity may be seen from the growth of her national income from 15,195 million marks to 49,501 million marks and of her foreign investments to over 30,000 million marks. Her national product *per capita* was growing at 21.6 per cent in each decade as compared with Britain's 12.5 per cent. The undistributed income of her joint-stock companies rose from 79 million marks in 1879 to 712 million marks in 1912. Her share of the world output of manufactured goods rose from 13 per cent in 1870 to 16 per cent in 1900, while that of Britain fell from 32 per cent to 18 per cent.

Germany made the most of her natural resources, such as coal in the Ruhr, iron-ore in Lorraine and potassium salts in Stassfurt and Wittelsheim. By 1913 Germany had overtaken Britain as a producer of pig-iron and steel, while her output of coal and lignite did not fall far short of that of Britain. And Germany had become a large exporter of woollen cloth and semi-manufactured woollens. She had also developed important new branches of manufacture such as the chemical, electrical and shipbuilding industries. In 1913 she supplied nine-tenths of the world's demand for synthetic dyes, while her exports of electrical appliances exceeded those of any other country. Her shipbuilding industry, her mercantile marine and her navy had greatly expanded from very small beginnings. Industrial progress had been stimulated by German inventions, such as the electric dynamo, aniline dyes and petrol and diesel engines.

Germany's industrial expansion had been achieved partly by private enterprise and partly by vigorous state intervention. Dynamic entrepreneurs like Werner Siemens, Emil Rathenau, August Thyssen, Emil Kirdorf, Wilhelm Cuno, Bernhard Dernburg, Albert Ballin and

Carl Fürstenberg built up great industrial, commercial and financial empires. On the other hand the Reich (or the Federal States) managed most of the railways and inland waterways, as well as extensive landed estates and forests. In 1906 Prussia operated 39 nationalized mines, 12 ironworks, 5 saltworks and 3 stone quarries. Various states owned banks, breweries, amber works, tobacco factories, porcelain workshops and medicinal baths.

For 20 years after the founding of the German Empire Bismarck was imperial chancellor, and his economic policy was directed towards stimulating industry and agriculture. As minister president of Prussia in the 1860s he had been concerned mainly with political problems such as the constitutional conflict and with foreign policy — the struggle with Austria and the unification of Germany. Economic problems had been left largely in the hands of ministerial colleagues and senior officials. But if necessary he was prepared to take action himself. Thus he insisted that all members of the customs union who wished to renew their Zollverein treaties would have to accept the tariff included in the Franco-Prussian commercial treaty of 1862. And after 1867 he tried to extend the powers of the Customs Parliament in the hope of turning this assembly into a German Reichstag.

It has been argued that as a Prussian landowner Bismarck was much better acquainted with the agrarian economy of the great estates east of the Elbe than with the new industrial economy that had recently developed in the Rhineland, Westphalia, Upper Silesia and Saxony. In fact he lived in cities for most of his life and he was well aware of the rise of great manufacturing regions in Germany. He saw that the industrial revolution was making the country richer and more powerful and was raising the standard of living of the workers. His confidential discussions with Lassalle in 1863 and his visit to Alfred Krupp at Essen in 1864 suggest that he appreciated the significance of the economic and social changes that were taking place in Germany at that time.

After 1871, as chancellor of the united Reich, Bismarck devoted more attention to economic and social questions. In his view Germany was now a satiated power with no territorial ambitions. Her interest lay in the maintenance of peace. Henceforth German diplomacy was devoted to the construction of a system of alliances on the Continent that, in the unlikely event of war, would guarantee Germany either the active support or the benevolent neutrality of at least two great powers.

At home Bismarck tried to strengthen the economic links between Prussia and other German states so as to cement the political unification secured in 1871. And he tried to foster the expansion of both the industrial and the agrarian sectors of the economy. He considered that economic growth was essential if Germany were to support the cost of increased armaments and of the new welfare services. His railway policy, his tariff policy, his colonial policy and his social policy were all directed towards stimulating economic expansion.

Two developments in the 1870s influenced the means by which Bismarck sought to achieve his aims on the home front. The first was the economic crisis of 1873. He was determined that there should be no repetition of the collapse of the stock market, the spate of bankruptcies, the rise in unemployment or the financial scandals. The encouragement given to the formation of cartels and the revision of the Company Law to give greater protection to investors illustrate this aspect of his policy. Again, the rise of the Social Democrat Party filled him with foreboding. In his view a party that advocated the abolition of capitalism and the establishment of a socialist state threatened the very existence of the empire that he had played a leading part in creating. His attempt to crush the party by his Anti-Socialist Law failed, but his policy of meeting his opponents halfway by laying the foundations of a welfare state was more successful. His schemes for sickness and accident benefits and old-age pensions were eventually copied by many other nations.

In view of the remarkable expansion of the German economy between 1873 and 1913 and the growing prosperity of the country it is a little surprising that some contemporaries and some historians have regarded the first part of the period — the years 1873 to 1896 — as a 'great depression'. In Britain many of those who were engaged in industry, commerce or finance — and many farmers — were convinced that times were hard. They pointed to dramatic falls in prices, profits, dividends and interest rates. They complained of keen competition in overseas markets. On the other hand, as Musson observes, although prices undoubtedly fell,

> . . . almost every other index of economic activity — output of coal and pig-iron, tonnage of ships built, consumption of raw wool and cotton, import and export figures, shipping entries and clearances, railway freight and passenger traffic, bank deposits and clearances, joint-stock company formations, trading profits, con-

sumption per head of wheat, meat, tea, beer, and tobacco — all
these showed an upward trend.

In Germany too the period 1873-96 has been called 'the great
depression'. But Hans Rosenberg, who uses the term, produces ample
evidence to suggest that this was a very curious sort of depression. As
in Britain, so in Germany, prices, profits and interest rates fell and
there was a reduction in the rate of growth of capital investment in the
private sector of the economy. But industrial output increased and
there was an expansion in overseas trade. Moreover real wages rose,
as there was a tendency for retail prices to fall more quickly than money
wages. Treitschke, writing in 1874, observed: 'The transformation
of our national economy has given to the working class a great increase
of wages, without parallel in German history. Therewith they secured,
as aforetime the English working classes, the possibility of permanently
improving their standard of life, and of approximating more nearly to
the habits of the middle classes.' And looking back on the 'depression'
the economist Julius Wolf declared in 1888 that 'despite unemployment and frequent — though not universal — wage reductions, this
has been much more a crisis for the rich than for the poor.'

Although the term 'great depression' is an unhappy one, there can
be no doubt that between 1873 and 1896 German industrialists had
to cope with conditions far less favourable than those that had existed
in the 1850s and 1860s. It is to their credit that they boldly met the
challenge of falling prices, low interest rates and reduced profits.
Despite unfavourable circumstances that might have retarded economic
expansion, Germany's industry made remarkable progress in the last
quarter of the nineteenth century. At the end of 1898 the British
commercial attaché in Berlin wrote that 'today is seen on all sides a
prosperity hardly dreamed of by the most enthusiastic patriots twenty
years ago'. Germany's experience in this respect was not unique. The
industrial revolution in Britain had taken place under equally difficult
conditions. The wars of the French Revolution and of Napoleon could
hardly be regarded as favourable to industrial expansion. Both in
Britain between 1792 and 1815 and in Germany between 1873 and
1896 entrepreneurs made remarkable progress in periods which — for
very different reasons — were inimical to economic growth.

One aspect of Germany's rapid economic growth in the last quarter
of the nineteenth century was the significant role played by the Reich,
the Federal States, and the provincial and municipal authorities in

promoting the expansion of industry, agriculture, forestry and commerce. Public authorities were responsible — either entirely or in part — for the provision of communications, energy, land improvements, educational institutions and health facilities. Public undertakings included railways, collieries, ironworks, shipyards and various manufacturing enterprises. According to the industrial census of 1907 these enterprises accounted for about a tenth of all the mines, factories and transport facilities in the country. And it has been estimated that in the early years of the twentieth century between 20 and 25 per cent of investments in Germany were made through public authorities or nationalized undertakings. In other highly industrialized countries the public sector of the economy was a good deal smaller at this time.

Another unusual feature of Germany's rapid economic expansion after 1873 was the failure of those sections of the population primarily responsible for the industrialization of the country to secure the degree of political influence that they enjoyed in Britain, France or the United States. In Britain effective political power was wielded by the House of Commons in the nineteenth century and successive Reform Acts gave the vote first to the middle classes and then to the workers. In Germany, on the other hand, the chancellor and the ministers of state were responsible to the emperor and not to the popularly elected Reichstag. In Prussia, by far the largest of the Federal States, the lower house was still elected by the undemocratic three-class system. It was this system that made it possible, early in the nineteenth century, for 161 landowners or farmers and only 17 representatives of trade and industry to be elected as deputies to the lower house. The owners of the great estates east of the Elbe continued to exercise a powerful influence over the political and social life of the country. Yet their economic power was declining. The more Germany became industrialized, the weaker became the position of the landed gentry. A situation in which a social group exercised political power that bore no relation to its contribution to the economic development of the country was fraught with danger for the future.

15   Cartels and Banks

In the middle of the nineteenth century industrialization had been fostered in Germany by the development of joint-stock companies. After 1873 a number of firms expanded and became linked in cartels, while at the same time six great banks secured for themselves a dominant position in the world of finance. Large concerns and cartels working in close association with the great banks — these were the twin pillars of the German economy in the last quarter of the nineteenth century.

The rate of growth of some large firms was accelerated. Krupp, for example, developed into a huge vertical combine producing iron and steel, rails, armaments and much else. It controlled sources of coal and iron-ore. Its activities were extended to shipbuilding and to other undertakings that used its iron and steel products. By 1887 it had 12,600 workers on its pay-roll. Nationalized as well as private undertakings expanded. The Prussian State, for example, embarked upon a policy of purchasing private railway companies, so that by 1914 nearly the whole Prussian railway network had been nationalized.

Another way in which industrial enterprises expanded was by the amalgamation of firms that had formerly competed with one another. As early as 1836 some coalmining firms merged to form the United Wurm Company. The expansion of large-scale industry was associated with the growth of mammoth enterprises. The number of undertakings with a capital of over 10 million marks rose from 74 in 1886 to 229 in 1909. In the Ruhr in 1893 the coal produced by the ten largest colliery companies accounted for over one-third of the output of the region. By 1910 the ten largest colliery companies — including giants like Gelsenkirchen, Harpen, and the Gutehoffnungshütte — produced nearly 60 per cent of the output of the coalfield.

The great manufacturing and mining firms, shipping companies and banks not only expanded but drew more closely together in associations known by various names — 'interest groups', 'pools', 'rings', 'trusts', 'syndicates', and 'cartels'. These organizations sometimes developed from earlier unions of employers, which were pressure groups engaged in campaigns in favour of such things as a higher tariff or lower freight charges.

The first German cartel was the Neckar Salt Union of 1828, which included the nationalized saltworks of Württemberg and Baden and a private saltmine at Ludwigshalle. In 1836 all the alum works in Prussia agreed to sell their entire output through the state-owned Overseas Trading Corporation (Seehandlung). In the 1840s the Oberlahnstein Association was formed to control the sale of pig-iron produced in Nassau. In 1870 six cartels were in existence.

During the slump that followed the speculation mania of 1872-3 a few more cartels — mainly in the heavy industries — were set up and then the new type of industrial organization gradually spread to other branches of manufacture, such as plate-glass, cement and chemicals. It was not until the 1880s that the cartel movement gathered momentum. Of the 275 cartels in operation in 1900 nearly 200 had been founded between 1879 and 1890. The history of some of the cartels was a stormy one. When cartel agreements came up for renewal there were sometimes bitter struggles between members concerning output quotas, share of profits and the allocation of markets. And one type of industrial enterprise — the 'mixed' undertaking — sometimes found itself in a quandary when cartels were established. Thus a steel company that owned a colliery and joined both a steel and a coal cartel might find itself involved in a conflict of loyalties if the interests of the two cartels clashed.

A number of the cartels were 'horizontal cartels' linking firms making the same products, but there were also 'vertical cartels' uniting firms engaged in different stages of production from the raw material to the finished article. Among the larger cartels were the Rhenish-Westphalian Coal Syndicate, the Steelworks Union, the German Potash Syndicate, the Siemens-Schuckert group of electrical companies, the AEG (*Allgemeine Elektrizitäts* AG) and the Dye Cartel (I.G. *Farben*). The State—the Reich and the Federal States—favoured the development of cartels in the interest of industrial efficiency. The law regarded a cartel agreement in the same light as any other commercial contract. In 1910 the Prussian parliament passed a law setting up a 'compulsory cartel' of potash firms when it seemed inevitable that there would be cut-throat competition in the industry if the existing voluntary cartel was not renewed.

There were four main types of cartel agreements. First there were compacts to share the market by which certain regions or customers were allocated to particular cartel members. Secondly there were agreements that fixed prices for sales at home and abroad. Thirdly there were agreements fixing the total volume of production of cartel firms, with a quota of the output allocated to each member. Finally there were agreements to share profits in accordance with a predetermined formula. Some associations were content to try to achieve only one of these objectives while others were more ambitious and sought to achieve several objectives at the same time.

A successful cartel might eventually bring its members even closer together by an agreement to form a holding company controlling a majority of the shares of all the firms concerned. And the process of cooperation might culminate in a complete merger of the members of the cartel into a single company. It took only 3 years for the profit-sharing cartel formed in 1904 by the Gelsenkirchen Mining Company, the Rote Erde ironworks of Aachen and the Schalk Mining and Smelting Company to be turned into a single concern.

Firms hoped to derive substantial advantages by coming together to form a cartel. They considered that a cartel would increase efficiency by concentrating output in a smaller number of factories or mines. The least efficient and the least favourably-located plants could be closed. A cartel would enable by-products to be used more effectively. In certain industries, where progress depended upon scientific research, costly laboratories—too expensive for individual firms to maintain—could be financed by the cartel. It was also hoped that a cartel would promote exports by establishing agencies abroad that might be beyond the means of member firms. Above all the larger the cartel the greater would be its share of the market. Agreements on the volume of output and the level of prices might be expected to secure an increase in profits.

Since, with only a few exceptions, cartels were first established just after the crisis of 1873, some contemporaries regarded them as emergency organizations—'children of the financial storm'—that would help hard-pressed companies to survive at a critical time but would disappear when conditions improved. But these early cartels were not wound up when trade took a turn for the better. Moreover it was soon seen that cartels were being established when the economy was in a flourishing condition—between 1888 and 1890 for example—and in these cases the 'children of the financial storm' explanation for the establishment of cartels could not be put forward.

The fact that a number of cartels were formed shortly after the adoption of a protectionist tariff in 1879 suggested that another reason for setting up such associations was a determination to expand sales in the home market at a time when foreign competitors were at a disadvantage. Other reasons for founding cartels were the desire to monopolize the use of new patents or to maintain research establishments. Sometimes banks holding large blocks of shares in companies put pressure on those firms to sign a cartel agreement. The cartels in the electrical industry were generally founded in this way. Yet another reason for the formation of cartels was self-preservation. If the producers of a raw material or a fuel formed a cartel it would be in the interest of their customers to establish cartels themselves to strengthen their bargaining power over prices. Thus a cartel of colliery companies could call into existence cartels of private firms and public bodies that consumed coal. An association of railway undertakings or gasworks would be in a stronger position than a single company to argue about prices with a coal cartel. The Potash Syndicate was an exceptional case since it was formed by four undertakings — two state-owned and two privately owned — to exploit a natural monopoly. The main potash deposits in the world were at Stassfurt and Wittelsheim and by signing a cartel agreement the potash firms were able to take full advantage of this situation. By 1908 the membership of the potash cartel had grown to fifty firms.

German firms joined not only national but also international cartels. One of the earliest was the International Railmakers Association of 1883, which was joined by German, British and Belgian firms. In 1892 the Hamburg-America Line and the North German Lloyd joined with the Holland-America and the Red Star Lines to set up the first North Atlantic shipping pool. By 1910 German firms were members of about a hundred international cartels and a dozen shipping conferences.

As an illustration of the establishment and working of industrial cartels a brief description may be given of the formation and development of the Rhenish-Westphalian Coal Syndicate. Since 1858 the colliery owners in the Ruhr had been cooperating to promote their common interests through the Ruhr Mineowners Association. In the slump that followed the speculation mania of 1872-3 coal prices fell and profits vanished. In 1876 losses amounting to 12.8 million marks were sustained by 109 coal companies in the Ruhr. Between 1878 and 1886 various attempts were made to reach agreement on the restriction of output, the fixing of prices and the sharing of markets but they all failed. Some agreements were too limited in scope, such as the Bochum Sales Association. Others quickly collapsed because there were too many violations of the agreement. But price agreements concerning particular types of fuel — such as gas-coal and coking-coal — were more successful.

After 15 years of experiments in controlling the Ruhr coalmining industry an agreement that proved to be permanent was at last reached. According to W.F. Bruck it was established 'by the ingenious collaboration of Emil Kirdorf, the representative of the coal interests, and the leaders of the *Disconto-Gesellschaft*'. In 1893 colliery owners responsible for producing 86 per cent of the coal in the Ruhr not only signed a cartel agreement to regulate output, prices and sales but also set up and financed a new company called the Rhenish-Westphalian Coal Syndicate. It was originally formed to buy and sell coal, coke and briquettes, but in 1904 its functions were extended to include 'the preparation of coal for the market and the acquisition of coal lands and mining installations, and the conduct of such undertakings as might aid in the storage, sale, and transport of coal'. Each member of the cartel had a production quota based upon its output in 1891-2, which had to be delivered to the syndicate. All orders for coal had to be passed on to the syndicate.

Between 1893 and 1914 the syndicate came to be dominated by the larger companies. Membership declined in these years from 96 to 62. Over one-third of the output in 1904 came from the 6 largest firms. A high proportion of the coal handled by the cartel — about 70 per cent — was used directly for industrial purposes. Although the output of coal by members of the cartel increased considerably at this time the amount produced was not always sufficient to fulfil all the orders it received. In 1906 the syndicate had to import some coal from England.

When the syndicate was established in 1893 nearly all the members were purely coalmining concerns. Most of the Ruhr steel companies that owned collieries had no need to join the syndicate, since they normally consumed all the coal their mines produced. Subsequently the output of these 'tied mines' expanded and by 1900 it amounted to about one-fifth of the total production of the Ruhr. The coal produced by the 'tied mines' that was surplus to the requirements of the steel plants was sold on the open market — sometimes at a price lower than that fixed by the syndicate. In 1899 the steel companies that owned collieries joined the syndicate on terms very favourable to themselves.

There were significant reactions on the part of wholesale and retail coal merchants and of large and small consumers of coal to the price maintenance policy of the syndicate. Wholesale coal merchants and carriers of coal soon formed their own cartels to strengthen their bargaining position. The coal syndicate, however, was generally represented on the boards of directors of these combines. Retail coal merchants formed associations that undertook the bulk purchase and the storing of coal on a cooperative basis. Large consumers of coal — steelworks, power stations, chemical companies, gasworks, shipping firms and large municipalities — purchased or leased coalmines so as to be independent of the syndicate. Domestic consumers joined cooperative societies that handled large quantities of coal for sale to the general public.

On the whole the policy of the syndicate was successful in eliminating seasonal variations in the output of coal. It also seems to have reduced the effects of cyclical fluctuations of trade, though these could not be entirely eliminated. From time to time the syndicate was able to sell abroad stocks of coal that might otherwise have accumulated at the pithead and so caused a decline in output. Between 1893 and 1913 the syndicate gradually raised coal prices from 7.50 marks per ton to 12 marks per ton. It was not possible to secure a more substantial increase owing to the competition from other fuels and from power plants. The higher prices benefited the coalminers, whose wages rose more rapidly than coal prices.

Cartels were not confined to industrial firms. The organization of the banks in Germany followed a very similar pattern to that of manufacturing companies. The great banks not only grew by merging with smaller banks but they frequently collaborated in a very similar fashion to the cartel agreements of industrial enterprises. Besides the Reichsbank, the Prussian Seehandlung and a few federal state banks, there were six major banks in Germany in the early twentieth century. They were the four 'D' banks — the Deutsche Bank, the Dresden Bank, the Discount Bank (Disconto-Gesellschaft), the Darmstadt Bank — and the Schaaffhausen Bank and the Commercial Company (Handelsgesellschaft) of Berlin. The largest was the Deutsche Bank, with share capital and reserves of over 300 million marks in 1908. A dozen important provincial banks were associated with the Deutsche Bank. The capital and reserves of the whole Deutsche Bank group amounted to 785 million marks. The total capital and reserves of the six great German banks and their associated houses was over 2,500 million marks.

There were groups of banks that regularly cooperated to raise public loans. A separate 'consortium' of banks — virtually a temporary cartel — was set up for each loan but many finance houses appeared again and again in associations formed for this purpose. There was a Prussian consortium, led by the Overseas Trading Corporation (Seehandlung), which placed Prussian state loans on the market. The first was a loan raised in connection with the mobilization of the army at the time of the Italian war of 1859. There was a Reich consortium, led by the Reichsbank, to handle imperial loans. The Rothschild consortium raised loans for the government of Austria-Hungary. The Asiatic consortium, led by the Disconto-Gesellschaft, handled public loans in China, Japan and Korea.

One way in which the banks influenced the expansion of the German economy was by promoting the establishment of mergers and cartels in various industries. The great banks were very active in the coal and iron industry. The Discount Company helped to establish the Rhenish-Westphalian Coal Syndicate. The Darmstadt Bank stood behind the Deutsch-Luxembourg Mining and Iron-smelting Company, while the Schaaffhausen Bank held a majority of the shares of the *Internationale Bohrgesellschaft* and operated the sales office of the Union of German Wire Manufacturers. The power of the banks was seen in 1904, when Bleichröder and the Commercial Company of Berlin together successfully resisted an attempt by the Prussian government to nationalize the Hibernia coalmining company. Nearly all the joint-stock companies in the electrical industry were founded with the aid of one or more banks and it was pressure from their financial backers that led to the establishment of the first two cartels in this industry.

German banks were also closely associated with the promotion of foreign investment, the export drive and the expansion of Germany's economic interests overseas. The construction of the Berlin-Bagdad railway was supported by several banks. In 1889 the Deutsche Bank and the Dresden Bank cooperated to set up the Anatolian Railway Company, while in the following year a group led by the Deutsche Bank and a Vienna bank (the *Wiener Bankverein*) acquired Baron von Hirsch's shares in the Oriental Railway Company.

In the German colonies the Deutsche Bank helped to finance the East Africa Company. The Discount Company (Disconto-Gesellschaft) was associated with the German Commercial and Plantation Company of the South Sea Islands and with the founding of the New Guinea Company and the Otavi Mining and Railway Company of South West

Africa. German banks helped to finance the German East Africa Bank, the German West Africa Bank and the Cameroons Railway Company.

The mammoth industrial concerns, the giant cartels and the great banks did not have to cope with the public hostility that the American trusts had to face. In the United States the Interstate Commerce Act and the Sherman Anti-Trust Act were passed in the hope of curbing the powers of the great combines. In Germany the opposition to cartels did not come from one of the large powerful political parties. It came from a relatively small radical group whose influence in the Reichstag was declining. Eugen Richter, the leader of the *Deutsche Freisinnige* party, was one of the main critics of cartels but he could not hope to achieve very much without any support from conservatives or socialists.

In 1879 Richter denounced manufacturers who sold locomotives and rails abroad more cheaply than at home. In the years that followed ample evidence was forthcoming to show that cartels were adopting a ruthless policy of 'selling at all hazards at the best possible price'. But the government believed that the great combines and cartels were playing an essential part in stimulating Germany's economic advance. The attitude of the leaders of the Social Democrat Party is more difficult to fathom. One might have expected that men like Bebel and Liebknecht would have denounced cartels as organizations of capitalists who were filling their pockets at the expense of the workers. The failure of the German Socialists to mount an effective campaign against cartels may perhaps have been due to the fact that they realized that if ever they came into power it would be much easier for them to nationalize an industry dominated by a few cartels than to take into state-ownership an industry in which there were a large number of relatively small firms.

16   New Industries

Chemical Industries

The rapid growth in the manufacture of chemical products was one of industrial Germany's greatest successes. Although employing a relatively small number of workers, these industries are of great significance in the development of a modern industrial economy. By 1913 Germany was producing three-quarters of the world's synthetic dyes and her exports of dyestuffs were valued at 195 million marks. There were two main branches of the chemical industry, one producing 'heavy' and the other 'light' chemicals. The former produced alkalis for the manufacturers of soap and glass, while the latter made synthetic (aniline) dyestuffs for the textile industry as well as pharmaceutical products, perfumes, cosmetics, photographic materials and plastics for sale to the general public.

Two factors contributed to the remarkable expansion of the chemical industries in Germany. The first was the existence in Germany of certain raw materials such as rock salt (for sodium), potassium salts (for potash), iron pyrites (for sulphuric acid) and coal-tar (for aniline dyes). The output of potassium salts from the Stassfurt deposits rose from 2,400 tons in 1861 to 8,311,700 tons in 1910. The second factor was the establishment of research laboratories by chemical firms, by universities and by technical colleges in which scientists discovered new products such as drugs and synthetic dyes.

Early in the twentieth century Dr Steigel boasted that in the chemical industries 'empiricism has absolutely disappeared from present day methods of production . . . . The large factories have well-equipped and often model laboratories for scientific research in which it is a pleasure to work. Nowhere is the alliance between science and technology so intimate as in Germany, and no one doubts that this accounts for the pre-eminence of the German chemical industry.'

As early as 1840 Dr John Bowring had observed that in Germany 'chemical research in its various branches is further advanced than with us'. In the middle of the nineteenth century several university departments of chemistry in Germany were in charge of scientists with international reputations, such as Justus von Liebig, the 'father' of agricultural chemistry. But in those days young German chemists had few opportunities to carve out careers for themselves at home and men like Heinrich Caro, Ludwig Mond and Philipp Pauli secured posts with English chemical firms. Others obtained teaching appointments — August Wilhelm Hofmann in London, Carl Schorlemmer in Manchester and Wilhelm Dittmar in Glasgow. Schorlemmer's main researches were on the normal paraffins, and he showed that all of them, however they were derived, formed a single series. Hofmann became director of the Royal College of Chemistry in London, where he discovered how to make benzene by distilling coal-tar. In 1856 one of his pupils, William Henry Perkin, produced tyrian purple, the first of the aniline dyes. Soon afterwards Hofmann himself produced blue and violet coal-tar dyes. At industrial exhibitions held in London (1862) and Paris (1867) English cloths impregnated with brilliantly coloured synthetic dyes were much admired. But the British chemical industry failed to hold the lead in the manufacture of synthetic dyestuffs that it might have secured, because of the discoveries of Perkin and Hofmann and because it had easier access than continental rivals to anthracene, an essential raw material in the production of coal-tar dyes. German firms forged ahead and eventually dominated world markets not only in aniline dyes but in other chemical products as well, such as drugs and fertilisers. Hofmann's return to his native land in 1865 later came to be regarded as a turning-point in the fortunes of the chemical industry in Germany. Before long the scientists whom he had trained were making their mark in the research laboratories of German firms.

The firms that came to dominate the chemical industry in Germany were Friedrich Bayer & Co of Elberfeld; Meister, Lucius & Brüning of Höchst-am-Main; the *Badische Anilin- und Sodafabrik* of Ludwigshafen; and the *Actien-Gesellschaft für Anilin-Fabrikation* (AGFA) of Berlin. Many important discoveries were made in the laboratories of the leading chemical firms. Landmarks in the expansion of the aniline dye industry were the discovery of alizarin, the colouring matter of the madder root, by Graebe and Liebermann and the preparation of synthetic indigo by Adolf Baeyer. In the pharmaceutical branch of the chemical industry a number of new drugs were produced, such as aspirin, insulin, several antibiotics and liver extracts to combat anaemia. Agriculture benefited from Rudolf Frank's discovery of the value of potassium salts as fertilizers and from the researches that resulted in a very substantial increase in the saccharine content of sugar beet.

The work of the laboratories of German chemical firms may be illustrated from the achievements of Carl Duisberg and A. Laubenheimer. At first the firm of F. Bayer & Co (Elberfeld) engaged four foremen, trained at the Krefeld Trade School, to supervise both production and research. Then in the 1870s university graduates were introduced into the laboratory. The most outstanding chemist was Carl Duisberg. He was soon devoting all his time to research — he discovered three new aniline dyes — and to training young chemists. His activities expanded as the firm extended its range of products to include heavy chemicals, drugs, ointments and photographic accessories. An important aspect of his work was the maintenance of close links between his laboratory and the chemistry departments of the universities of Berlin and Würzburg. In 1912 Duisberg was appointed managing director of F. Bayer & Co. In 1883 Laubenheimer gave up an academic career to join the firm of Meister, Lucius & Brüning. Ten years later he took charge of a new central laboratory, a post he held for 30 years. Much of his research was concerned with the production of new drugs to combat diphtheria, tetanus, dysentery and foot-and-mouth disease.

The rapid expansion of the chemical industry began in the boom that followed the Franco-Prussian War. The years 1870 to 1874 saw the establishment of 42 chemical companies with a capital of 42 million marks. By 1896 Germany had 108 chemical firms with a capital of 332 million marks. But almost from the first the industry was dominated by a few large firms. By the early twentieth century they had become highly prosperous undertakings. For example, Meister, Lucius & Brüning of Höchst had been founded in 1863 with a capital of 66,450 gulden. In 1880, when the firm became a joint-stock company, its capital had grown to 8.5 million marks. By 1904 the capital was 22.5 million marks. The reserves were 6.7 million marks, the turnover was 40 million marks and the net profits were 6.7 million marks. Between 1896 and 1904 dividends of between 20 per cent and 30 per cent had been declared. Despite the prosperous condition of the industry there were those who felt that there were dangers if the fierce competition between chemical firms continued. In 1903 Carl Duisberg of F. Bayer & Co visited the United States where he studied the great trusts that had developed there. He returned convinced that the large German chemical firms should be united in a single cartel.

Duisberg argued that if this were done the industry could be rationalized. Costs could be reduced and cut-throat competition at home and abroad could be largely eliminated. Above all money could be saved if there were cooperation, instead of rivalry, in research programmes to produce new aniline dyes and drugs. But formidable obstacles prevented the realization of Duisberg's grandiose plan at this time. When the Ruhr coalowners had formed their cartel they had to plan the production and sale of a single commodity — coal. But the output of chemical firms was quite different since it included a great variety of products such as dyes, drugs, fertilizers, perfumes, cosmetics and photographic accessories. To plan the output and sale of so many products would be an extremely complicated and difficult task.

No cartel covering the whole of the German chemical industries was established in 1904 as a result of Duisberg's efforts. Instead two associations of chemical firms were set up. The first was between F. Bayer & Co, the *Badische Anilin- und Sodafabrik*, and the *Actien-Gesellschaft für Anilin-Fabrikation* (AGFA). The second consisted of Meister, Lucius & Brüning (or *Höchster Farbenwerke*), Kalle & Co AG, and Leopold Cassella & Co. In the second group the *Höchster Farbenwerke* virtually took over the other two firms. It was not until the First World War that the two groups joined to form a 'community of interests' (1916), which developed into a still closer union (I. G. Farben) in 1925. When Carl Duisberg was appointed chairman of the board of directors of I. G. Farben, his dream of 1904 had at last come true. Hermann Levy, writing in 1935, declared that I. G. Farben was 'not only the most important trustification in German industry, but indeed one of the most important trusts in the international economic sphere'. In sharp contrast to the experience of the electrical industry, the initiative for the establishment of cartels in the chemical industry came from within the industry itself. The great banks had little influence over the cartel movement in the chemical industry.

Electrical Industries

The electrical — like the chemical — industries made rapid progress in Germany in the last quarter of the nineteenth century. Clapham considers that 'beyond question the creation of this industry was the greatest single achievement of modern Germany . . . . Her success was rewarded by a foreign trade in electrical appliances which no other nation could approach.' Germany's exports of electrical products — about half of the world's trade in these goods — were valued at nearly

220 million marks in 1913. The growth of the industry was made possible by scientific research and by financial support from the great banks. Inventions such as the dynamo and the white filament electric bulb were as important to the electrical industry as was the discovery of synthetic dyes to the chemical industry.

The electrical industry included several different branches of manufacture each turning out a variety of products. The output of the 'heavy' section consisted of generators, accumulators, transformers and other equipment for power stations, factories and tramway undertakings. The 'light' section of the industry manufactured cables, lamps, telephonic and telegraphic equipment and various appliances for use in the home. The generation of electricity in power stations and the maintenance of cables to take power and light to industrial and domestic consumers could be regarded as another branch of the electrical industry. The feasibility of electric traction was demonstrated in the 1880s when an electric tram ran in a Berlin suburb, but it was the introduction of electric trams (with overhead wires) in Halle-an-der-Saale in 1891 that opened a new era in municipal transport — an era called into being by the electrical industry. In 1907 there were 3,719 kilometres of tramways in Germany. At first it was private enterprise that promoted the growth of the electrical industry, but before long certain undertakings — especially those operating tramways and street lighting — came to be owned and operated by public authorities. A study of 87 municipalities in 1910 showed that 58 of them had their own power stations.

Although the first German electrical firm — Siemens & Halske — had been founded as early as 1847 the boom in the industry did not occur until the 1880s. A visit to the Paris electrical exhibition of 1881 convinced Emil Rathenau that there was a great future for the electrical industry. In 1883 he set up the German Edison Company — Germany's first electrical joint-stock company — with help from the banks and this became the Allgemeine Elektrizitäts-Gesellschaft (AEG) four years later.

As the demand for electrical power and electric light grew, Rathenau's example was followed by a number of other entrepreneurs, who also received support from the banks. In 1891 the first electric cable to transmit power over a long distance was laid by the Allgemeine Elektrizitäts-Gesellschaft (AEG). This was between Lauffen on the River Neckar and Frankfurt-am-Main (175 kilometres). The advantage of the electric generator over the steam-engine could now be seen. Electricity could be used far from the power station but steam-power could be used only quite near the steam-engine.

By 1896 there were 39 electrical companies in Germany with a total capital of 195 million marks. But a handful of big firms dominated the industry. In 1900 there were seven large groups of electrical companies, each supported by several banks. They constructed dynamos and transformers, built power stations and supplied light and energy to industrial establishments. In 1900 they proudly displayed their products at the Palace of Electricity at the Paris exhibition. But only a year later the electrical industry in Germany faced a serious crisis. Keen competition, price cutting and overproduction led to a dramatic fall in prices, profits and dividends. Several electrical firms were in grave difficulties. The banks, which had invested heavily in the industry, became alarmed and put pressure on electrical firms to pool their resources to avoid disaster. Two large cartels were formed — the Siemens Schuckert group and the Allgemeine Elektrizitäts-Gesellschaft (AEG). At the head of these cartels were the two men who had played a decisive role in the establishment of the electrical industry in Germany — Werner Siemens and Emil Rathenau.

Werner Siemens was born near Hanover in 1816. A brilliant member of a large and talented family, he joined the Prussian army as a cadet and attended the United Engineering and Artillery School in Berlin. On the completion of his studies he was appointed a second lieutenant in the artillery. His interest in the relatively new science of electricity was shown in 1842 when he patented a galvanic process for gilding and plating. His brother William sold the English patent right of electroplating to a Birmingham firm for £1,500. Siemens realized the potentialities of the electric telegraph — the most recent form of rapid communication — and he invented a process for insulating telegraph wires with gutta-percha. This method was successfully used in 1847 on the overhead telegraph lines of the Berlin-Potsdam railway and on the underground line between Berlin and Grossburen. Dial and printing systems patented by Werner Siemens were also used on these lines.

In the same year Werner Siemens went into partnership with the mechanic Johann Georg Halske to set up a small workshop (the *Telegraphen Bauanstalt*) in the Schöneberger-Strasse in Berlin to make dial telegraphs, ringing devices and electro-medical inductors. At first the firm employed only three workers. Financial backing was secured from Werner's cousin Johann Georg Siemens, who provided a loan of £1,000. As Werner Siemens was a serving officer he could devote only part of his time to the firm, but it was agreed that he could become an active partner whenever he left the army. Such was the genesis of a firm that eventually grew into a huge combine employing some 60,000 workers in 1914.

In 1848, during the war against Denmark, Siemens was responsible for defending Kiel harbour from a Danish naval attack by laying submarine mines with electric detonators. Next he was seconded from the army to the newly created Prussian Ministry of Commerce to supervise the construction of the first long telegraph line in Europe. This underground telegraph ran from Berlin to Frankfurt-am-Main, where the German National Assembly was sitting. The successful completion of the line towards the end of 1849 encouraged the Prussian government to authorize the laying of an underground telegraph line between Berlin and Cologne with an extension to Verviers in Belgium, which was linked with Brussels by an overhead telegraph.

Werner Siemens resigned his commission in 1849 so as to be able to devote all his time to the firm of Siemens & Halske, which now employed twenty workers. Unfortunately the partners almost immediately suffered a setback. The Berlin-Frankfurt telegraph, successful at first, broke down and Siemens wrote a pamphlet blaming officials of the Ministry of Commerce for ignoring his advice. The Prussian authorities, annoyed at this unwelcome criticism, placed no further orders for telegraphic apparatus with Siemens & Halske and the firm had to rely upon orders from private railway companies in Germany and from foreign railway administrations. Siemens & Halske were already supplying the Russian government with appliances for the telegraph from St Petersburg to Moscow and this was followed by many other orders from abroad. The reputation of the firm as one of the leading electrical enterprises in Europe was enhanced by the award of a Council Medal at the Great Exhibition at the Crystal Palace in 1851.

In the next 30 years Siemens & Halske went from strength to strength. Subsidiary companies were set up in England and in Russia and were run by two brothers of Werner Siemens. The English enterprise, which became an independent firm in 1858, was in the capable hands of William Siemens. It secured a government contract to prepare and test submarine cables. William Siemens thereupon built a cable works at Woolwich. In 1865 Halske, alarmed at early losses in the cable side of the business, withdrew from the English subsidiary, which was reconstituted under the name Siemens Brothers. This firm had a twin-screw cable ship, the *Faraday*, built on the Tyne. It was launched in 1874 and in the same year began to lay a direct cable from Ireland to the United States. It remained in service until 1922. Meanwhile in Russia the St Petersburg subsidiary, with Carl Siemens in charge, had built many telegraph lines in the Czar's dominions and by 1858 it was earning 80,000 roubles a year for managing and maintaining them.

Meanwhile the parent firm in Berlin never lacked orders for erecting telegraph lines and laying submarine cables. In 1867 a new company called the Indo-European Telegraph Company was established in London to construct and operate an overland telegraph line from Britain to India by way of Prussia, Russia and Persia. The line was constructed by the three Siemens firms. At the end of 1867 Halske retired and the firm fell entirely into the hands of the Siemens family. Werner Siemens explained in his memoirs:

> We three brothers decided accordingly upon an entire reform of the business connection of our different firms. A joint business was formed which embraced them all. Each firm retained its independence as regards administration and financial methods, but its profit and loss account was carried over to the joint business, of which we three brothers were the sole proprietors and partners. The St. Petersburg concern was placed under an able manager, whilst Carl went to England to undertake the special management of the London firm.

In 1876 Siemens & Halske built a cable factory in Berlin in order — with Felton & Guilleaume — to supply cables to the German post-office for its new underground telegraph network.

In addition to his work in connection with the steady expansion of his business interests in three countries Werner Siemens continued his scientific experiments. He devised numerous electrical appliances. His greatest achievement was the invention of the electric dynamo, which was shown at the Paris international exhibition in 1867. In the 1870s and 1880s he successfully applied electric power to a variety of purposes. He made improvements to Bell's telephone; he installed electric lights in the Leipziger-Strasse in Berlin; he built a miniature electric railway and a full-scale electric trolley bus; and he constructed an electric lift. Electric trams, built and operated by Siemens & Halske, went into service at Lichterfelde (by Berlin) in 1881 and the following year saw the beginning of the manufacture of electric bulbs.

It was electric bulbs that first brought Werner Siemens into conflict with Emil Rathenau. Siemens had imagined that he had a clear field for the sale of his carbon filament bulbs, which gave a white light. It came as a disagreeable surprise when he realized that Emil Rathenau — who had not made electrical appliances before — was planning to put on to the market Edison incandescent bulbs that gave a yellow light. So long as the electrical industry had been virtually confined to what was later called the 'light' branch of the industry — mainly the production of telegraphic equipment and electric cables — Werner Siemens had, to a considerable extent, dominated the scene in Germany. But now that the 'heavy' branch of the electrical industry was being established — the erection of power stations to provide lighting for towns and power for tramways and industrial establishments — Siemens had to face a determined challenge from a ruthless rival. Emil Rathenau's bid for a share in the German market for electric bulbs was only a beginning. Before people needed bulbs they had to have power stations and transformers as well as cables to take the current to streets, shops, public buildings and private houses. And most of them were constructed by the 'heavy' side of the industry. Moreover the voltage required by tramway undertakings and industrial enterprises was far greater than that needed to send messages by telegraph or cable. Werner Siemens was an acknowledged expert in the manufacture of telegraph cables but he was a newcomer to the production of the appliances required by the 'heavy' branch of the electrical industry.

There were few signs in Emil Rathenau's early career that he was destined to become one of Germany's leading industrialists. Born in Berlin in 1838, he studied engineering at the technical colleges of Hanover and Zürich and gained experience as a draughtsman in the drawing offices of Borsig, the famous locomotive firm. He then went to England, where he held various posts with engineering firms, including one with the British and Continental Improvements Co (London) at a salary of £4 a week.

On his return to Berlin he (and a partner) purchased a small engineering plant in a converted dance hall in the Chausseestrasse, which employed between forty and fifty men. The workshops produced steam-engines, equipment for gasworks and waterworks, as well as stage equipment for the Royal Opera House. He later recalled that, on taking over the plant, he was commissioned to build a stage ship for a performance of Meyerbeer's *Die Afrikanerin*. He was determined to expand the range of products made in his workshops and he succeeded in securing orders from the military and naval authorities. Thus he constructed a movable metal artillery tower capable of holding two 50-centimetre cannons. During the Franco-Prussian War he hastily reorganized the plant to make torpedoes for the navy. He also claimed to have been the first to manufacture corrugated-iron sheets in Germany. A second engineering plant was built at Martinikenfelde and Rathenau boasted that there was not another like it in Berlin.

During the speculation mania that followed the Franco-Prussian War, Rathenau was approached by banks anxious to finance the reorganization of the firm as a joint-stock company. At first he rejected their offers. But eventually his partner persuaded him to accept a very favourable offer from one of the banks to take over the engineering works. Rathenau refused to accept any shares in the company and insisted upon being paid in full in cash. He agreed to continue to supervise the plant but when the company ran into difficulties in the economic crisis of 1873 he completed the construction of the Martinikenfelde plant, paid all the creditors and left the company, which eventually went into liquidation. He refused an offer to buy back the engineering works for a much smaller sum than he had received for them and, although he was only 35 years of age, he went into retirement.

Ten years elapsed before Emil Rathenau was back in harness again. He devoted himself to the study of recent technical advances and visited several international exhibitions for this purpose — Vienna in 1873, Philadelphia in 1876 and Paris in 1878 and 1881. His visit to the Paris electrical exhibition in 1881 proved to be the turning-point in his career, for it was there in the American section that he first saw Edison's incandescent electric bulb. Walther Rathenau, in an oration delivered at his father's funeral in 1915, declared that when Emil Rathenau

> . . . saw this little bulb alight for the first time, he had a vision of the whole world covered with a network of copper wire. He saw electric currents flowing from one country to another, distributing not only light but also power — energy that would become the life blood of the economy and would stimulate its movement and growth. In his mind's eye he saw changes in the structure of populations as communications took on a new form — changes which have not yet been fully realized. Looking into the future he saw the possibility of extracting metals and other rare materials from

the bowels of the earth by the force of electric power. He vowed that he would devote his life to electricity. He saw many things that have not yet come to pass but that will come about in the future. Such was his gift of prophetic vision.

So convinced was Rathenau of the unlimited possibilities of electricity in the future that he immediately secured an option on the European rights of the Edison lamp. A company was formed to undertake research into the provision of electric light and power on a commercial scale. Rathenau backed the company with some of his own money — the proceeds of the sale of his engineering plant — and he received financial support from Jacob Landau, the Gebrüder Sulzbach and the National Bank of Germany. He showed the results of his efforts at the electrical exhibition at Munich in 1882. The director of the Bavarian Royal Theatre commissioned Rathenau to install electric lights in the theatre, saying: 'Do the job at your own risk. If it works you will get your money. If it doesn't, that's your bad luck.' Rathenau lit the theatre successfully.

By April 1883 Rathenau had made sufficient progress to encourage him to set up the German Edison Company with the same financial backers as before. The greatest danger came from Siemens & Halske, whose bulbs were popular because they were cheap. Rathenau's bulbs were regarded as a luxury that only theatres, large stores and high-class restaurants could afford. In an attempt to placate its most serious rival the German Edison Company came to an agreement with Siemens & Halske. It was agreed that Siemens & Halske should have the sole right to manufacture carbon filament (white) bulbs, while the German Edison Company should have the sole right to make incandescent (yellow) bulbs. Rathenau also agreed to purchase the dynamos and cables that he needed from Siemens & Halske. At this time Werner Siemens showed no inclination to build power stations but was content to dominate the market in electrical machinery.

In its early days the German Edison Company built small electric installations for light and power in sugar refineries, weaving sheds and corn-mills. Rathenau's first power station was erected in Berlin by the Municipal Electricity Works, an offshoot of the German Edison Company. This subsidiary company secured a concession from the municipal authorities to supply Berlin with electricity at a fixed tariff for 30 years, after which the city had the right to purchase all its installations. The company began operations in the autumn of 1884 on

a very modest scale. By 1887 little progress had been made either by
the German Edison Company or by the Municipal Electricity Works.
Rathenau considered that the situation could be remedied only by
raising more capital, by installing larger dynamos in his power
stations, and by finding a new director for the Municipal Electricity
Works.

So Rathenau embarked upon a radical reconstruction of both the
German Edison Company and the Municipal Electricity Works.
The German Edison Company was reorganized as the Allgemeine
Elektrizitäts-Gesellschaft and its capital was increased from 7 to 12
million marks. The banks that raised the money included not only
the former backers but also the Berlin Commercial Company,
Delbrück, Leo & Co and the Deutsche Bank. Siemens & Halske subscribed 1 million marks and Arnold von Siemens (son of Werner
Siemens) secured a seat on the board. The agreement of 1883 between
Siemens and Rathenau was modified so that Rathenau could now
build small dynamos himself. But larger dynamos and cables still had
to be purchased from Siemens & Halske. In return Siemens & Halske
agreed that if any company that operated power stations approached
Siemens & Halske with a view to establishing a joint enterprise, such
a request should be passed on to Rathenau. Both the agreements of
1883 and 1887 could have led to closer collaboration between Siemens
and Rathenau. But this did not happen. Siemens made no attempt
to influence the policy of the Allgemeine Elektrizitäts-Gesellschaft,
although his son Arnold was one of its directors. Emil Rathenau's
biographer Riedler considers that the agreements between Siemens
and Rathenau — which restricted both of them but led to no closer cooperation — in the end benefited only the other large electrical firms,
such as Schuckert & Co of Nürnberg, the Helios Electrical Company
of Cologne, Wilahmeyer & Co of Frankfurt-am-Main, and O. L.
Kummer & Co of Dresden.

At the same time that the German Edison Company was being
turned into the Allgemeine Elektrizitäts-Gesellschaft its subsidiary,
the Municipal Electricity Works, was reorganized as the Berlin Electricity Works. The concession granted by the municipal authorities
to the defunct company was passed on to the new firm. The Berlin
Electricity Works proved to be a successful undertaking. Rathenau recognized that previous failures had been — at any rate partly — due to
the use of a series of smaller dynamos to produce the required current. Instead of dynamos of only 500 horse-power, as recommended

by both Edison and Siemens, Rathenau ordered dynamos of 600 and 1,000 horse-power from Siemens & Halske. When Edison visited the engineering works in the Spandauer-Strasse in which these large dynamos were being made, he declared: 'Your plant is an excellent one.' The new dynamos proved to be efficient and contributed to the success of the Berlin Electricity Works.

Despite competition from several new electric firms Rathenau's *Allgemeine Elektrizitäts-Gesellschaft* (AEG) flourished in the 1890s. Its reputation was enhanced in 1891 when it laid a power cable between Lauffen and Frankfurt-am-Main. One of the reasons for the expansion of the AEG was Rathenau's belief that, in the electrical industry, success depended upon production on a very large scale. He organized his plants efficiently and his output was of the highest quality. He was always alive to the importance of encouraging research to secure improvements in his electrical products. He aimed at securing high profits so that he could pay his investors high dividends. In his view only high dividends could ensure the continued support of the banks, which was essential for the continued progress of his business.

By 1900 the competition between rival electrical firms had become so severe that the banks intervened to bring about cartel agreements between groups of firms. In the years immediately before the First World War the AEG and Siemens & Halske gradually became linked with a number of other electrical firms. In 1903, for example, the Siemens-Schuckert Works were set up to operate the whole high-voltage side of the business of Siemens & Halske and Schuckert & Co. In 1908 the AEG and the Siemens-Schuckert group came together to establish the Electrical Trust Company (Electro-Treuhand-Gesellschaft). By 1914 the AEG and Siemens-Schuckert dominated the entire electrical industry in Germany.

Shipbuilding and the Mercantile Marine

Shipbuilding
Another industry that expanded with astonishing rapidity in the last quarter of the nineteenth century was shipbuilding and marine engineering. For centuries shipbuilding had been of small account in Germany. Since Britain was building about three-quarters of the world's tonnage it might have seemed hopeless for Germany to attempt to become an important shipbuilding nation. Yet in only 15

years — between 1892 and 1907 — Germany succeeded in increasing her share of world shipbuilding from 7.3 per cent to 13.8 per cent.

The years following the establishment of the Zollverein saw the modest beginnings of a modern shipbuilding industry both in the North Sea ports of Hamburg and Bremen and in the Baltic ports. Thus Ferdinand Schichau of Elbing and Danzig built the first German steam-dredger in the 1840s and Prussia's first iron-screw propelled steamship in 1855. At Bremerhaven — the outport of Bremen — shipbuilding yards were established by R. C. Rickmers (1839), J. L. Tecklenborg (1841) and G. Seebeck (1855). After the founding of the united Reich more shipyards were opened. In Hamburg the firm of Blohm & Voss was set up in 1877, while in Kiel the Germania yard was taken over by Krupp in 1896. Nevertheless even in the 1880s most ships flying the German flag had been built in foreign yards. From 1881 onwards, for example, the North German Lloyd ordered a number of fast steamers for the Atlantic run from John Elder & Co of Glasgow. Meanwhile the Vulkan shipyard in Stettin had been building locomotives for some time for lack of orders to build ships.

But the situation was changing. Unless Germany was prepared to allow its growing passenger — including emigrant — traffic and its ever expanding foreign trade to be carried in foreign ships, it was necessary to increase the capacity of the German mercantile marine. More vessels were required and in the 1880s shipowners began to place more orders with German yards. In 1887 the Vulkan shipyard received a contract for its first large ocean-going liner. In the previous year the secretary of the English boiler-makers' trade union had told the Royal Commission on the Depression of Trade and Industry that the shipbuilding industry on the Tyne was 'in a most deplorable condition' and that 'one third of our members who are usually engaged in shipbuilding [are] out of employment'. The chairman of the Commission observed that 'the German yards, we hear, are in full operation, whereas ours are idle'. Some of the more important German shipyards that were expanding in the 1880s were the Vulkan works at Stettin, F. Schichau at Elbing and Danzig, the (Krupp) Germania dockyard at Kiel, R. C. Rickmers at Bremerhaven, and Blohm & Voss, the *Howaldtswerke* and the *Deutsche Werft* at Hamburg.

By the 1890s German shipowners were placing a number of their contracts with German shipyards. In 1894, for example, 54 out of the 74 ships built for the mercantile marine were constructed at home. In 1899, 9 out of the 14 steamers under construction for the Hamburg-

America line were being built in German yards. In 1900 German shipyards built 215 steamships of 255,000 tons and 170 sailing ships of 30,300 tons. On the stocks were 64 steamers, 19 warships, 42 sailing ships and 57 river-craft. These included foreign orders for 12 steamers, 9 warships and 4 sailing ships. On the other hand in the same year 25 steamers and 13 sailing vessels were being built abroad for German shipowners.

Various factors contributed to the expansion of Germany's ship-building industry. As the growth of the industry began in the 1880s many shipbuilders were able to concentrate at once on building iron and steel steamships, leaving the building of sailing ships to older and smaller yards. Many German shipyards did not have to make the painful transition from sail to steam and from wood to iron and steel. They seldom had to phase out their shipwrights, carpenters, caulkers and sailmakers to make room for platers, riveters, boilermakers and marine engineers. Often with help from the banks, the new ship-building companies invested heavily in docks and engineering work-shops, in which they installed the most modern equipment. They aimed at achieving the highest standards of efficiency. Their engineers, foremen and craftsmen were trained at special colleges at Hamburg and Kiel or at the technical colleges of Charlottenburg, Danzig and Bremen. German shipbuilders prided themselves on their ability to compete successfully with British rivals in the construction of ever larger and faster liners. Bernhard Hulderman claimed that the *Imperator* class liners of the Hamburg-America Line were 'a triumph of German shipbuilding and engineering skill; and when the *Vaterland* was launched the senior partner of Messrs Blohm & Voss stated with just pride that she was the biggest vessel in existence; that she was built on the biggest slip; that she had received her equipment under the biggest crane, and that she would be docked in the biggest floating dock in the world'. German steamers, built at Stettin, captured the blue riband of the Atlantic — the *Auguste Victoria* in 1888, the *Kaiser Wilhelm der Grosse* in 1897 and the *Deutschland* in 1900. A few years later the *Imperator* (1912) and the *Vaterland* (1914) were among the largest and fastest liners in the world.

Moreover the chief raw materials required by the modern ship-building industry — iron and steel — were available in Germany and close links were forged between the steel and engineering companies and the leading shipbuilding firms. Krupp had its own shipyard at Kiel. Inventions — and improvements to existing appliances and machines — also played a part in fostering the development of ship-building in Germany. Rudolph Diesel's heavy oil engine, first applied to the propulsion of ships by Burmeister and Wain of Copenhagen, was a particularly significant innovation. A fleet of motor vessels was used by the Danish East Asiatic Company. The Hamburg-America line purchased one of them. This type of vessel came into its own during the First World War when some shipowners were unable to secure British bunker coal.

The Reich encouraged shipbuilding in various ways. It established state naval dockyards. Until 1898 it allowed shipbuilders to import their raw materials free of duty. It subsidized certain shipping lines on condition that their new ships were built in German shipyards. The building of river-craft in inland harbours was encouraged by local authorities. That Wilhelm II took a lively interest in the development of the German shipbuilding industry may be seen from the fact that, even before his accession, he asked the Prussian minister to Hamburg to make urgent representations to the directors of the Hamburg-America company to entrust the building of one of their first fast Atlantic liners to a German rather than to an English yard. As a result the *Auguste Victoria* was built at Stettin.

In the twentieth century the shipbuilding industry in Germany continued to expand. The tonnage built rose from 240,000 tons in 1899 to 390,991 tons in 1906. By 1914 the capacity of her shipyards was about 400,000 tons of merchant ships. In addition warships were being built for the growing navy, while river-craft were being constructed in inland harbours. German shipowners from time to time still placed orders abroad. On the other hand German shipyards were receiving orders from foreign shipowners.

Mercantile Marine
The growth of the German mercantile marine was as spectacular as that of the shipbuilding industry. When the German black-white-red maritime flag was adopted in 1867 the mercantile marine was quite small. Since Germany had no navy some shipowners registered their vessels abroad. Ships registered in the Holstein port of Altona, for example, enjoyed the protection of the Danish navy. In 1871 the German mercantile marine had 4,350 sailing ships (982,355 tons) and 150 steamers (81,994 tons).

Traffic on the high seas and the inland waterways increased considerably in the next 40 years. There were more steerage passengers (mainly emigrants) and cabin passengers, while the volume of freight also expanded with the success of Germany's export drive. In the circumstances Germany's merchant shipping and liners had to be increased unless the country was prepared to follow the example of the United States and allow the bulk of her passenger traffic and overseas trade to be carried in foreign vessels. The boom that followed the Franco-Prussian War saw the tonnage under steam rise to 420,000 while the increase in emigration in the 1880s — 220,000 in 1882 alone — gave further opportunities to German shipowners. By 1897 total tonnage had risen to 1,650,000 tons, of which a million were steam tonnage, and it was estimated that the book value of the steam fleet was about £15,000,000. This growth occurred entirely in the North Sea ports of Hamburg and Bremen and their outports. The tonnage registered at Baltic ports declined from 449,000 to 270,000 between 1871 and 1897.

In the early twentieth century German steamships were plying on every ocean in the world. Their tonnage had overtaken that of the United States in 1884 and that of France in 1889. By 1908 German shipowners were operating the world's second largest merchant navy — though it was, of course, very much smaller than that of Britain. While German firms owned just over 11 per cent of the world's steam tonnage, British shipowners owned 50 per cent. In 1910 the steam tonnage of the German mercantile marine was 2,397,000 and this included several of the finest liners on the Atlantic run. At this time the German shipping industry was dominated by the Hamburg-America Line and the North German Lloyd which together owned 289 steamers in 1908. The other major shipping companies were the Kosmos Steamship Company, the German Levant Line, the German East Africa Line, the Hamburg-South America Steamship Company, the German-Australian Steamship Company and the Argo, Hansa, Neptun and Union Lines.

The State fostered the expansion of all branches of the shipping industry in various ways. Wilhelm II took a close personal interest in the fortunes of the great shipping companies — such as the North German Lloyd and the Hamburg-America Line — and he considered that successes on the North Atlantic route — such as winning the blue riband — added to Germany's prestige as a world power. The State reserved the coastal trade to ships of its own flag. From 1894 onwards postal subventions were granted to the North German Lloyd and to the German East Africa Line with respect to their regular sailings to

German colonies in East Africa and New Guinea as well as to ports in Australia and eastern Asia. But these subsidies — £370,000 in 1909 — were smaller than those granted by the French government (£ 2,650,000) and by the British government to the Cunard Line alone (£ 1,700,000). The State gave financial assistance (over £ 3 millions) to enable Hamburg and Bremen to build large free ports, when they joined the customs union in the 1880s. Indirectly the expansion of the German navy promoted the growth of the mercantile marine. The prospect of naval orders encouraged shipbuilders to extend their dock facilities and repair workshops, which benefited German shipowners. The construction of the Kiel Canal, opened in 1895, was undertaken largely to enable warships to move quickly between the Baltic and the North Sea. But the new waterway also improved facilities for Germany's coastal traffic.

The traffic on Germany's inland waterways also expanded after 1871. Improvements were made in river navigation and important new canals were built. Berlin's links with the Baltic and the River Oder were strengthened by the completion of the Havel-Oder, the Spree-Oder, the Berlin-Stettin, and the Teltow canals. The Ruhr was served by the Rhine-Herne Canal from Ruhrort to Bochum and by the Ems-Weser Canal from Bergeshövede to Minden and Hanover. The latter was the western portion of the Mittelland Canal which, it was hoped, would one day link the Rhine and the Elbe, but the eastern portion was not completed until 1938. At the same time extensions were made to the major inland harbours. W. H. Lindley, writing in 1909, observed that the usefulness of the German waterways

> . . . had been greatly increased and the cost of transport by water diminished by shortening as much as possible the time necessary for loading and unloading the boats. Some of the new harbours, for instance at Duisburg, Kosel and others, have been equipped with very complete arrangements for this purpose, consisting of coal chutes and tips, hydraulic steam and electric cranes, depots served by elevated lines of rail, fixed and movable grain-elevators, granaries and sheds, and all arrangements for handling bulk goods in the most rapid and cheap manner possible.

At the beginning of the twentieth century Germany had 13,800 kilometres of navigable waterways, of which four-fifths were rivers and one-fifth canals. In 1912 nearly 30,000 cargo vessels, with a capacity of 7,400,000 tons were in operation on the rivers and canals.

Despite competition from the railways the volume of goods carried on the inland waterways — particularly on the Rhine, the Elbe and the Oder — rose from 21 per cent to 25 per cent of Germany's total freight traffic. One reason for this was the introduction of more powerful tugs and barges. The expansion of traffic on Germany's rivers and canals was due partly to private enterprise and partly to state action. Private firms normally operated freight and passenger services. Fourteen new companies engaged in the business of river transport were established in the 1880s and six in the 1890s. (The Prussian State, however, monopolized the provision of tugs on the Kiel Canal.) On the other hand canal building and river improvements were undertaken by the Federal States and by provincial and municipal councils. In 1905 the Prussian Diet sanctioned the expenditure of nearly £17,000,000 for these purposes.

One of the leading architects of the spectacular revival of the German shipping industry was Albert Ballin. He was born in Hamburg in 1857. His father was a partner in the firm of Morris & Co, an emigration agency. Ballin entered the service of the agency in 1874 and his father died in the same year. A few years later his father's partner retired and Ballin was left in charge of the business. He boldly embarked upon a policy of expansion and during the emigration boom of the early 1880s his firm secured about a third of that part of the emigrant business concerned with arranging passages for those crossing the Atlantic from non-German ports.

In 1881 Ballin became the general representative in Hamburg of an English steamship company, the Carr Line, which carried steerage passengers as well as cargo from Hamburg to the United States. In 1883 the Carr Line, largely as a result of Ballin's untiring efforts, carried 16,000 emigrants. A rate-war broke out among the companies engaged in the Atlantic emigrant traffic and Ballin played an important part in bringing it to an end in 1885 by negotiating an agreement on steerage fares. The Carr Line was taken over by the Hamburg-America Line.

By this time Ballin had switched his allegiance to the Hamburg-America Line and had become the head of its North American passenger department, which handled the firm's emigrant traffic to the United States. Ballin was determined to challenge the position of the North German Lloyd of Bremen as the leading shipping company in the business of carrying emigrants from Germany to New York. He was appointed a director in 1888 and later managing director.

Before long he had made great improvements in the accommodation and food provided for steerage passengers. And he persuaded the directors to increase their fleet with four new fast steamers that were built to carry not only cabin and steerage passengers but some cargo as well. By securing all-purpose steamships for the North Atlantic route he was adopting a different policy from that pursued by rival companies, which operated different ships for passengers and cargo.

There was keen competition on the Atlantic route at this time and in 1886 Ballin wrote a memorandum in which he supported a suggestion made by the Red Star Line for the establishment of a shipping pool (or cartel) of the companies engaged in the Atlantic emigrant business. The pool would fix fares and allocate profits on a predetermined ratio. Eventually the North Atlantic Steamship Lines Association was set up, though at first without British participation. From Ballin's point of view the agreement could hardly have come at a worse time since in 1892 there was a cholera epidemic in Hamburg and this paralyzed the trade and shipping of the port. When normal trading conditions had been restored, Ballin put pressure on the English shipping companies by competing with them for the emigrant traffic from the Scandinavian countries, with the result that in 1895 the British firms joined the North Atlantic shipping pool. The agreements were renewed from time to time and lasted until 1914.

The next threat to the stability of the Atlantic emigrant traffic came from the International Mercantile Marine Company, popularly known as the Morgan Trust. The American banker, Pierpont Morgan, had conceived the idea of forming a syndicate of businessmen to finance a great expansion of American mercantile marine by buying up some European lines and he hoped that the government would assist the project by granting subsidies to shipping companies. He began by acquiring the Atlantic Transport Company and the Leyland Line of Liverpool, which had itself recently absorbed the West India and Pacific Line. Eventually Morgan controlled nine American and English shipping companies. In 1902-3, after protracted negotiations, in which Ballin was actively engaged, agreements were reached between the two chief German Lines (the Hamburg-America and the North German Lloyd), the Holland-America Line and the Morgan Trust. The German companies secured exclusive rights in German ports as far as passenger traffic was concerned, in return for giving up their share of the Atlantic cargo traffic. There was also an agreement on the sharing of profits and on the chartering of vessels if a member of the pool was short of passenger space. The Cunard company, however, refused to join in these arrangements and even withdrew from the North Atlantic shipping pool. A rate-war broke and Cunard's profits dropped from £248,563 in 1903 to £61,588 in 1904. But the Hamburg-America Line and the North German Lloyd also suffered heavy losses.

The Hamburg-America Line expanded under the inspired leadership of 'the uncrowned King of Hamburg'. In 1886, when he joined the company, it had 22 ocean-going steamers of 60,531 tons. In 1913 the company had 172 steamers of 1,028,762 tons. In the same period the capital of the firm had increased tenfold, from 15 million marks to over 157 million marks. The average dividend paid to shareholders had been just over 7 per cent. In 1886 the Hamburg-America Line had been concerned mainly with the North Atlantic route but by 1913 its steamers were also operating regular services to South America, Australia and the Far East as well.

As the war clouds gathered over Europe in the years before 1914 Ballin urged the German government to make a real effort to come to an agreement with Britain to halt the naval arms race. His efforts came to nothing and the First World War saw his life's work destroyed as German merchant shipping was swept off the high seas. A staunch patriot, he did not survive Germany's defeat in 1918. He died of an overdose of sleeping pills on the afternoon of 9 November, the day on which militant workers took to the streets in Berlin and Hamburg.

17   Economic and Social Policy

After the unification of Germany Bismarck tried to promote economic expansion and also to alleviate some of the social evils brought about by industrialization. At the same time he sought to strengthen the influence of the central government over the economic development of the nation and to prevent the particularism of some of the German states from holding up the economic and social reforms that he considered necessary. Among his earliest reforms were a reform of the currency, the introduction of the gold standard and the establishment of a central bank. Next came the attempt to nationalize the railways, the adoption of the policy of protection, the establishment of colonies, the introduction of old-age pensions and a national health scheme.

Railway Nationalization

One of Bismarck's most ambitious projects was to bring all the German railways under the control of the central government. Since postal and telegraph services were nationalized, it seemed reasonable to unify and to nationalize the railways as well. Bismarck's proposal was not a new one, since the idea of bringing Germany's network of railways under state supervision had been put forward by Friedrich List in his pamphlet on the Leipzig-Dresden railway and by those who drew up the draft German constitution of 1849.

At this time there were over 60 railway administrations in Germany. The length of the railway network was 27,956 kilometres. Some lines were owned and operated by the various Federal States (12,062 kilometres); some were run by joint-stock companies (12,641 kilometres); while some were privately owned but operated by one of the Federal States. The railways of Alsace and Lorraine (863 kilometres) were owned by the Reich. The three southern states had nationalized most of their lines but in Saxony only 264 kilometres of nationalized lines had been opened between 1863 and 1876 as compared with 848 kilometres of private railways. In Prussia over half the lines (9,183 kilometres) were in private hands, while the rest were either nationalized lines (4,281 kilometres) or private railways under state administration (2,736 kilometres). Among the many drawbacks caused by the multiplicity of railway administrations was the existence of at least 1,500 different freight tariffs.

Bismarck's attempt to nationalize the German railways failed because there were three controversies that could not be resolved at this time. First, there was the controversy between those who argued that private railway companies should continue to exist side by side with public railways and those who advocated the nationalization of all railways. Secondly, if nationalization were decided upon, there was controversy as to whether the central authority or the various federal authorities should own and operate the railways. Bavaria and some other states firmly refused to allow their state railways to be absorbed into a unified railway system owned by the Reich. Local patriotism and the desire to enjoy the revenues earned by profitable federal lines lay behind this attitude. Prussia's offer to hand over her state railways to the Reich evoked no response from the opponents of Bismarck's plan. The third controversy was the dispute concerning the way in which freight charges should be fixed. Some railways charged freight by value, some by the amount of waggon space used and some by a combination of the two. Most of them were complicated and it proved to be impossible to secure agreement on a system that would be acceptable to all the railway administrations. In 1873 the private companies agreed on a uniform tariff, but this was based upon principles diametrically opposed to those governing the freight tariff in force on the Prussian state railways.

In 1873 public concern over the operation of existing railways and the promotion of new ones came to a head. When Lasker had exposed some of the scandals connected with recent railway promotions Dr Elben presented a bill to the Reichstag to establish a Reich Railway Office to exercise a general supervision over all the railways. Bismarck welcomed the bill, hoping that it would give practical effect to those articles of the imperial constitution that were concerned with the railways. He compared these articles to a loaded gun without a firing pin and he asked the Reichstag to provide the pin. Article 4 of the constitution stated that the central authority had the right to legislate on matters concerning the railways. Articles 42 to 45 — which did not apply to Bavaria — laid down some rather vague general principles concerning the relations between the State and the railways. It was, for example, the duty of the central government to ensure that the railways were administered as 'a united network'. In practice, however, the Federal States retained complete control over the railways within their own territories. Dr Elben's bill became law in June 1873, but the new Railway Office was only an advisory body and had no power to enforce its recommendations.

The economic crisis of 1873 did not merely bring to light some serious irregularities in the promotion of new railway companies, it also caused a drop in railway revenues and a decline in the value of railway shares. In 1874 the railway administrations raised their freight charges by 20 per cent. Some interpreted this as meaning that the maximum increase was to be 20 per cent, while others raised their charges by an average of 20 per cent. There were vigorous protests from industrialists. W. T. Mulvany, a leading member of the Ruhr Mineowners Association, denounced the raising of railway freight charges. He claimed that the reduction of these charges in the 1860s had stimulated the expansion of Germany's industries and he declared that any increase would be a retrograde step, harmful to the future growth of the economy. In 1877 the higher railway freight rates were reduced, though at the same time a supplementary loading fee was charged.

In March 1874 and in April 1875 the Railway Office made public proposals for draft laws that would have strengthened its hand when dealing with state and private railways. These modest suggestions were, however, greeted with such a storm of protest from the railway companies and from some of the Federal States that they were not submitted to the Reichstag. In the autumn of 1875 Albert Maybach, who was president of the Railway Office between 1874 and 1878, hinted that the government was considering laying new proposals on railway nationalization before the Reichstag.

On 11 December 1875, at a parliamentary reception, Bismarck confirmed that he hoped to submit to the Reichstag a plan to nationalize the whole railway network. Bismarck's views received wide publicity in the press and aroused strong protests in Bavaria, Württemberg and Saxony. It was clear that the governments of these states, supported by public opinion, were prepared to oppose tooth and nail any attempt by the Reich to take over their railways. Only from Hesse-Darmstadt was support forthcoming for Bismarck's plan.

In June 1876 the Prussian parliament passed a law that authorized the government to negotiate with the Reich concerning the sale of Prussia's state railways to the Reich. But no other German state followed suit by offering to sell its lines to the Reich. So the Prussian law remained a dead letter. Although the proposal to nationalize the entire German railway system was discussed in the press from time to time in later years, Bismarck realized that his plan had no hope of success.

Discussions on the reorganization of Germany's numerous railway administrations were revived in 1879, when a trade recession again threatened the revenues of the railways. Bismarck appreciated that in view of the hostile reception of his plan to place all the railways under the control of the Reich, it would be useless to revive this scheme. So he adopted an alternative policy. This was to nationalize as many private lines in Prussia as possible. The new plan was confined to Prussia and was not concerned with lines in any other German state. It was a revival, under different circumstances, of the policy pursued in the 1850s by von der Heydt, when he was Prussian minister of commerce. By 1857 about half of the Prussian railways had been either nationalized or brought under the administration of the State. Looking ahead, Bismarck saw that if eventually all the railways in Prussia were nationalized, the state lines of Prussia, Bavaria, Baden and Saxony would be in a dominant position. Only a handful of private lines might be expected to retain their independence. The nationalized lines of course would be owned and operated by Prussia and certain other Federal States and not — except for those in Alsace and Lorraine — by the Reich. This would fall short of Bismarck's plan of 1876 to bring all the lines under the control of the central authority, but the new policy of 1879 at least had the merit of securing a much simpler railway structure than that in operation in the 1870s.

The task of nationalizing nearly 10,000 kilometres of private lines in Prussia fell to Maybach who, having been in charge of the Railway Office and subsequently minister of commerce in 1878, was appointed minister of public works in Prussia in 1879, a post which he held for 13 years. By the autumn of 1879 he had brought to a successful conclusion his negotiations with the companies owning the following railways — Berlin-Stettin, Berlin-Magdeburg, Magdeburg-Halberstadt, Cologne-Minden, Hanover-Altenbeken, Deutz-Giessen and the Rhenish railway. The total length of these lines was 5,000 kilometres. The negotiations had been conducted in great secrecy in the hope of avoiding speculation in railway shares on the stock exchanges.

Maybach secured the cooperation of some of the banks—particularly the official Overseas Trading Corporation (Seehandlung) and the Disconto-Gesellschaft—in buying railway shares before the negotiations began. Company directors were converted to the idea of nationalization by promises of golden handshakes or well-paid posts in the Prussian railway administration.

As Maybach was anxious that the Prussian railway administration should secure control over the private lines as soon as possible, he sometimes agreed that during an interim period—which might be as long as 6 years—the railway should continue to be privately owned, while being operated by the State. Shareholders generally obtained a guaranteed fixed dividend during the interim period and then exchanged their shares for state bonds or sold their shares to the State for cash. Holders of railway shares on which the company had paid no dividend for many years were naturally treated less favourably than holders of shares on which dividends had been paid regularly.

In October 1879 the draft law nationalizing the first seven lines was submitted to the Prussian parliament and was accompanied by a memorandum in which Bismarck explained once more why a reform of the Prussian railway system was urgently needed. He declared that since there were so many private lines in Prussia, the cost of running the railways was very high. There were so many directors, managers and officials who all had to be paid. There was an unnecessary duplication of lines, stations and rolling-stock. There were still far too many different freight tariffs and both passenger and goods traffic suffered from excessive competition between rival lines. The establishment of a single nationalized railway system in Prussia would remove many of these drawbacks. In December 1879 both houses of the Prussian parliament passed a law giving effect to Maybach's agreements with the seven railway companies.

After this initial success Maybach vigorously pursued the policy of nationalizing as many railway companies in Prussia as possible. In 1882 another 3,145 kilometres of private lines and in 1884 a further 3,766 kilometres came under state ownership. By 1895 the process of nationalizing Prussia's railways was nearly complete. In 1897 Prussia and Hesse-Darmstadt came to an agreement to nationalize the Ludwig Railway and to run it in partnership. This railway lay partly in Prussia and partly in Hesse-Darmstadt. Just as Hesse-Darmstadt had been the first German state to set up a customs union with Prussia (the first step towards the establishment of the Zollverein) so now Hesse-Darmstadt was the first state to come to an arrangement with Prussia concerning the joint administration of one of her principal railways. In 1901 Prussia, Hesse-Darmstadt and Baden agreed that the Main-Neckar Railway should be operated by the administration responsible for running the Ludwig Railway. Meanwhile other German states, such as Bavaria and Saxony, had followed Prussia's example and had nationalized their private lines.

On the eve of the First World War nearly all the Prussian railways were owned by the State (37,400 kilometres) and only 2,900 kilometers remained in private hands. There were now seven state railway networks in Germany administered by the governments of Prussia, Bavaria, Baden, Württemberg, Oldenburg and Mecklenburg-Schwerin. Only a few lines (3,600 kilometres) were still privately owned. The state railways in Germany were all prosperous, making a profit of 786 million marks in 1917. In Prussia nearly one-fifth of the state's revenues came from the profits of the railways. And these profits — £293 million between 1887 and 1906 — were not subject to parliamentary control. In 1906 the Essen chamber of commerce observed that 'the prosperity of our entire state finances is largely dependent upon the prosperity of our railway finances'. In the same year the Prussian parliament passed a resolution urging the railway administration to reduce its charges on goods traffic but this advice was not followed because the government had come to rely upon the substantial contribution that railway profits made to the public revenue.

Efficiency in the administration of the railways was to some extent a product of the military discipline imposed upon the staff. The railways and the post-office were discribed as 'simply the civilian sections of the army'. An engine driver or a guard might vote for a socialist candidate at a general election, but he stood smartly to attention when he was receiving orders from his superiors. In 1919 the policy advocated by Bismarck in 1876 was at last carried out and all the German railways were owned and operated by the Reich.

Protection

The economic crisis of 1873-5, which showed how urgent was the need to reform the administration of the railways, also focused attention on Germany's fiscal policy. As early as 1818 the Prussian tariff, devised by Maassen, had been the most liberal in Europe. In

1862 the Franco-Prussian commercial treaty had substantially lowered the import duties of the Zollverein. When Germany was united in 1871 she had a free-trade tariff, similar to that of Britain. In 1873 almost her last protective import duties—those on pig-iron, steel ingots, and ships—were abolished. The remaining iron duties were due to be repealed in 1877. Most deputies in the Reichstag and the Prussian parliament, as well as leading Reich and Prussian ministers and civil servants, were free-traders. So were the owners of the great estates east of the Elbe and the merchants of the major ports and commercial cities. At that time the policy of protection had little support outside the ranks of the ironmasters and the millowners.

In the 1870s there were moves towards a return to protection on the continent. In France the Third Republic was gradually abandoning the liberal fiscal policy of the Second Empire. In the negotiations for a peace treaty after the Franco-Prussian War, France declined to renew the commercial treaty of 1862. Article 11 of the Treaty of Frankfurt placed Franco-German trade on a most-favoured-nation basis. But this was a most-favoured-nation clause with a difference. It was a permanent arrangement with no provision for its modification at any time in the future. And instead of applying to trade with all countries it was restricted to concessions made by either party to the following countries: Great Britain, Russia, Austria-Hungary, Holland, Belgium and Switzerland. In the 1870s Russia and Austria-Hungary had very high protective tariffs, so that Germany was surrounded by states that levied higher import duties than her own. In Europe only Britain and some of the smaller countries such as Switzerland and Belgium remained faithful to free trade.

Soon after the abolition of the import duties on pig-iron and steel ingots some of the ironmasters inaugurated a campaign in favour of extending the remaining iron duties beyond 1877 when they were due to be repealed. This inaugurated a protectionist reaction against free-trade that culminated in the passing of a new tariff law by the Reichstag in 1879. There was a slump in the sale of iron and steel products after the collapse of the boom of 1871-2. The firm of Krupp, for example, laid off some four thousand men between 1874 and 1876. A Union of Iron and Steel Manufacturers, established in 1873, soon embarked upon an agitation in favour of the postponement of the repeal of the last of the iron duties. The ironmasters were supported by the influential Union for the Promotion of the Common

Economic Interests of the Rhineland and Westphalia, whose president
(W. T. Mulvany) and secretary (A. H. Bueck) supported the maintenance of import duties on iron. The ironmasters claimed that their
industry was in a depressed state and was suffering from low prices
and low profits. The situation was aggravated by increased foreign
imports and by the recent 20 per cent increase in railway freight
charges. It was alleged that a collapse of the iron and steel industry
would threaten Germany's ability to defend herself in time of war.

At first the ironmasters made little headway, although they were
asking only for the maintenance of an existing import duty and were
not as yet demanding any radical change in Germany's fiscal policy.
Most of the farmers, particularly the influential junkers in the eastern provinces, still considered that their interests would be best
served by adhering to their traditional policy of free trade. In 1875
the Congress of German Farmers supported the repeal of the remaining iron duties. Most ministers of state and senior civil servants had
little sympathy with the ironmasters. When the emperor asked for
his views on the subject Delbrück submitted two memoranda firmly
rejecting any concession to the protectionists. He argued that the
troubles of the ironmasters were of their own making. They were
paying the penalty of their own folly during the boom of 1871-2,
when they had recklessly expanded the capacity of their plants. The
emperor, however, was far from satisfied. He declared that he could
not understand why Germany should abolish her iron duties, while
the French 'prospered by adhering to their old system of protection'.

By 1876 the advocates of protection were making some headway.
They had secured allies from the ranks of the textile, paper, leather
and chemical manufacturers. Support for import duties came from
large cotton-spinning companies in southern Germany, though not
from small weaving firms or handloom weavers. In the chemical
industry it was the manufacturers of soda and not the manufacturers
of synthetic dyes who were beginning to turn to protection. Industrialists who needed foreign raw materials or semi-manufactured
products — yarn and anthracene for example — ramained faithful
to free trade. But what had begun as a demand for the maintenance
of a few surviving iron duties was now developing into an agitation
in favour of a general revision of the tariff on protectionist lines. A
new organization, the Central Association of German Manufacturers, established in 1876, was an alliance between the iron and
steel industry and the textile industry. By appointing Bueck as its

secretary, the Central Association secured a valuable personal link with both the Union of German Iron and Steel Manufacturers and the Union for the Promotion of the Common Economic Interests of the Rhineland and Westphalia. Indeed the influential north-western section of the Union of German Iron and Steel Manufacturers became affiliated to the Central Association of German Manufacturers. In 1876 the Central Association collected some sixty thousand signatures to a petition in favour of the retention of the remaining iron duties.

The free-trade cause suffered a setback in April 1876 when Delbrück, President of the Imperial Chancellery, resigned. He had been largely responsible for carrying out the liberal fiscal policy of the Zollverein and his departure marked a decline in the influence of the free-traders in the highest government circles. The minister of the Hansa towns in Berlin wrote that Delbrück's unexpected resignation had been a political sensation and added: 'There is a feeling that this is not just a question of personalities, but a change of system.'

The change, however, was not an immediate one. In December 1876 Windthorst, the leader of the Catholic Centre Party, made a last-minute appeal to the Reichstag to reprieve the remaining iron duties, which were due to be abolished on 1 January 1877, but his proposal was rejected and the last of the iron duties were abolished. In April 1877 the Reichstag also turned down a proposal that Germany should levy an import duty on iron products imported from France, equivalent to the export bounty paid by the French government. But it proved to be a Pyrrhic victory for the free-traders.

At a conference held in June 1877 the Central Association of German Manufacturers passed a resolution that advocated not merely the revival of the iron duties, which had just been repealed, but also the appointment of a commission to enquire into the state of German industry, with a view to recommending a complete reform of the tariff. This resolution received the support of the Union of German Iron and Steel Manufacturers. Next the Central Association of German Manufacturers set up a committee to prepare the draft of a proposed new tariff. In February 1878 a draft tariff was approved by the Central Association. It was suggested that substantial import duties should be levied on iron and steel products and on textiles. The discussions on the proposed tariff showed that the interests of the different branches of the iron and textile industries varied considerably. While the large firms producing pig-iron and steel ingots favoured protection, the cutlers of Solingen and Remscheid did not. While the owners of large cotton spinning-mills demanded high import duties on foreign yarn, the weaving firms (except in Saxony) did not. Again the firms that manufactured mixed cloths in Krefeld and Elberfeld objected to the imposition of any duty on foreign yarn because most of the yarn they used came from abroad. Similarly in the new chemical industry the soda manufacturers demanded protections, but the firms which produced synthetic dyes did not. Although the protectionists were far from united, they secured two successes in 1878. In February Otto von Camphausen, the Prussian minister of finance, who was a staunch free-trader, was forced by Bismarck to resign. In June two official commissions were appointed. One was to examine the state of the iron industry, the other the cotton and linen industries. The protectionists expected the commissions to recommend the imposition of import duties to safeguard these industries. No doubt the appointment of a commission to examine all German industries would have been even more welcome, but at any rate the government had tacitly admitted that a case had been made out for a limited enquiry.

By January 1879 the appetites of both the Central Association of German Manufacturers and the Union of German Iron and Steel Manufacturers had grown considerably. Whereas in December 1877 the protectionists would have been satisfied with an import duty of 6 marks per ton on pig-iron, they now demanded one of 10 marks. The Central Association tried to influence public opinion through its journal the *Deutsche Börsen-und Handelszeitung* which conducted a vigorous campaign in favour of the introduction of a new tariff. The climax of the agitation came during the Reichstag general election of June 1878, when candidates prepared to vote for the imposition of new import duties received strong support from the protectionist pressure groups.

It may be doubted whether the industrialists who were clamouring for tariffs would have achieved their aims so quickly had they not gained support from the owners of great estates and from the farmers — particularly of the eastern provinces. For many years grain had been grown in these provinces for export. And manufactured goods from abroad had been bought in exchange. In the circumstances the junkers had favoured a liberal tariff and had supported the free-traders. In the 1870s, however, they saw wheat prices fall from 216 marks per ton to 198 marks per ton, while rye fell from 159 to 133 marks per ton. At the same time foreign markets for German grain were being lost. By 1879 Germany was sending hardly any grain to Britain, which was now drawing 68 per cent of her requirements from the United States and Canada. Even the home market appeared to be in danger from American, Russian and Hungarian cereals, especially when German railways carried foreign grain at reduced freight charges.

In 1877 the Economic and Fiscal Association, supported by over four hundred landowners, adopted a protectionist policy. The long-standing hostility between the junkers from the eastern provinces and the industrialists of western Germany delayed the formation of a political alliance between them. By 1878, however, both had realized that the time had come to bury the hatchet and to cooperate to defeat the free-traders and to secure the adoption of a protectionist tariff. It would be an oversimplification of a complex situation to label all the owners of great estates and farmers and all the manufacturers as supporters of protection for agriculture at this time. A good many farmers, particularly in the south, continued to support free-trade in food. Similarly there were manufacturers who objected to the inclusion of farm products in the proposed new tariff. They argued that if agriculture were protected in this way, food prices would rise and the workers would demand higher wages to meet the increased cost of living. The veteran protectionist Moritz Mohl was a leading politician who advocated the imposition of import duties on manufactured products but objected to import duties on foodstuffs.

Bismarck's attitude towards the controversy between the free-traders and the protectionists was of crucial importance to the outcome. In 1875 he had described himself as 'a comparative layman' in fiscal matters. For many years he had accepted the free-trade views of his fellow junkers in the eastern provinces. As minister president of Prussia in the 1860s he had generally accepted the advice of his ministers and senior civil servants on fiscal matters. But if an economic issue was also a political issue Bismarck would relate it to his policy of securing German unification under Prussian leadership. He had supported the Franco-Prussian commercial treaty of 1862 and the tariff reductions it entailed, as much on political as on economic grounds. He had realized that a low Zollverein tariff would effectively prevent Austria from pressing forward with her plans to enter the German customs union and to challenge Prussia for the economic leadership of Germany. But after the Franco-Prussian War, the speculation mania and the subsequent economic crisis, he began to have misgivings concerning the wisdom of Germany's liberal fiscal policy. His doubts were confirmed by the swing towards protection in neighbouring countries, such as France, Austria and Russia. He considered that free-trade might be an admirable policy if it were pursued by all the major industrial countries in the world. But he doubted the wisdom of retaining the existing liberal tariff if other countries were pursuing a very different fiscal policy. For many years Delbrück and Otto von Camphausen had assured him that Germany's best interests lay in the maintenance of free-trade but when they left office he listened more and more to advisers who advocated the imposition of import duties on both manufactured and agricultural products.

Yet what weighed most with Bismarck was an aspect of the problem that had little to do with the merits of either the free-trade or the protectionist cause. This was the effect that additional revenues from new import duties would have upon the national finances. On the establishment of the united Reich it had been arranged that indirect taxes should provide a revenue for the central authority, while direct taxes should provide a revenue for the Federal States. Article 71 of the imperial constitution provided that if indirect taxes failed to meet the expenses of the central authority, the deficit would be met by annual contributions from the Federal States. These were called 'matricular contributions'. Starting at over 82 million marks in 1872, they declined to nearly 52 million marks in 1875 and then rose again to 70 million marks in the financial year 1878-9. During the depression that followed the speculation mania of 1871-2 the smaller states found it increasingly difficult to raise the money to pay their matricular contribution to the central authority. Between 1875 and 1879 the amount paid in matricular contributions was 90 million marks less than what had been requested by the central authority. Consequently the larger states had to increase their contributions. Prussia paid 41.7 million marks in 1879, as compared with only 7.9 million marks in 1871. At the same time Bavaria's contribution rose from 14.6 million marks to 19.1 million marks. And if there was a strain on the finances of the Reich, the Federal States were also experiencing difficulties in making ends meet. Prussia had to borrow 200 million marks between 1877 and 1880 to balance her budget.

Bismarck disliked a system that placed the central authority at the mercy of the Federal States. In 1872 he told the Reichstag: 'An empire that is dependent upon the contributions of individual states lacks the bonds of a strong and common financial institution.' And in 1879 he declared that it was degrading that the central authority should have to pass a begging bowl from one federal state to another to secure revenues essential to its requirements. Bismarck supported the raising of existing import duties and the imposition of new ones in order to increase the revenue that was levied by the central authority and was under its control. Moreover Bismarck had always regarded indirect taxes as being superior to direct taxes. As a young man he had expressed a distinct preference for indirect taxes in a speech to the Prussian parliament in February 1851. Now he argued that those who paid direct taxes were bearing too heavy a burden. He claimed that three out of every four estates in Prussia were in financial difficulties owing to the heavy mortgage repayments that had to be paid every year.

In 1878 when the controversy between the protectionists and the free-traders came to a head, German politics were in a state of flux. Bismarck had decided that he could no longer work with the National Liberals in the Reichstag, if only because they believed that — as in Britain — ministers of state should be responsible to parliament and not simply to the Chancellor. By coming to an agreement with Pope Leo XIII in 1878 concerning his dispute with the Roman Catholics (the *Kulturkampf*) Bismarck paved the way for a reconciliation with the Catholic Centre Party. This party was no longer in permanent opposition to the chancellor and might indeed be expected to support some of Bismarck's proposals in the Reichstag. Bismarck used the alleged danger to the State from the socialists to gain support both from Conservatives and from Roman Catholics. In 1876 two Socialist groups — known as the 'Eisenachers' and the 'Lassalleans' — had joined to form the Social Democrat Party, under the leadership of Bebel and Liebknecht. At the general election held in January 1877 the Socialists polled 493,000 votes (over 9 per cent of the votes cast) and gained 12 seats in the Reichstag.

Bismarck was determined to crush the socialists. He thought that his chance had come when an attempt was made in May 1878 to assassinate the emperor but the deputies of the National Liberal Party and the Progressive Party combined to defeat an anti-socialist bill in the Reichstag. On 2 June there was a second attempt on the life of the emperor, this time by Karl Nobiling. Bismarck promptly had the Reichstag dissolved and there was another general election on 30 June. During the campaign the conservatives attacked the liberals and the progressives for voting against the anti-socialist bill. There was a swing to the right. The conservative parties gained 37 seats, the liberal parties lost 29 seats and the socialists lost 3 seats. Bismarck now had a majority in the Reichstag for a new anti-socialist law. At the same time he had a majority for a new tariff law that would impose additional import duties. On 15 December 1878 Bismarck stated in a message to the Bundestag that the government would submit a new tariff for the approval of the Reichstag.

After some hard bargaining behind the scenes between various pressure groups the tariff was approved by the Reichstag in July 1879. It had a free list which included most raw materials (except oil, tallow and timber), all scientific instruments, as well as sea-going vessels and ships plying on the inland waterways. Import duties were imposed upon a wide range of industrial products, the rates varying according to the quality of the goods concerned. Pig-iron paid 10s a ton, manufactured iron £1.50, fine steel goods £12 and sewing needles £30. Cotton yarn paid from £6 to £24 a ton, cotton goods £40 and knitwear £60. A duty of 10s a ton was levied on flax but this was abolished in April 1880. Most of the import duties were moderate. Had they been calculated by value they would have been between 10 and 15 per cent. Many of them were the same as those levied in 1865 before the reductions, made as a result of the Franco-Prussian commercial treaty of 1862, had come into force. The pig-iron duty was the same as that levied between 1868 and 1870. Import duties were also levied on paper, leather, glass, earthenware, wooden goods and certain metal and chemical products. And this by no means exhausted the list of dutiable goods. The new import duties on agricultural products were also low. Barley and maize paid only 5s a ton, wheat, rye and oats 10s and malt 12s. Fairly high import duties continued to be levied for revenue purposes on tea, coffee, spirits, wines, petrol and tobacco.

Bismarck had expected the Reich to keep the whole of the additional revenues to be collected from the new import duties. But his intention was frustrated by the Reichstag, which accepted an amendment to the tariff law, proposed by Freiherr zu Frankenstein. This placed a limit on the amount of customs revenue to be retained by the Reich. If the customs revenue exceeded 130 million marks, the surplus was to be divided among the Federal States in proportion to their population. Bismarck had never disguised the fact that his main object in supporting the protectionists had been to secure urgently needed additional revenues for the Reich. Now he found that these revenues had been strictly limited. Although the yield from the tariff rose from 2.62 marks per head in 1878 to 7.30 marks per head in 1890 he soon had to seek new sources of revenue for the Reich.

The tariff was revised in 1885 and again in 1887. Duties on cereals and livestock were raised in 1885. Wheat and rye now paid £1.10s a ton instead of 10s, oats 15s instead of 10s and barley 15s instead of 5s a ton. The import duty on flour went up from £1.10s to £3.15s a ton. Horses now paid £1 instead of 10s and cattle from 6s to 9s instead of 4s to 6s. Only minor changes were made with regard to import duties levied on industrial products.

Two years later there was a further increase in the duties on grain and livestock. Wheat and rye now paid £2.10s a ton and oats paid £2. The protection given to agriculture led to higher food prices. For 20 years before 1870 wheat had cost £2.2s a ton less in Prussia than in England but in 1890 the price of wheat in Prussia was £2.4s higher than in England.

The next important change in the German tariff came in December 1891, when Caprivi, Bismarck's successor as chancellor, completed negotiations for commercial treaties with Austria-Hungary, Italy, Belgium and Switzerland. Treaties with Serbia (1892) and Rumania (1893) followed, as well as one with Russia — after a tariff war — in 1894. The more industrialized Germany became, the greater was her need to secure access to foreign markets for her manufactured goods. But many countries had recently increased their import duties to protect their own industries. The high McKinley tariff in the United States (1890) was a case in point. The Germans began to realize that if they imposed high duties on imports, foreigners could retaliate by levying high duties on German goods. Caprivi recognized that some tariff concessions — mainly a reduction of import duties on agricultural products — would have to be made to foreign countries to persuade them to lower their tariff barriers. He told the Reichstag: 'We must export. Either we export goods or we export men. The home market is no longer adequate.' He had to face considerable opposition from the agrarians, who objected to tariff concessions to benefit manufacturers at their expense.

Caprivi's policy was to have two types of tariff. First there was what was called the 'autonomous' tariff that applied to countries having no commercial treaty and no most-favoured-nation agreement with Germany. Secondly there were several so-called 'conventional' tariffs, each applicable to a particular country with which Germany had signed a commercial treaty. The import duties fixed by commercial treaties were lower than those of the 'autonomous' tariff. The treaty with Austria-Hungary, for example, provided for reductions in German import duties on certain agricultural products from Austria-Hungary. The duties on wheat and rye were cut from 5 marks to 3.50 marks a ton, and on oats from 4 marks to 2.80 marks a ton. Any concession in a commercial treaty was automatically passed on to all countries that had signed most-favoured-nation agreements with Germany. One merit of Caprivi's commercial treaties was that they were to last for 12 years. This introduced a valuable element of stability into Germany's commercial relations with a number of her neighbours and it enabled German industrialists to plan ahead, knowing that there would be no new hostile tariffs to surmount for some time to come.

In 1899 the British commercial attaché in Berlin described the German tariff as

> . . . moderate, very simply constructed in comparison with those of some other Continental Powers, but is well able to accomplish its object of conferring upon national industries and undertakings sufficient protection from foreign competition where it is thought necessary. At the same time it merely gives the producer a small advantage in the home market and does not appear to any appreciable extent to impair his natural activity in competition, nor to prevent his using every effort to keep down the cost of production and every other expense incidental to a keen struggle for the markets of the world . . . . In consequence of the higher price, rendered possible at home from the protective duty, the German manufacturer can afford to sell abroad the surplus of his output at a lower price than he could otherwise do.

Caprivi's commercial treaties were due to expire at the end of 1903. As early as 1897 the question of their renewal was raised in the Reichstag, which set up an economic committee to report on the question. When Bernhard von Bülow became chancellor in October 1900 the landowners and farmers—now organized in the powerful Agrarian League (1893)—made it clear that when negotiations for new commercial treaties were undertaken they would expect the import duties on all agricultural products to be raised. When the bill to revise the tariff was submitted to the Reichstag in July 1901 the government stated that although Germany would never be able to do without imported cereals altogether it was nevertheless highly desirable that 'the greater part of the nation's requirements' in grain should be produced at home.

It was not until the end of 1902 that Bülow's tariff was at last approved by the Reichstag. A feature of the new tariff was the high minimum duties levied upon farm produce that could not be reduced in negotiations with other countries. These import duties, however, did not come into effect until March 1906. The new minimum rate for wheat was £2.15s a ton. Rye and oats were to pay at least £2.10s a ton. (In 1879 import duties on these cereals had been only 10s a ton.)

As far as industrial products were concerned, raw materials generally remained on the free list, though import duties were imposed upon timber and linseed. Goods in the earlier stages of manufacture continued to pay only low duties. Cotton yarn, for example, paid the same duty as before. But at the later stages of manufacture the duties were progressively raised, sometimes by as much as 50 per cent.

Bülow's tariff classified goods in much greater detail than had been customary in earlier tariffs. When products had been defined in large groups there was nothing to stop a country that enjoyed most-favoured-nation status from claiming that it was entitled to a tariff concession on a large group of products, because Germany had made a reduction on a single item within this group to a third party in a commercial agreement. But when products were more precisely defined this was no longer possible.

It is not possible to determine the extent to which the adoption of the fiscal policy of protection contributed to the expansion of Germany's international trade between 1880 and 1914. Many factors played their part in stimulating the growth of foreign commerce in those years and the fiscal policy adopted by Bismarck in 1879 — and developed by Caprivi and Bülow —was not necessarily the most important. Free-traders argued that Germany would have been even more prosperous if she had maintained the tariff in force in 1878. They pointed out that as far as farming was concerned the new import duties on cereals and livestock did not save German agriculture from declining in the last quarter of the nineteenth century. Socialists complained that the import duties on food pushed up the cost of living for the workers. Bülow, on the other hand, claimed that his tariff of 1902 had been a great success. He wrote:

Side by side with foreign trade, advancing with such might strides, the maintenance of a strong home industry was secured . . . .

German agriculture, under the influence of the new tariff and of
the commercial treaties based on it, has experienced a decade of
vigorous development . . . . Compared with the agriculture of
other countries, ours has developed quite extraordinarily in the
last decade . . . . But the agricultural development has not taken
place at the cost of the expansion of our industrial export trade
or of our commerce.

He added that in negotiating treaties of commerce 'we could expect
concessions because we were such excellent customers to foreign
countries . . . . Under the commercial treaties based on the tariff of
1902 commerce and industry have steadily continued their brilliant
development.'

German Colonies

The agitation in favour of protection was not the only attempt in
the 1870s to persuade Bismarck to change his mind on an important
aspect of national policy. While the protectionists were demanding
the imposition of import duties, the colonial enthusiasts were trying
to persuade the public that Germany should establish an overseas
empire and enjoy what Wilhelm II later called her 'place in the sun'.

Just as Bismarck changed his mind on fiscal policy, so he changed
his mind on colonial policy. For years he had opposed the acquisition
of overseas possessions. In 1871 he declared that 'for Germany to
acquire colonies would be like a poverty-stricken Polish nobleman
providing himself with silks and sables when he needed shirts'. Ten
years later he stated categorically that 'while I am chancellor, we will
carry out no colonial policies'. For Bismarck there were positive advantages in not having colonies. If Germany were at war she could
use all her resources to defend her own frontiers without having to
defend distant colonies as well. Without a colonial empire she would
save the cost of building and maintaining a navy to protect her overseas territories. Again, if she had no colonies, Bismarck's system of
alliances would not be endangered by disputes concerning overseas
possessions. And she could spend at home the money that would
otherwise be spent on conquering colonies and administering them.

Advocates of colonial expansion, such as Missionary Inspector
Fabri, did not lack persuasive arguments. They claimed that the rapid
growth of manufactures made it necessary that Germany should

acquire colonies. She needed territories overseas that would help to supply her factories with essential raw materials and her people with tropical foods. A colonial empire might be expected to develop into a market on which some of her manufactured goods could be sold. It was also hoped that overseas possessions would provide new homes for Germans who wished to emigrate. Since 1815 hundreds of thousands of Germans had settled in the United States, where they had become American citizens and had been lost to the fatherland. If Germany were a colonial power it might be possible for some emigrants to settle in territories in which they could retain their nationality and not be absorbed into an alien society. It was also argued that Germany should share the 'white man's burden' with other colonial powers and should help to bring law and order to regions rent by tribal warfare and to preach the gospel to the heathen. Supporters of colonization complained that, without overseas possessions and gunboats to protect them, Germans trading in some parts of the world were at a disadvantage as compared with foreign rivals. The colonial enthusiasts urged Bismarck to act quickly. The 'scramble for Africa'—and the scramble for possessions in south-eastern Asia and the Pacific — had begun and before long there would be no territories left to colonize. If Germany were to become a colonial power there should be no delay in claiming such territories as were still available.

German merchants, explorers and missionaries had long been engaged in activities that might be expected to pave the way to the establishment of overseas territories. Three Hamburg merchants had been pioneers in developing Germany's trade in Africa and the Pacific — William O'Swald in Zanzibar, Carl Woermann in the Cameroons and Johann Cesar Godeffroy in Samoa. Several German explorers had helped to open up central Africa — von der Decken on Mount Kilimanjaro, Schweinfurth on the Upper Nile, Nachtigal on the River Shari, Junker in the region between Lake Chad and the Nile. German missionaries too, were active in Africa. The Barmen Rhine Mission had stations in south-western Africa, while the Basel Mission — a Swiss society largely run by Germans — worked in Togoland.

As Germany's commercial and shipping interests in Africa and the Pacific expanded in the 1870s, it became difficult for Bismarck to ignore appeals from merchants for protection when they came into conflict with nationals of other colonial powers, or when they traded with natives in regions not under the control of any European country. The refusal of the local British authorities to recognize the land claims of Germans in Tonga in 1874 led to lengthy diplomatic exchanges. When the house of Godeffroy, long dominant in the copra trade in Samoa, ran into financial difficulties in 1878, Bismarck submitted a bill to the Reichstag to provide some financial assistance so as to avert the danger of Godeffroy's trading stations falling into the hands of its English creditors — Baring Brothers of London. A new company (the *Deutsche Handels- und Plantagen-Gesellschaft*) had been founded to take over Godeffroy's establishments and the bill provided for a state guarantee to investors of 4 per cent on their shares. The most that the Reich would have been liable to pay was a mere 300,000 marks a year. Despite the swing to the right at the last general election, the opponents of any sort of colonial policy were able to defeat the Samoa Subsidy Bill in 1880. It was left to the banker Adolph von Hansemann of the Discount Company to mount a rescue operation and to raise the money to put the new company on a sound financial footing. Bismarck thanked Hansemann and his colleagues for their patriotic action. He wrote: 'His Majesty and the German government appreciate the great service that you have rendered the Fatherland by supporting the German enterprises in the South Seas.' The failure of the Samoa Subsidy Bill warned Bismarck of the opposition that would have to be overcome if he decided to found a colonial empire. For the colonial enthusiasts the events of 1880 proved to be only a temporary reverse. They redoubled their efforts to rally public opinion to their cause and to put continual pressure on the chancellor and on the Reichstag. In 1882 they founded the Colonial Society (*Kolonialverein*) and within three years over 10,000 members had been enrolled. Another colonial association was established by Carl Peters in 1884. This was the Society for German Colonization (*Gesellschaft für deutsche Kolonisation*), which aimed at raising funds to finance future colonial development in East Africa. The two associations joined together in 1887 to found the German Colonial Society (*Deutsche Kolonial-Gesellschaft*).

By 1884 Bismarck considered that he could safely pursue a policy of colonial expansion without risking a repetition of the rebuff that he had received from the Reichstag over the Samoa Subsidy Bill. But he was mistaken, for the Reichstag rejected a Steamship Subsidy Bill that would have granted subventions to German shipping lines providing regular services to south-eastern Asia and to Australia.

Only after a general election did the new Reichstag prove to be more amenable to a colonial policy. But imperial protection could be extended to overseas territories without consulting the Reichstag and this Bismarck was now prepared to do. The international situation was favourable, since Germany had concluded three alliances between 1879 and 1882 that assured her of either the active support or the benevolent neutrality of Russia, Austria and Italy in the event of war with France. Moreover a brief rapprochement with France in 1884 gave Bismarck a unique opportunity to pursue his colonial aims.

On 24 April 1884 he took the decisive step of placing under imperial protection the establishment of the Bremen merchant Adolf Lüderitz at Angra Pequeña in South West Africa. The coast of the Cameroons and Togoland and territories in northern New Guinea were similarly placed under imperial protection before the end of 1884. In February 1885 an imperial charter was granted to Carl Peter's Society for German Colonization in respect of an area of some 60,000 square miles in the hinterland of east Africa between Pangani and Kingani. In 1885 Germany came to an agreement with Britain concerning the establishment of German colonies in Kaiser Wilhelmsland (New Guinea), the Bismarck Archipelago and the Marshall Islands. And in March 1885 the Steamship Subsidy Bill — rejected by the previous Reichstag — was passed by the new Reichstag. It provided an annual grant from the State to steamship lines operating regular services to south-eastern Asia and Australia. The services were operated by the North German Lloyd shipping company. Moreover in 1884-5 the Congo (West Africa) Conference was held in Berlin. The fact that Bismarck presided over an international gathering to determine the future of a vast region in central Africa added to his prestige and showed the world that Germany had definitely entered the ranks of the colonial powers.

By 1890 a series of treaties with other colonial powers had fixed the frontiers of most of Germany's overseas possessions. The last was the Anglo-German agreement of 1890 by which — in return for giving up her claims to Zanzibar and Uganda — Germany secured the island of Heligoland as well as a corridor from south-western Africa to the River Zambezi (*Caprivizipfel*). Only minor extensions to the colonial empire were made later. They were the Caroline, Pelew and Marianne Islands (except Guam), which were purchased from Spain in 1898; the naval base of Kiao Chow, which was leased for 99 years from China in 1898; and the New Cameroons, which were acquired from France in 1911 in return for giving France a free hand in Morocco. In 1914 Germany had a colonial empire of over a million square miles, with an estimated population of about 14 millions.

From the first Bismarck stressed the commercial significance of the colonies. He wished to avoid the expense of administering overseas possessions and he proposed merely to grant imperial protection to chartered companies, which should themselves administer colonial territories. He told the Reichstag in June 1884: 'I would follow the example of England in granting to these merchants something like Royal Charters . . . . I do not wish to found provinces, but to protect commercial establishments . . . . We hope that the tree will flourish in proportion to the activity of the gardener, but if it does not, the whole responsibility rests with him and not with the Reich, which will lose nothing.'

Unfortunately for Bismarck the merchants who were trading in Africa and the Pacific were not prepared to accept the role that he had designed for them. The German firms in business on the eastern and western coasts of Africa refused to have anything to do with Bismarck's schemes for the establishment of chartered companies with sovereign rights. No companies enjoying such powers were ever set up in the Cameroons, Togoland or South West Africa. It was only with considerable difficulty that a company was induced to accept sovereign powers in Kaiser Wilhelmsland (New Guinea) and that the Jaluit Company was persuaded to pay for the cost of administering the Marshall Islands. In East Africa a charter was originally given not to a trading company but to a virtually penniless colonisation society.

This was no auspicious inauguration of a policy of colonial government by chartered companies. Bismarck's plan failed completely. The chartered companies operating in East Africa and New Guinea had surrendered their administrative functions by 1890 and the Jaluit Company followed suit in 1906. The South West Africa Company did not accept a charter and soon gave up the few administrative functions that it had exercised. The responsibility and the cost of conquering and ruling the colonial empire fell upon the Reich.

The failure of Bismarck's plans had unfortunate results, since the former chartered companies survived as commercial companies that enjoyed many privileges. They secured large grants of land and received exclusive rights to build railways and to exploit mines. They received generous cash payments in return for giving up administrative functions that had sometimes been exercised for only a very short time. And several companies that had never wielded administrative powers secured substantial concessions. In South West Africa, for example, nine companies owned nearly one-third of the entire territory in 1903.

The economic development of Germany's overseas possessions was disappointing. By 1913 deficits on colonial budgets had cost the German taxpayer over 1,000 million marks ánd only two small territories — Togoland and Samoa — were self-supporting. The suppression of insurrections, such as the Herero revolt in South West Africa and the Maji-Maji rising in East Africa, proved to be costly in lives and money. Neither as reservoirs of raw materials, nor as markets for manufactured goods did the colonies play a significant part in Germany's economic life. In 1913 the colonial trade of the Reich was only 0.5 per cent of her total external trade. Germany pursued the policy of the open door and made no attempt to monopolize the commerce of her overseas territories. Some German firms benefited from contracts to supply materials for major public works in the colonies, such as the railway from Dar-es-Salaam to Kigoma in East Africa. And the North German Lloyd shipping company enjoyed subsidies for its regular services to south-east Asia and to Australia. Only a few regions in the colonies, such as parts of South West Africa and the Usambara highlands in German East Africa, proved to be suitable for white settlement. German emigrants still preferred to settle in the great cities of the United States rather than in the wide open spaces of Africa. In 1913 there were only 23,500 Germans in the colonies, a number of whom were officials and not permanent settlers.

Welfare State

At the same time as he was reforming the tariff and establishing a colonial empire, Bismarck also embarked upon the task of laying the foundations of the welfare state. Germany was the first great industrial country to do this. Nearly a quarter of a century elapsed before Britain followed suit. In the 1880s Germany was confronted with a more serious 'social question' than in the 1860s. Social distress had followed in the wake of rapid industrialization. Although the living standards of certain workers had gradually improved, particularly during the short boom of the early 1870s, the poor-law authorities, the churches and various charitable organizations were fighting an uphill battle against the effects of low wages, long hours, unemployment, sickness and bad housing conditions. Few workers could save enough money to support their families if they were off work owing to an illness, and accident or the loss of a job. Many old people did not have a sufficient income to live on and were dependent upon their children. Efforts had been made by friendly societies, by trade unions and by savings banks to help people to save money. Prussia, for example, had some 5,000 friendly societies with 800,000 members in 1874. Moreover some enlightened employers such as Krupp and Stumm were providing admirable welfare services for their workers.

Bismarck realised that the very magnitude of the problem made state intervention — sometimes called 'state socialism' — inevitable. The duty of the State to help those who could not provide for themselves had long been recognized in Germany. The Prussian Code of 1794 specifically laid it down that the State was responsible for relieving the destitute, for finding work for the unemployed and for providing forced labour for the work-shy. When Bismarck was accused of preaching the socialist doctrine of the 'right to work' he retorted that this principle had been practised by the Prussian State from time immemorial.

Bismarck's policy of providing welfare services was part of his campaign to wean the workers from the Social Democrat Party, which was the largest socialist party in the world at that time. Bismarck regarded with abhorrence the Marxist doctrines preached by the socialists and he considered that the continued growth of socialism would endanger the survival of the State, the family and the Christian religion. In 1878 the Reichstag had passed the 'Exceptional Law against the universally dangerous endeavours of Social Democracy'. This law banned the Social Democrat Party and prohibited nearly all its political activities. Its newspapers were suppressed. A state of minor siege was proclaimed in Berlin and some other large cities. The Socialist Party was driven underground. But the party was not crushed. Its propaganda was soon revived and a socialist newspaper, printed first in Switzerland and then in England, was widely distributed in Germany. The anti-socialist law did not prevent socialist candidates from seeking election to the Reichstag and those who were successful were able to use the Reichstag as a platform from which to denounce Bismarck and all his works. The socialist vote fell at the Reichstag elections of 1878 and 1881 but then increased at a surprising rate.

Having used a stick to beat the socialists with little success, Bismarck tried the effect of a few carrots. He presented to the Reichstag comprehensive schemes for compulsory state insurance against sickness, accidents and old age. At first he proposed to pay for these services by money raised from a tobacco monopoly but this scheme was rejected by the Reichstag and other methods of financing the welfare schemes had to be devised.

The Health Insurance Law of 1883 compulsorily insured factory workers, miners and the lower-paid black-coated workers. Subsequent legislation extended the scheme to farm workers, craftsmen, apprentices and casual workers. The number of persons covered by the scheme rose from 4.6 million (10 per cent of the population) in 1885 to nearly 14 million (21.5 per cent of the population) in 1910. Certain persons were excluded from the scheme because they were already covered by schemes operated by the Reich, the Federal States or the municipalities. The scheme was operated through friendly societies. A worker who was liable to compulsory insurance had to join an approved friendly society, but he was not required to join any particular society. Seven different types of friendly societies were recognized under the Health Insurance Law. The most important were the Local Health Associations (*Ortskrankenkassen*), which operated in a town or a rural area. Factory Health Associations were organized by firms employing over fifty workers. The Miners Friendly Societies (*Knappschaften*) — old-established mutual-aid associations in the mining industry — were brought into the scheme. The Building Health Associations were joined by those employed by contractors on public works, such as roads or fortifications. The Gild Health Associations were supported by self-employed craftsmen. The Free Associations (*Hilfskassen*) were formed by groups of people who were prepared to pay larger contributions in return for higher benefits if they fell ill. Finally there were the Communal Sick Associations, which provided a safety net for those who, for any reason, could not find any other friendly society that was prepared to accept them. Both the contributions and the benefits varied somewhat from one friendly society to another. Normally two-thirds of the contribution was paid by the worker and one-third by his employer. Self-employed persons and voluntary members paid the full contribution themselves Benefits generally included free medical attention and a weekly payment during sickness. Some friendly societies maintained convalescent homes by the sea or in the mountains in which members could recover from illnesses after being discharged from hospital.

The Accident Insurance Law of 1884 covered 13 million workers in 1889 and nearly 24 million in 1909. Employers had to pay the full cost of insuring workers against accidents. This gave employers a strong incentive to make their factories and mines as safe as possible. In manufacturing industry, in building, in shipping and in agriculture and forestry, groups of employers (*Berufsgenossenschaften*), generally organized on a regional basis, were required to impose upon member firms an annual levy to meet all accident claims. In case of injury at work an insured person could claim a weekly payment after his benefits from the health-insurance scheme had been exhausted. If he were permanently disabled he could be granted a pension for life. If a worker died as the result of an accident while at work — and 15.6 per cent of industrial accidents were fatal in 1888 — his widow was entitled to a burial grant, a weekly pension and an allowance for each dependent child.

The scheme for old-age and disability pensions was passed by the Reichstag in 1889. Like the other two schemes it covered factory workers, miners and some black-coated workers. Certain small employers and independent craftsmen could join as voluntary members. The fund from which pensions were paid was made up of equal contributions from employers and workers, to which was added a grant of 50 marks a year from the Reich in respect of each insured person. The cost of the subsidy to the taxpayer was between 5 and 6 million marks when the scheme started. An old-age pension was paid at the age of 70, while a disability pension was paid if a worker became incapacitated for any reason other than an industrial accident. The number of invalidity pensions rose from 55,983 in 1895 to 152,882 in 1903. Then the administration of the scheme was tightened — the inspectorate was increased — and there was a considerable decline in the number of disability pensions that were approved.

In 1889 Professor Luzzatti, a distinguished Italian economist, discussed the new German social-insurance schemes before an international congress in Paris. He described Bismarck's achievement as '*une oeuvre gigantesque forgée au marteau d'un cyclope social*'. Other foreign observers echoed these sentiments. But in Germany the welfare schemes met with considerable criticism. There were employers who complained of the heavy financial burden placed upon industry. Nearly 14.5 million marks were paid out to meet accident claims in 1889 and this charge fell entirely upon the employers. Moreover in the same year employers paid 300,000 marks in safety precautions to prevent accidents. The health scheme cost 71 million marks in

1889 and the employers were paying one-third of the contributions to the fund from which sickness payments were being made.

The socialists denounced the welfare services on various grounds. They claimed that the workers' contributions to the health and old-age pensions schemes — an enforced reduction in wages in effect — were too high, while the benefits were too low. They demanded the payment of old-age pensions at the age of 65 instead of 70 on the ground that few workers ever reached the age of three score and ten. And if a worker did live to celebrate his seventieth birthday his pension of about 125 marks a year could only be described as a miserable pittance.

In so far as the welfare services had been introduced to wean the workers from socialism, they failed in their objective. At the Reichstag general elections the socialist vote rose from 549,000 in 1884 to 1,427,000 in 1890. Moreover the socialists had strengthened their position, because they now controlled an important group of trade unions and also a number of new friendly societies that had been called into existence by Bismarck's health scheme. Shortly after Bismarck's fall from office the anti-socialist law was allowed to lapse.

Whatever mistakes Bismarck may have made when introducing his welfare schemes, there can be no doubt that in the long run they were successful. Over the years the three insurance laws proved their worth and their provisions were extended to workers not insured under the original schemes. In 1911 the Insurance Consolidation Law brought the three schemes within the scope of a single statute. The schemes gave workers a feeling of security, since an accident at work or a prolonged illness no longer plunged a family into poverty. The health of the workers improved, since friendly societies provided free medical attention and hospital treatment when necessary. The only serious gap in Bismarck's schemes was the lack of any insurance against unemployment. This was because unemployment could not be accurately forecast, while the number of deaths, industrial accidents and illnesses that were likely to occur in the future could be forecast with reasonable accuracy. It was not until 1926 that German workers were insured against unemployment. The first steps towards a welfare state that Germany took in the 1880s, particularly the health scheme, were a factor that contributed to the welcome fall in the annual death rate in Germany from 25.4 per 1,000 of the population in 1881-5 to only 16.2 per 1,000 in 1910. Eventually other industrial countries followed Germany's example and adopted schemes very similar to those introduced by Bismarck between 1884 and 1889.

18 *The Age of Wilhelm II, 1888-1914*

In 1913, when Wilhelm II celebrated the twenty-fifth anniversary of his accession, his subjects could look back upon a reign that had seen Germany advance to the forefront of the industrial nations of the world. The continued growth of the population — 66 millions in 1913 as compared with 48 millions in 1888 — increased both the labour force and the number of consumers. Industrial expansion and rising living standards were reflected in a sharp fall in the number of emigrants. Only 28,000 Germans left the country in the first decade of the twentieth century, as compared with 134,200 in the 1880s. The population was becoming more and more concentrated in large industrial towns and ports. In 1910 Germany had 23 great cities of over 200,000 inhabitants each. Their total population was 8,677,000. Three of them — Essen, Duisburg and Dortmund — were in the Ruhr. The occupational structure of the population was changing. In 1882 the number of persons engaged in industry and commerce on the one hand and in agriculture and forestry on the other was approximately equal, but in 1907 nearly twice as many people were engaged in industrial occupations as in farming.

Many factors had helped to bring about the astonishing progress of German industry and commerce. The unifying influence of the customs union, the economic and social achievements of Bismarck, the influence of the credit banks and the growth of joint-stock companies and cartels were of particular significance. Scientific and technical progress played their part in carrying Germany forward on the road to industrial expansion. Werner Siemens's electric dynamo, Otto's gas engine, Diesel's heavy oil engine and the discovery of synthetic dyes by Caro and others were but a few of the many inventions that contributed to Germany's rapid development as a manufacturing country. Much scientific research took place in laboratories maintained by large firms, universities and technical colleges.

The development of an efficient transport system contributed to the expansion of industry. Germany's railways came increasingly under the ownership of Prussia and a few other Federal States. Prussia's nationalized lines were well managed and were run at a profit. The railway network grew from 37,190 kilometres to 60,521 kilometres between 1885 and 1912. The inland waterways were extended and improved. A Prussian law of 1905 provided for a substantial expansion of Prussia's navigable waterways. Canals opened in Wilhelm II's reign included the Kiel Canal, the Dortmund-Ems, the Rhine-Herne, the Ems-Weser and the Berlin-Stettin canals. A quarter of the goods traffic of the Reich was carried by inland waterways in 1910.

Keynes declared that 'the German empire was built more truly on coal and iron, than on blood and iron'. It was the coal, iron, steel and engineering industries that were the backbone of the German economy. Germany had nearly caught up Britain as a producer of coal in 1913. The output of the Reich was 190 million tons as compared with 60 million tons in 1887. In addition Germany produced 87 million tons of lignite as compared with only 16 million tons in 1887. Net exports of coal and coke amounted to 20 million tons. The number of coalminers had increased from 120,000 in the 1860s to over half a million in 1913.

The principal coalfields were in the Ruhr, the Saar, Upper Silesia and Saxony. By far the most important was the Ruhr. Over 114 million tons of coal were mined in this region in 1913 and this represented more than half of the total German output. Upper Silesia produced nearly 44 million tons in 1913 and the Saar produced 13 million tons.

The amount of coal mined in the valley of the River Ruhr itself declined from half of the total output of the coalfield in 1850 to only 10 per cent in 1900. The opening of the Rheinpreussen mine on the left bank of the Rhine in 1875 and of the Wene mine north of the River Lippe in 1903 marked the extension of the mining area far to the west and to the north of the original coalfield. The Ruhr was dominated by a few great mining companies, which had absorbed many smaller collieries. The Gelsenkirchen Mining Company and the Harpen Mining Company had each acquired fourteen mines between 1873 and 1907. Mines producing about one-fifth of the output of the Ruhr were owned by steelworks. After 1893 most of the Ruhr mining companies were brought together in the powerful Rhenish-Westphalian Coal Syndicate. The great increase in the output of coal, coke and briquettes stimulated the expansion of the industrial sector of the economy. The steelworks, the railways, the merchant ships, the navy, the power stations, the gasworks and the factories all needed coal, while many products of the chemical industry — such as synthetic dyes — were derived from coal tar.

The expansion of the iron and steel industries was also of fundamental significance to the continued expansion of the German economy. Before 1870 these industries were based upon scattered iron-ore deposits, of which the most important were those of the Siegerland, Upper Silesia, Luxembourg and the Lahn-Dill and Ilsede-Peine districts. In the 1860s, when total output amounted to about 2 million tons Silesia's output of iron-ore had declined, while that of western Germany had expanded. The annexation of Lorraine greatly increased Germany's iron-ore resources, since the output of the province was 684,000 tons (1872). This *minette* ore was phosphoric but once the process invented by Thomas and Gilchrist was introduced, the output of iron-ore in Lorraine — and also in Luxembourg — rapidly increased. Germany's output of iron-ore grew from 6.7 million tons in 1887 to over 28 million tons in 1913. But this was not sufficient for Germany's needs and in 1913 her net imports of iron-ore amounted to 11.4 million tons. In 1901 the Ruhr drew 43 per cent of its iron-ore from German mines, while nearly 22 per cent was imported from Sweden and 17.5 per cent from Spain.

There were a few blackband deposits in Germany and Luxembourg, but normally iron-ore and coal were not found together. So it was necessary either to take the ore to a coalfield or to transport the coke to an ironfield. Some ironworks and steelworks were situated on the ironfields. The de Wendel works at Hayange (Lorraine), the Iselder works at Peine (Hanover), and the Deutsch-Luxembourg Company at Differdange (Luxembourg) were examples of steelworks that used local iron-ore and secured coke for smelting from the Ruhr and other coalfields. On the other hand many ironworks were established on the coalfields, such as the Ruhr and Upper Silesia, and they drew their ore from ironmines that might be a long distance away. There were also some ironworks at the ports that smelted Swedish iron-ore with English coal.

In 1860 Germany's output of pig-iron was still only just over half a million tons, as compared with Britain's 3.8 million tons and France's 898,000 tons. With the introduction of Bessemer converters and open-hearth furnaces the iron and steel industries rapidly expanded. The annexation of Alsace-Lorraine gave Germany not only a new ironfield but also great ironworks and engineering plants. Immediately after the Franco-Prussian War the iron trade experienced a great boom and a large number of new iron companies were established. In 1875 Germany's output of pig-iron had risen to 2 million tons.

A sharp recession followed this boom. In the 1880s, however, the industry recovered, although rival industries abroad were either stagnant or making little progress. A small import duty had been imposed in 1879 and the introduction of the Gilchrist-Thomas process enabled the vast *minette* resources of Lorraine and Luxembourg to be fully exploited. By 1913 Germany's output of pig-iron had risen to 19.3 million tons, of which 8.2 million tons were produced in the Ruhr and 6.4 million tons in Lorraine and Luxembourg. Germany was now the second largest producer of pig-iron in the world. In the same year Germany's output of steel ingots and castings amounted to 18.9 million tons of which 10.1 million tons came from the Ruhr. The iron and steel industry, like the coal industry, was dominated by very large firms (such as Krupp) and thirty of them — mainly in western Germany — were linked in a powerful cartel.

To a considerable extent the German iron industry was producing for the home market. 'Its development was closely connected with the increasing industrialization of Germany, with the growth of large towns and with building, with the extension of the network of tramways and railways . . . . The external market for raw materials and partly-manufactured as well as foundry goods was very small.' On the other hand Germany exported a quarter of her rolling-mill products. Even more important were the exports of the finished products of the engineering industry. The value of her exports of machinery rose from 52.8 million marks in 1887 to 680.3 million marks in 1913.

The textile industries also expanded, though their progress was somewhat uneven. The number of persons employed in these industries did not change very much. In 1907 the number was just over a million, as compared with 910,000 twenty-five years before. Yet the volume of output and the value of exports showed a considerable increase.

The manufacture of cotton had developed on modern factory lines at Elberfeld-Barmen (Wuppertal), Chemnitz, Augsburg and elsewhere in the middle of the nineteenth century. After the Franco-Prussian War the annexation of Alsace substantially increased the number of spinning-machines, powerlooms and textile operatives in the Reich. In the early 1870s Germany was importing over 100,000 tons of raw cotton a year. Power weaving was introduced more slowly than mechanical spinning. In 1875 about two-thirds of the German weavers were still domestic outworkers. Twenty years later there were only 50,000 such workers left and the vast majority of the weavers were to be found in large factories. In 1913 the German cotton industry — measured in terms of raw cotton imports — was about half the size of the British cotton industry. German cotton-mills drew much more of their raw material from India than was customary in Lancashire. Consequently the quality of much German cloth was not so good as that manufactured in Britain. German spinners did not produce enough yarn to satisfy the demands of the weaving establishments. Before the First World War the value of Germany's annual imports of yarn and twist — mostly fine English yarns — was about 100 million marks. Exports of German cotton piece goods and yarns were worth 500 million marks in 1913.

The manufacture of woollens also developed as a great modern industry. There were many woollen centres and few signs of geographical concentration. At one time German sheep farmers had produced enough wool not only to supply the home market, but to sell abroad as well. The fine wools of Saxony had commanded a ready sale in foreign markets. In the 1860s, however, a fall in world wool prices led to a sharp reduction in the home clip and to an expansion of imports from Cape Colony and the Argentine. The decline in sheep farming continued, so that the German woollen industry came to depend almost entirely upon imported raw wool. By 1900 'no great nation was so dependent on the outside world for the raw material of its warm clothing'. The modern spinning-mills and weaving sheds used imported wool while, for a time, the domestic craftsmen continued to work with local wools. There were still 28,000 domestic weavers in Germany in 1895. The weaving factories drew some of their fine yarns from Britain though, at the same time, coarse German yarns were being exported to Austria-Hungary and the Balkans. The combed-wool branch of the industry expanded rapidly after 1870. The combing of wool became a specialized activity and the number of wool-combers rose from 5,800 in 1882 to 21,600 in 1907. Both combing and worsted spinning-mills were usually operated as joint-stock companies and not as family businesses. Germany's exports of woollen goods and yarns were valued at 361 million marks in 1913.

The silk industry, with exports valued at just over 200 million marks in 1913, had greatly changed since 1887, when exports had amounted to only 16 million marks. The rapid modernization of the industry can be seen from the growth of powerloom weaving in

Krefeld, which was the greatest silk centre in the country. In 1890 there were only 5,400 silk and velvet powerlooms in the town. But there were 25,000 handlooms. In 1909, however, there were only 2,700 handlooms left, while the number of powerlooms had increased to 9,900. German silk manufacturers were now able to compete with their French rivals in the markets of the world.

The linen industry has been called 'one of Imperial Germany's failures'. In the eighteenth century German linens had been among the best in the world and they had been exported in large quantities. In the nineteenth century less flax was grown in Germany and more was imported. It was a long time before the linen industry was re-organized on a factory basis. The domestic spinners and weavers of Silesia persisted in their efforts to survive despite the competition of Ulster and Belgian machine-made linens. Eventually modern heck-ling and spinning-machines and powerlooms were introduced and factories were established. But in 1913 Germany was still an importer of both linen yarn and fine linens.

An account has already been given of three new industries that developed after 1870. The rapid expansion of shipbuilding and the making of marine engines at Hamburg, Bremen and Stettin was a particularly remarkable achievement. So was the phenomenal growth of the mercantile marine. In 1913 no less than a quarter of Germany's merchant ships were less than 5 years old. Liners of the Hamburg-America company and the North German Lloyd had firmly estab-lished themselves on the North Atlantic route. Two other new branches of manufacture were the electrical and chemical industries. The high quality of their products had won for Germany a leading place in international markets.

By 1914 Germany had become one of the leading trading nations in the world and in the previous 25 years her overseas commerce had been expanding more rapidly than that of her rivals. The imports and exports of the Reich (excluding bullion) had increased from 6,472 million marks in 1888 to 20,776 million marks in 1913. The pattern of Germany's overseas trade was what was to be expected in an advanc-ed industrial country. Over 70 per cent of her imports in 1913 con-sisted of raw materials for industry as well as food, drinks and tobacco. A quarter of her imports were semi-manufactured and finished goods. Three-quarters of her exports were manufactured (or semi-manufactured) products, 15 per cent were raw materials and 10 per cent were foods and drinks. The expansion of her exports of manufactured goods had, to some extent, taken place at Britain's expense. German goods were sold in markets in Latin America, Africa and Asia, where British exporters had formerly not had to face much competition. It has, however, been pointed out that

> . . . increased trade rivalry between Britain and Germany . . . at the turn of the century did not — with few exceptions — produce political repercussions in either country. The Atlantic shipping pool, agreement on the continuation of the building of the Bagdad railway, the relations between British and German, British and North American banks in South America, prove that at this time there were growing possibilities of trade and profit for all.

Germany was exporting not only goods but capital as well. A country that Voltaire had thought would be condemned to everlasting poverty was now rich enough to invest money abroad. Until about 1860 Germany had been a borrower rather than a lender. In the 1820s, for example, two loans raised on the London money market had put the Prussian government on its feet after the Napoleonic Wars. In the boom of the 1850s foreign investors had helped to establish new collieries and ironworks in the Ruhr, while English financial houses had extended generous 'open credits' to Hamburg merchants and shippers. The 1860s were a period of transition. On the one hand English capital was helping to extend the network of railways in Germany. On the other hand some German private banks were investing in American railways. In the 1870s and 1880s the great joint-stock banks began to invest heavily abroad. In Europe German investors put their money in Russian and Austrian loans. In 1887 Bismarck in effect banned Russian government bonds from the German money market for political reasons. Between 1887 and 1890 heavy investments were made in securities in the Argentine and in loans to the governments of Italy and Turkey.

In 1913 Germany's overseas investments were estimated to amount to 23,500 million marks. Just over half of them were in Europe and the Ottoman Empire. Elsewhere Germany's largest investments were in North and South America and in Africa. Herbert Feis states that 'despite a prevailing conception to the contrary, substantially more than half of the foreign investment was in fixed interest-bearing securities, especially in the bonds of foreign governments. A large part of the investment of variable return was not in the hands of individual investors but of the great banks.' Those German foreign investments that were not in government bonds were in the shares of railway companies, public utilities, iron-ore mines, oilfields and colonial plantation and trading companies. Germany had an adverse balance of commodity trade, but she was able to pay her way in international trade because of her invisible exports, which included interest from foreign investments and payments received from foreign investments and payment received for banking, insurance and shipping services.

Karl Helfferich, a director of the Dresden Bank, estimated that Germany's national income had increased from 23.5 thousand million marks in 1896 to 43 thousand million marks in 1913. The total wealth of the country had increased from 200 thousand million marks in 1895 to over 300 thousand million marks in 1913. The increase in the national income and in national wealth was reflected in rising living standards. In 1912 Germany consumed — per head of the population — 52 kilogrammes of meat, 21.4 kilogrammes of sugar, 2.4 kilogrammes of coffee, 3.5 kilogrammes of rice and 7.5 kilogrammes of cotton. There had been a substantial increase in the consumption of these — and many other — commodities in the previous 25 years. Helfferich observed that the statistical information available disposed of the myth that Germany was becoming a 'plutocracy' before the First World War. On the contrary his investigations showed that many people whose incomes had formerly been so low that they were not liable to income tax had now improved their financial position and had entered the group earning between 900 and 6,000 marks a year. The average annual wages of coalminers had risen from 863 marks to 1,755 marks in the Ruhr between 1888 and 1913 and from 516 marks to 1,053 marks in Upper Silesia. Deposits in German savings banks had risen from 6,800 million marks in 1895 to 17,800 million marks in 1911. Such evidence suggests that the industrial workers were sharing in the national prosperity in the reign of Wilhelm II.

The industrialization of Germany had taken place in a remarkably short space of time. A man born in 1834, when the Zollverein was established, who reached the age of 80 would have witnessed the whole process in his own lifetime. As a boy he might have been present at the opening of one of the railways that spanned the country and stimulated trade between distant regions. As a young man in his twenties he would have seen the first industrial boom of the 1850s, when new towns sprang up like mushrooms on the major coalfields.

In middle age he would have lived through the era dominated by Bismarck when great new branches of manufacture — the electrical, chemical and shipbuilding industries — had joined the older iron, engineering and textile industries to make Germany the leading industrial state on the Continent. And in his old age in the reign of Wilhelm II he would have witnessed the worldwide expansion of Germany's trade abroad and the increasing improvement of the standard of living of the workers at home. On his eightieth birthday he could look back upon economic and social changes that had turned his fatherland from a relatively underdeveloped country into one of the world's industrial giants.

Bibliography and Index

Bibliography

Part I: The Dawn of the Industrial Era, 1834-1851

1 Introduction

For early signs of industrialization in Germany see W. O. Henderson, 'The Genesis of the Industrial Revolution in France and Germany in the 18th Century', in *Kyklos*, II (1956), pp. 190-206. For the economic development of Germany between 1834 and 1850 see Sir John Clapham, *The Economic Development of France and Germany 1815-1914*, (3rd edn. 1928), ch. 4-7; A. Sartorius von Waltershausen, *Deutsche Wirtschaftsgeschichte 1815-1914* (1923), part III; Pierre Benaerts, *Les origines de la grande industrie allemande* (1933); and Martin Kutz, *Deutschlands Aussenhandel von der französischen Revolution bis zur Gründung des Zollvereins* (1974).

2 The Customs Union

For the German customs union (Zollverein) see W. O. Henderson, *The Zollverein* (1939 and 1959) and 'Deutscher Zollverein', in *Handwörterbuch der Sozialwissenschaften*, part 52 (1964); C. F. Nebenius, *Der deutsche Zollverein* (1835); G. Höfken, *Der deutsche Zollverein in seiner Fortbildung* (1842); H. A. J. Richelot, *L'association douanière allemande* (1845); F. Honth-Weber, *Der Zollverein seit seiner Erweiterung durch den Steuerverein* (1861); J. Falke, *Die Geschichte des deutschen Zollwesens* (1969); H. Festenberg-Packische, *Geschichte des Zollvereins* (1869); W. Weber, *Der deutsche Zollverein* (1969); W. Roscher, *Zur Gründungsgeschichte des Zollvereins* (1870); Karl Braun, *Die Männer des Zollvereins* (1881); B. Bab, *Die öffentliche Meinung über den deutschen Zollverein zur Zeit seiner Entstehung* (1930); A. H. Price, *The Evolution of the Zollverein* (1949); W. Fischer, 'The German Zollverein. A Case Study in Customs Union', in *Kyklos*, XIII (1960). For documents on the founding of the German customs union see W. von Eisenhart-Rothe and A. Ritthaler, *Vorgeschichte und Begründung des deutschen Zollvereins, 1815-1834*, 3 vols. (1934). For the controversy on free trade and protection see Margaret E. Hirst, *Life of Friedrich List* (1909) and W. O. Henderson, *Britain and Industrial Europe*, 3rd edn (1972), ch. 7: 'Prince Smith and Free Trade in Germany'.

3 Railways

The standard work on the history of German railways is Arthur von Mayer, *Geschichte und Geographie der deutschen Eisenbahnen von ihrer Entwicklung bis 1890* (2 vols bound together, 1891). See also H. Klomfass, *Die Entwicklung des Staatsbahnsystems in Preussen* (1900); A. van D. Leyden, 'Eisenbahnen', in *Handbuch der Staatswissenschaften* (1909); E. Kech, *Geschichte der deutschen Eisenbahnpolitik* (1911); Max Hoeltzel, *Aus der Frühzeit der Eisenbahnen* (1935); the centenary publication *Hundert Jahre deutscher Eisenbahnen* (Reichverkehrsministerium, Berlin, 1935); W. O. Henderson, *The State and the Industrial Revolution in Prussia, 1740-1870* (1958), ch. 8: 'The Genesis of the Prussian Railways 1815-48' and ch. 9 : 'von der Heydt and the Prussian Railways 1848-70'. For Friedrich List and German railways see Friedrich List, *Schriften, Reden, Briefe*, III (1) and (2) 'Schriften zum Verkehrswesen' (Scientia Verlag Aalen, 1971).

4 Industrial Expansion

For the coal industry see Maurice Baumont, *La grosse industrie allemande et le charbon* (1928) and *La grosse industrie allemande et le lignite* (1928). For iron, steel and engineering see L. Beck, *Die Geschichte des Eisens*, 5 vols (1884-1903); N. J. G. Pounds and W. N. Parker, *Coal and Steel in Western Europe* (1957); Alfred Schröter and Walter Becker, *Der deutsche Maschinenbau in der industriellen Revolution* (1962) and Horst Wagenblass, *Der Eisenbahnbau und das Wachstum der deutschen Eisen- und Maschinenbauindustrie 1835 bis 1860* (1973). For the textile industries see Hans Mottek (ed.), *Studien zur Geschichte der industriellen Revolution in Deutschland* (1960) (see particularly Horst Blumenberg's essay on the German linen industry, 1834-70, pp. 65-143); Martin Schumacher, 'Die Bielefelder Leinenindustrie im Umbruch 1836-1839', in the sixty-fifth *Jahresbericht des historischen Vereins für die Grafschaft Regensburg*, Jahrgang 1966-7 Bielefeld (1968), pp. 121-38; Horst Blumenberg, *Die deutsche Textilindustrie in der industriellen Revolution* (1965); this book deals with the woollen industry. For the industrial revolution in Berlin see Lothar Baar, *Die Berliner Industrie in der industriellen Revolution* (1966), Otto Büsch, *Industrialisierung und Gewerbe im Raum Berlin-Brandenburg 1800-1850* (1971) and Hartmut Kaelble, *Berliner Unternehmer während der frühen Industrialisierung* (1972).

For foreign influences on the industrialization of Germany see W. O. Henderson, *Britain and Industrial Europe* (1972); Martin Schumacher, *Auslandsreisen deutscher Unternehmer 1750-1851 unter besonderer Berücksichtigun von Rheinland und Westfalen* (1968). For the major industrial regions (Ruhr, Upper Silesia, Saar, Saxony) see Anton Hasslacher, *Das Industriegebiet an der Saar und seine haupt-*

sächlichen Industriezweige (1879); N. J. G. Pounds, *The Ruhr* (1952); R. Forberger, 'Zur Aufnahme der maschinellen Fertigung durch sächsische Manufakturen', *Jahrbuch für Wirtschaftsgeschichte* (1960), part I; Konrad Fuchs, *Vom Dirigismus zum Liberalismus. Die Entwicklung Obeschlesiens als preussisches Berg- und Hüttenrevier* (1970). For documents on the process of industrialization see W. Treue, H. Pöniche, Karl-Heinz Manegold (eds), *Quellen zur Geschichte der industriellen Revolution* (1966); *Documents of European Economic History*, I, *The Process of Industrialization, 1750-1870,* eds. S. Pollard and C. Holmes (1968).

5 *The Role of the State*
For the role of the State in the industrial revolution in Germany see articles in the *Journal of Economic History*, supplement X (1950); Conrad Matschoss, *Preussens Gewerbeförderung und ihre grossen Männer* (1921); W. O. Henderson, *The State and the Industrial Revolution in Prussia* (1958); U. P. Ritter, *Die Rolle des Staats in den Frühstadien der Industrialisierung* (1961); Wolfram Fischer, *Der Staat und die Anfänge der Industrialisierung in Baden 1800-1850* (1862); Wolfram Fischer, 'The Strategy of Public Investment in nineteenth century Germany, (6th International Economic History Conference, Copenhagen, August 1974), Ilja Mieck, *Preussische Gewerbepolitik in Berlin 1800-1844* (1865). For the Prussian Overseas Trading Corporation see Paul Schrader, *Die Geschichte der Königlichen Seehandlung (Preussische Staatsbank . . .)* (1911); Hermann Schleutker, *Die volkswirtschaftliche Bedeutung der kgl. Seehandlung* (1920); and a book issued to celebrate the 150th anniversary of the corporation entitled *Die Preussische Staatsbank (Seehandlung), 1772-1922* (1922).

6 *Revolution and Reaction*
For the German revolution of 1848 see J. G. Legge, *Rhyme and Revolution in Germany, IV* (1918); V. Valentin, *Geschichte der deutschen revolution von 1848-9,* 2 vols (1930-1); L. B. Namier, *1848: the Revolution of the Intellectuals* (1944); T. S. Hamerow, *Restoration, Revolution, Reaction. Economics and Politics in Germany 1815-71* (1958), part II; F. Eyck, *The Frankfurt Parliament 1848-9* (1968); R. J. Rath, *The Viennese Revolution of 1848* (1957).
For the economic and social aspects of the revolution see Karl Marx (should be Friedrich Engels). *Revolution and Counter Revolution; or Germany in 1848,* ed. Eleanor Marx (1952); P. Albrecht, *Die volkswirtschaftlichen und sozialen Fragen in der Frankfurter National Versammlung* (1914); W. Schneider, *Wirtschafts- und Sozialpolitik im Frankfurter Parlament* (1923); R. Stadelmann, *Soziale und politische Geschichte der Revolution von 1848* (1948); P. H. Noyes,

Organisation and Revolution: Working Class Associations in the German Revolution of 1848 (1948); L. O'Boyle, 'The Democratic Left in Germany 1848', *Journal of Modern History* (1961).
For Bruck's plan for a Central European customs union see R. Charmatz, *Minister Freiherr von Bruck. Der Vorkämpfer Mitteleuropas* (1916). For the Zollverein crisis of 1848-53 see Rudolph von Delbrück, *Lebenserinnerungen*, 2 vols (1905), chs. 9-14; and W. O. Henderson, *The Zollverein*, new edn (1959), pp. 190-228 and 'Deutscher Zollverein', in *Handwörterbuch der Sozialwissenschaften* (1964), part 52; Alfred Gaertner, *Der Kampf um den Zollverein zwischen Österreich und Preussen von 1849 bis 1853* (1911).

7 Germany at the Crystal Palace
See Utz Haltern, *Die Londoner Weltausstellung von 1851* (1971), pp. 134-47, 199-206 and 236-43.

Part II: The Rise of the Great Industries 1851-1873

8 Boom and Slump, 1851-57
See J. Becker, *Das deutsche Manchestertum* (1907); L. Katzenstein, *Die Zeit der preussischen Freihandelspolitik* (1913); Sartorius von Waltershausen, *Deutsche Wirtschaftsgeschichte, 1815-1914* (1923); Felix Pinner (Frank Fassland), *Deutsche Wirtschaftsführer* (1924); Pierre Benaerts, *Les origines de la grande industrie allemande* (1933), chs. 10-14 (Les débuts de la grande industrie); T. S. Hamerow, *Restoration, Revolution, Reaction . . .* (1958), part 3; William Carr, *A History of Germany, 1815-1914*, ch. 3 (Germany in the 1850s). For the commercial crisis of 1857 see Hans Rosenberg, *Die Weltwirtschafts Crisis von 1857-9* (1934). For joint-stock companies see Horst Blumberg, 'Die Finanzierung der Neugründungen und Erweiterungen von Industriebetrieben in Form der Aktiengesellschaften während der fünfziger Jahre des 19en Jahrhunderts in Deutschland am Beispiel der preussischen Verhältnisse erläutert', in Mottek, Blumberg, Wutzmer and Becker, *Studien zur Geschichte der industriellen Revolution in Deutschland* (Akademie Verlag, Berlin, 1960).

9 The Banking Revolution
The standard history of German banking is Jacob Riesser, *Die deutschen Grossbanken und ihre Konzentration . . .* , 3rd edn (1910): English translation — *The German Great Banks . . .* Washington, (1911). For the Crédit Mobilier see Tooke and Newmarch, *A History of Prices . . .* , VI (1857: reprinted 1928), pp. 104-34; M. Aycard, *Histoire du Crédit Mobilier* (1867); J. Plenge, *Gründung und Geschichte des Crédit Mobilier*; and Rondo E. Cameron, *France and the Economic Development*

of Europe 1800-1914 (1961), chs. 6 and 7; Rondo Cameron *et al.,
Banking in the Early Stages of Industrialization* (1967).

10 The Great Industries

A. Sartorius von Waltershausen, *Deutsche Wirtschaftsgeschichte 1815-
1914* (1923), pp. 156-80; J. H. Clapham, *The Economic Development
of France and Germany, 1815-1914* (1928); Pierre Benaerts, *Les origines
de la grande industrie allemande* (1933).

COAL

Maurice Baumont, *La grosse industrie allemande et le charbon* (1928)
and *La grosse industrie allemande et le lignite* (1928); N. J. G. Pounds,
The Ruhr (1952); Konrad Fuchs, *Vom Dirigismus zum Liberalismus*
(1970); this deals with coal and iron in Upper Silesia.

IRON AND STEEL

L. Beck, *Die Geschichte des Eisens*, 5 vols (1854-1903); Wilhelm Berdrow,
Alfred Krupp (1943); H. G. Heymann, *Die gemischten Werke im
deutschen Grosseisengewerbe* (1904).

ENGINEERING

A. Schröter and W. Becker, *Die deutsche Maschinenbauindustrie in der
industriellen Revolution* (1962).

TEXTILES

W. Lochmüller, *Zur Entwicklung der Baumwollindustrie in Deutschland*
(1906); R. M. R. Dehn, *German Cotton Industry* (1913); Horst Blumberg, *Die deutsche Textilindustrie in der industriellen Revolution*
(1965), which deals with the woollen industry; Mottek, Blumberg,
Wutzmer and Becker, *Studien zur Geschichte der industriellen Revolution in Deutschland* (1960), see Blumberg's essay on the linen industry.
For the Cotton Famine see W. O. Henderson, *The Lancashire Cotton
Famine*, 2nd edn. (1969), pp. 138-41.

11 The Struggle for Economic Supremacy 1862-5

Walther Lotz, *Die Ideen der deutschen Handelspolitik von 1860 bis 1891*
(1892); Ludolf Grambow, *Die deutsche Freihandelspartei zur Zeit ihrer
Blühte* (1903); J. Becker, *Das deutsche Manchestertum* (1907);
Oswald Schneider, *Bismarck und die preussische-deutsche Freihandelspolitik, 1862-76* (1910); L. Katzenstein, *Die Zeit der preussischen
Freihandelspolitik* (1913); W. Schüssler, *Bismarcks Kampf um Süd-
deutschland 1867* (1929); Eugen Franz, *Der Entscheidungskampf um
die wirtschaftspolitische Führung Deutschlands, 1856-67* (1933);
Walter Schübelin, *Das Zollparlament und die Politik von Baden, Bayern*

und Württemberg, 1866-70 (1935); W. O. Henderson, *The Zollverein* (1959), ch. 8.

12 Bismarck and Economic Unification

Georg Brodnitz, *Bismarcks Nationalökonomische Anschauungen* (1902); I. N. Lambi, *Free Trade and Protection in Germany 1868-1879* (*Vierteljahrschrift für Sozial-und Wirtschaftsgeschichte*, Supplement 44, 1963).

13 The Speculation Mania of 1871-3

For the speculation mania see F. Perrot, *Der Bank — Börsen — und Aktienschwindel* (1873); Otto Glagau, *Der Börsen — und Gründungs — Schwindel in Berlin*, I (1876) and *Der Börsen — und Gründungs — Schwindel in Deutschland*, II (1877); Rudolf Meyer, *Politische Gründer und die Corruption in Deutschland* (1877); Max Wirth, *Geschichte der Handelskrisen*, 4th edn (1890), ch. 15; K. Heinig, *Die Finanzskandale des Kaiserreichs* (1925); H. Gebhard, *Die Berliner Börse von ihren Aufängen bis 1905* (1928); Adolf Weber, *Depositenbanken und Spekulationsbanken*, 4th edn (1938); Jürgen Kuczynski, *Die Geschichte der Lage der Arbeiter unter den Kapitalismus*, part I, 3, ch. 1.
For Strousberg see his memoirs (*Dr. Strousberg und sein Wirken, von ihm selbst geschildert* (1876)) and Reitböck, 'Der Eisenbahnkönig Strousberg', in *Jahrbuch des Vereins deutscher Ingenieure*, 1924.

Part III: The Industrial Giant, 1873-1914

Accounts of Germany's industrial development between 1873 and 1914: E. E. Williams, *'Made in Germany'* (1896); Gastrell, *Development of Commercial, Industrial Maritime and Traffic Interests in Germany 1871 to 1898* (Foreign Office, January 1899); Ernst von Halle, *Die deutsche Volkswirtschaft an der Jahrhundertwende*, 2 vols. (1902); E. D. Howard, *The Cause and Extent of Recent Industrial Progress of Germany* (1907); W. H. Dawson, *The Evolution of Modern Germany* (1911); Karl Helfferich, *Germany's Economic Progress and National Wealth* (1913); A. Sartorius von Walterhausen, *Deutsche Wirtschaftsgeschichte 1815-1914* (1923), parts V and VI; W. G. Hoffmann, *Das Wachstum der deutschen Wirtschaft seit der Mitte des neunzehnten Jahrhunderts* (1965).

14 Introduction

For Bismarck's economic policy see Georg Brodnitz, *Bismarcks Nationalökonomische Anschaungen* (1902).
For the 'great Depression' in Germany see Hans Rosenberg, 'Political and Social Consequences of the Great Depression in Central Europe,

1873-96', in *Economic History Review* (1943) and *Grosse Depression und Bismarckzeit* (1967). For the depression in Britain see H. L. Beales, 'The "Great Depression" in Industry and Trade', in the *Economic History Review* (1934-5), pp. 65-75; A. E. Musson, 'The Great Depression in Britain, 1873-1896: a Reappraisal', in *Journal of Economic History* (June 1959), pp. 199-228 and S. B. Saul, *The Myth of the Great Depression, 1873-1896* (Economic History Society, (1969). Saul writes that 'the sooner the "Great Depression" is banished from the literature, the better'.

For the role of the State in the expansion of the German economy see Wolfram Fischer, 'The Strategy of Public Investment in the nineteenth Century in Germany' (sixth international conference of Economic History, Copenhagen, 1974).

15 Cartels and Banks

CARTELS

C. Goldschmidt, *Über die Konzentration im deutschen Kohlenbergbau* (1912); R. M. Michels, *Cartels, Combines, and Trusts in Post-War Germany* (1928); A. H. Stockder, *Regulating an Industry. The Rhenish-Westphalian Coal Syndicate* (1932); Robert Liefmann, *Cartels, Combines, and Trusts* (1913); Hermann Levy, *Industrial Germany* (1925). Official enquiries into German cartels were made in 1905 and in 1929-30. For reports issued by the second of these enquiries see *Ausschuss zur Untersuchung der Erzeugungs- und Absatzbedingungen der deutschen Wirtschaft: Verhandlungen und Berichte*.

INTERNATIONAL CARTELS

Robert Liefmann, 'Internationale Kartelle' in *Weltwirtschafts-Archiv* (1927).

BANKING

J. Riesser, *The German Great Banks* (United States National Monetary Commission, Washington (1911).

16 New Industries

CHEMICAL INDUSTRIES

H. Baron, *Chemical Industry on the Continent* (1909); E. Bäumler, *Ein Jahrhundert Chemie* Farbenwerke Hoechst, AG, (1963); H. J. Flechtner, *Carl Duisberg, Vom Chemiker zum Wirtschaftsführer* (1959 and 1960).

ELECTRICAL INDUSTRIES

Werner von Siemens, *Inventor and Entrepreneur. Recollections of Werner von Wiemens* (1966); Karl Helfferich, *Georg von Siemens*, 3 vols.

(1921-3), ch 3 and 4 (on the German electrical industry); W. O. Henderson, *The Industrialisation of Europe, 1780-1914* (1969), pp. 89-92 (on Werner von Siemens); A. Riedler, *Emil Rathenau und das Werden der Grosswirtschaft* (1916).

SHIPBUILDING AND THE MERCANTILE MARINE
Bernhard Huldermann, *Albert Ballin* (1922); G. Leckenbusch, *Die Beziehungen der deutschen Seeschiffswerften zur Eisenindustrie an der Ruhr in der Zeit von 1850 bis 1930* (1963); L. Beutin, *Bremen und Amerika* (1953).

17 *Economic and Social Policy*
RAILWAY NATIONALIZATION
Arthur von Mayer, *Geschichte und Geographie der deutschen Eisenbahnen von ihrer Entwicklung bis 1890* (1891); *Hundert Jahre deutsche Eisenbahnen* (Reichsverkehrsministerium, Berlin, 1935); Edwin Kech, *Geschichte der deutschen Eisenbahnen* (1911); F. Jungnickel, *Albert von Maybach* (1910).

PROTECTION
Max Sering, *Geschichte der preussisch-deutschen Eisenzölle von 1818 zur Gegenwart* (1882); Walther Lodz, *Die Ideen der deutschen Handelspolitik von 1860 bis 1891* (1892); Max Schippel, *Grundzüge der Handelspolitik* (1902); W. H. Dawson, *Protection in Germany* (1904); Max Nitzsche, *Die handelspolitische Reaktion in Deutschland* (1905); W. Treue, *Die deutsche Landwirtschaft zur Zeit Caprivis und ihr Kampf gegen die Handelsverträge* (1933); I. N. Lambi, *Free Trade and Protection in Germany, 1868-79* (Supplement 44 of the *Vierteljahrschrift für Sozial — und Wirtschaftsgeschichte*) (1963). The way in which Germany's tariff policy influenced the economic development of certain provinces is discussed in the following monographs — H. Haacke, *Handel und Industrie der Provinz Sachsen 1889-99 unter dem Einfluss der deutschen Handelspolitik* (1901); A. Friedrich, *Schlesiens Industrie unter dem Einflusse der Caprivischen Handelspolitik 1889-1900* (1902); T. Vogelstein, *Die Industrie der Rheinprovinz 1888-1900 . . .* (1902); S. Jonas, *Handelspolitische Interessen der deutschen Ostseestädte 1890-1900* (1902).

COLONIES
A. Zimmermann, *Geschichte der deutschen Kolonialpolitik* (1914); Kurt Herrfurth, *Fürst Bismarck und die Kolonialpolitik* (1917); Walther Stuhlmacher, *Bismarcks Kolonialpolitik* (1917); Mary Evelyn Townsend, *Origins of Modern German Colonialism, 1871-1885* (1921); Maximilan von Hagen, *Bismarcks Kolonialpolitik* (1923); Mary

Evelyn Townsend, *The Rise and Fall of Germany's Colonial Empire, 1884-1918* (1930); W. O. Aydelotte, *Bismarck and British Colonial Policy. The Problem of South West Africa 1883-85* (1937); A. J. P. Taylor, *Germany's first Bid for colonies, 1884-85* (1938); W. O. Henderson, *Studies in German Colonial History* (1962) and 'German East Africa, 1884-1918', in V. Harlow and E. M. Chilver (eds), *History of East Africa*, II, (1965), ch. 3; Hans-Ulrich Wehler, *Bismarck und der Imperialismus* (1969), 'Industrial Growth and early German Imperialism' (in R. Owen and B. Sutcliffe, *Studies in the Theory of Imperialism*, 1972, pp. 77-93) and 'Bismarck's Imperialism' in *Past and Present*, No. 48, 1970, pp. 119-55.

WELFARE STATE

C. D. Wright, *Compulsory Insurance in Germany* (Fourth Special Report of the Commissioner of Labor, Washington, 1893); W. H. Dawson, *Social Insurance in Germany 1883-1911* (1912).

18 *The Age of Wilhelm II, 1888-1914*

Karl Helfferich, *Germany's Economic Progress and National Wealth, 1888-1913* Deutsche Bank, (1913); Ernst von Halle, *Die deutsche Volkswirtschaft an der Jahrhundertwende*, 2 vols. (1902), I, ch. 2 'Deutschland am Ende des 19en Jahrhunderts': J. Riesser, *The German Great Banks* (Washington, 1911), part II, ch. 1, section ii (on the economic development of Germany between 1870 and 1905).

Index